THE EXPERIENCE OF INJUSTICE

NEW DIRECTIONS IN CRITICAL THEORY

NEW DIRECTIONS IN CRITICAL THEORY

Amy Allen, General Editor

New Directions in Critical Theory presents outstanding classic and contemporary texts in the tradition of critical social theory, broadly construed. The series aims to renew and advance the program of critical social theory, with a particular focus on theorizing contemporary struggles around gender, race, sexuality, class, and globalization and their complex interconnections.

For a complete list of books in this series, see pages 273–274

The Experience of Injustice

A THEORY OF RECOGNITION

Emmanuel Renault

TRANSLATED BY

Richard A. Lynch

Columbia University Press
New York

Columbia University Press
Publishers Since 1893
New York   Chichester, West Sussex
cup.columbia.edu

L'expérience de l'injustice
Reconnaissance et clinique de l'injustice
by Emmanuel Renault
© Editions La Découverte, Paris, France, 2004.

Cataloging-in-Publication Data is available from the Library of Congress.
ISBN 978-0-231-17706-1 (cloth)
ISBN 978-0-231-54898-4 (e-book)

Columbia University Press books are printed on permanent
and durable acid-free paper.

Printed in the United States of America

Cover design: Milenda Nan Ok Lee
Cover photo: Nikolas Georgiou / © Alamy

CONTENTS

PART II
The Politics of Identity and Politics in Identity

PART III
Social Suffering

TRANSLATOR'S NOTE

A few terms central to Emmanuel Renault's argument merit a brief discussion in advance—although quite succinctly expressed in French, they are difficult to render simply and concisely into natural English.

The first of these is *dominés et demunis*, of which Renault makes systematic use as a conceptual pair, and which is translated here either as "dominated and deprived," or frequently, as "the dominated and the deprived." In Renault's usage, *dominés* refers to individuals or groups living under domination or oppression, and *démunis* to those suffering the loss or deprivation of social resources, networks, and supports—including, but not merely limited to poverty, or loss of material resources. As Renault explains, one can be more or less endowed with resources for living under forms of domination and for facing life's hazards but also suffer from deprivation by being marginalized or excluded by forms of social domination; one can therefore suffer from deprivation quite independently of the fact of being oppressed. (Apart from preserving the alliteration, the English "dominated" seems preferable to "oppressed" because the latter can be both too strong and too narrow—not every space or state of domination is a space or state of oppression.) Similarly, "the deprived" seems preferable to "the poor," since it indicates that a poverty of social resources, and not merely material poverty, is intended. Renault uses *dominés et démunis* both as a pair and independently—the latter, "the deprived," is discussed in more detail below.

Another of Renault's central concepts that is difficult to express elegantly and succinctly in English is *dynamiques revendicatives*—the dynamics or process by which demands are developed and articulated, "the dynamics of formulating demands." The French noun *revendication* carries the sense of a demand or a claim, as in an actionable claim for justice; the adjectival form *revendicatif* carries a sense of dissent or protest. But the English "dissent" is closer to the French notion of *contestation* than *revendication*, and does not capture Renault's usage here (although he does use the adjectival *revendicatif*, in the sense of dissent or contestation, in other contexts). The phrase *dynamiques revendicatives*, "the dynamics of formulating demands," refers to the process by which negative experiences or feelings (of injustice) are cognitively transformed into normative and social demands (for justice, or for a new understanding of justice). One of the central tasks of the book is to explain this process, one that leads from a negative experience to demands, by distinguishing various practical dynamics (refusal, avoidance, or accommodation), cognitive processes (reinterpretation of a given context or norms), and normative dynamics (efforts to express what is at stake in these negative experiences).

Another important concept that is difficult to translate adequately and directly is *action protestataire* or *agir protestataire*—translated here as "action in protest" or "protest action." This term does not merely denote something like a strike or a protest march (though these can function as examples), but rather a broader category of action in resistance to something, action that pushes back against or refuses to accept a negative experience, whether that action is cognitive or social, whether it is carried out by an individual or a group.

Collective de travail (a concept that becomes significant in chapter 5), translated here as a "work collective," is yet another concept for which no direct English equivalent exists. The idea encompasses a team of workers—perhaps, for example, all the workers on a factory floor or on a shift, or all the employees at the same level of a corporate hierarchy. English terms that capture the idea partially but not fully, (but that could nevertheless help an American reader begin to see the term's extension, include "co-workers," "colleagues," "shift crew," and "project team." The notion of a "work collective" also encompasses some of the elements of solidarity represented in labor unions and collective bargaining units (though these are quite different institutional structures than a "work collective"): one can look to the other members of one's "work collective" for mutual respect, understanding, and recognition of one's skills, contributions, and accomplishments, even when the latter are overlooked or unrecognized by management. While "work collective" is a neologism in English (and one that might even misleadingly connote ideas of "collectivization" to American ears), this term has been employed in recent work by Renault and others (where it is briefly defined as "a number of coworkers who are brought together . . . by technical aspects of the tasks themselves"[1]), and so is also used here.

Two other related terms are the French expressions les "sans" (literally, "those without") and luttes des "sans" ("the struggles of those without"). Les "sans"—a fairly common term in French political theory—refers to people who have virtually no material or social resources, and encompasses groups such as the homeless (les sans-logement, "those without housing"), the unemployed (les chômeurs or les sans-travail, "those without work"), and undocumented immigrants (les sans-papiers, "those without [legal] documentation"). All are typically groups and individuals who have been marginalized, rendered invisible, and forgotten by society. At the author's suggestion, and in resonance with the pair "dominated and deprived" (discussed above), les "sans" is here glossed as "the deprived," and les luttes des "sans" as "the struggles of the deprived." While these English glosses do lose some of the vividness and directness of the French, they nevertheless fit within the conceptual landscape Renault is presenting here.

"Psychic suffering" (souffrance psychique—another critical concept in Renault's argument) may also sound a bit awkward in English; at first glance, "psychological suffering" would seem an easier, more familiar translation, one that avoids any unintended resonances with "psychics" or the paranormal, for example. However, souffrance psychique is a technical term in Renault's usage, denoting a particular form of psychological suffering (as is elaborated in more detail here and elsewhere[2]), and so "psychic suffering" is used here as well.

A final term that merits mention in advance is the idea of a porte-parole, translated here both as a "spokesperson" and as a "voice." Though the term itself does not appear until the later chapters of the book, the ideas behind it shape Renault's argument from the opening pages of the introduction, when he frames political philosophy's approach as a choice between seeking consensus or taking sides. Both English terms ("spokesperson" and "voice") capture something of Renault's usage here: he understands critical theory's role to be that of a spokesperson—giving voice to concerns in political or theoretical arenas where they would otherwise not be recognized. But in his view, the idea of the critical theorist as a "mere" spokesperson, who "speaks *for*" someone else, is still inadequate as a description. Critical theory must not simply "pass along" or enable the articulation of what is already thought, felt, or said by excluded groups, but must also actively contribute to the saying—and the self-understanding created in the saying. (In this respect, "voice" is a richer English term than "spokesperson.") Renault also situates his use of this term within historical context—in particular, that of the French revolution where the role of a "spokesperson" or "voice" was informally institutionalized, and a number of individuals played the role of a "spokesperson" or "voice" for revolutionary groups[3] (perhaps analogously to the way that lobbyists represent groups' interests in legislative halls today, except that of course lobbyists typically represent the interests of those who already have power and access and do not suffer from the kinds of marginalization and "invisible injustice" that Renault takes as the starting point for his reorientation of critical theory). Hence, "spokesperson" and "voice" are both used to render this idea of a *porte-parole*, with the choice between them in any given case determined by immediate context.

When citations are from texts originally written in English or available in English translation, I have generally used the available English version. In a few exceptional (and noted) cases, I have altered the English translation if the French text conveys a different sense than the standard English version. My notes (and citations added by the translator) are set as footnotes at the bottom of the page or in brackets within the author's notes; the author's notes are set at the back of the book.

For assistance and support with this translation, I would like to thank Cheryl Arnold, Christine Dunbar, Marcelo Hoffman, Stacy Klingler, Kevin Thompson, Jerry Zaslove, and everybody in the Interlibrary Loan department of the St. Ambrose University Library, and especially Joyce Haack, who managed to work through some difficult challenges finding source materials for me. This translation would be much poorer without the breadth of resources that interlibrary loan makes available. Finally, I owe a very special thanks to Emmanuel Renault for his generosity in answering many questions and making many useful suggestions throughout. It has been a great pleasure to work with him on this translation, and I hope that it does his voice justice.

PREFACE

The Experience of Injustice was originally published in 2004. Its objective was to bring out the critical potential of the paradigm of recognition as elaborated by Axel Honneth a little more than a decade earlier, and to show that the debates that traversed critical thinking, the social sciences, and political philosophy could profit from the latest developments in Frankfurt School critical theory. The task of this preface is to recall the general features of that context for the English-language reader and to indicate how it has led me along a path that I have subsequently tried to explore in different ways and which still seems to me to retain its philosophical and political pertinence.

DIVERGENT PATHS

The second half of the 1990s was marked by a dynamic revival of social critique accompanied by the emergence of an antiglobalist movement. In the landscape of political philosophy at the time, dominated by the debate between liberalism and communitarianism, Honneth stood in stark contrast because of his choices to start from social conflicts—the subtitle of his *The Struggle for Recognition* was *The Moral Grammar of Social Conflicts*—and to pay attention to labor and to domination.[1] His theoretical model appeared able to keep alive, after Jürgen Habermas, the initial program of critical theory[2] while also responding to two needs of the time: to contribute to the rekindling of social critique and to develop a critique of a newly resurgent post-Rawlsian normative political philosophy.

On the one hand, *The Struggle for Recognition* offered a way to contribute to this rekindling of social critique by adopting social movements' perspective on politics, at the very moment when the development of the antiglobal movement could lead one to think of social movements as one of the main political actors in its own right: Antonio Negri, for instance, spoke of a "movement of movements;" John Holloway of "changing the world without taking power." On the other hand, Honneth stressed that his theory of recognition approached the question at the heart of the resurgence of normative political philosophy—that is, justice—from the perspective of what he sometimes described as a "phenomenology of negative social experiences" in an Adornian vein that seemed equally capable of reviving certain themes in Marxian critiques of politics and political philosophy.[3] The methodological negativism employed in *The Struggle for Recognition*, which investigates the normative content of negative social experiences, made possible a critical approach to the silences of moral philosophy and mainstream[i] politics, as well as a reformulation *from below* of such fundamental topics as rights and justice.

The political context of the 1990s in France gave rise to specific effects in the social sciences and philosophy, effects that surely influenced the reception of this theory of recognition. From all sides, and in particular in the works of theorists such as Pierre Bourdieu,[4] Luc Boltanski,[5] and Christophe Dejours,[6] the social sciences attempted to contribute to the rekindling of social critique. But political philosophy seemed for the most part to remain on the sidelines, tending instead toward what was called the "return of political philosophy" (what was, in fact, the propagation of Rawlsian political liberalism) and the "revival of moral philosophy." Other important philosophical interventions supported radical political projects, as with Alain Badiou and Jacques Rancière, while Foucauldian and Deleuzian theorizations claimed large audiences, but all most often kept their distance from an effective critique of neoliberalism, content to cast a disdainful eye upon the resurgence of normative political philosophy. Although this has become less the case over time, a series of demands nevertheless went unanswered: for a philosophical expression of the social conflicts proper to the neoliberal epoch; for an immanent critique of the way in which social injustices were thematized by the dominant philosophical paradigms; for a social philosophy prepared to take account of new developments in critical social sciences. The theoretical model of *The Struggle for Recognition* seemed to be able to answer these demands.

i. Transl.: "Mainstream" is in English in the original.

Thus, in the opening years of the 2000s, a French adaptation of this model emerged.[7] It was challenged implicitly by Paul Ricoeur in 2004,[8] the very year *L'Expérience de l'injustice* was published. *The Experience of Injustice* was based upon significant aspects of Honneth's oeuvre: his work to revive the critical theory tradition through his articles on Georg Lukács and Theodor Adorno,[9] through his desire to actualize a theory of reification[10] and ideology[11] (and even the thematic of the contradictions of capitalism);[12] and his work to undertake a critique of the hegemony of political liberalism both by revisiting the debates about liberalism and communitarianism[13] and by opposing struggles against injustice to theories of justice[14] and social pathologies to social injustices.[15] His defense of social philosophy was thus understood as an interdisciplinary enterprise, by way of the establishment of social diagnostics starting with critical syntheses of contemporary research in the social sciences,[16] and by the revival of interdisciplinary research projects at the Institut für Sozialforschung, such as projects on the paradoxes of capitalist modernization.[17] As such, it also constituted a powerful source of inspiration. The development of these differing orientations figured among the intentions of *The Experience of Injustice*.

At the same time, and without realizing it, this book set out upon an inverse path to that which Honneth began to pursue. This was at the same time that Honneth took some steps away from his initial program. Initially quite discretely, but increasingly explicitly in the course of the 2000s, he abandoned George Herbert Mead for Émile Durkheim, at the same time as he made a return to Habermas. To make this evolution perceptible, it is probably helpful to recall the manner in which he had begun by claiming the primacy of negative social experiences. The primacy of negative experiences is an element of an espoused methodological negativism (inspired by Adorno and Michael Theunissen[18]) and of an effort to introduce Adornian elements into contemporary social theory. In a televised interview with Ian Angus and Jerry Zaslove, which initially aired in 1998,[19] Honneth explained that his theory "would start with phenomena which are experienced by ordinary people as disturbing, negative, unjust."[20] He reiterates that "the basis of critical theory" as he conceives it is "to start really with everyday experiences"—in particular, "negative experiences."[21] Starting with negative experiences—more precisely, "moral injuries"—constituted a revival of Adorno's approach to moral philosophy, especially in *Minima Moralia*, which consisted of "a kind of careful phenomenological description of certain moral tragedies."[22] The "careful description of the internal structure of those [negative] experiences" allows one to identify "tendencies towards [a] better society" which should contribute to "the foundation of your own normative theory of society."[23] Honneth also explains that this return to Adorno distinguishes his project from Habermas's as well as from the dominant orientations in moral and political philosophy.[24] He maintains that "all forms of social criticism have to be based in some form of moral theory,"[25] but "[t]he starting point is to describe what moral injuries are, or what is injustice, instead of the other way around[, i]nstead of starting positively with a developed idea of morality or some principles of justice. . . ."[26] Hence it is necessary to overcome the opposition between models of rational social critique, transcendent with respect to their context as in John Rawls, and models of hermeneutic critique "starting with the given social norms or the given moral principles and then trying to show that certain developments, institutional developments, in that culture do not fit any longer to the given principles or norms."[27] To this internal critique, which he attributes to communitarianism, he opposes a model of immanent critique, inspired by Hegel, founded upon the view that the normative expectations that structure social experience "are sometimes much richer, and morally richer, normatively richer than, what is explicit, let's say, what is known to the subjects themselves."[28]

It isn't difficult to draw certain consequences from this for a social theory and political philosophy that endeavors to begin from an expectation of recognition that is the arterial blood for social experience. Within the framework of social theory, we come to the two following theses: the first thesis is that expectations of recognition (of being recognized, recognitive expectations) need not be conceived, according to a Habermasian model, as normative presuppositions of social life or as quasi-transcendental conditions of social life, but rather, according to a model that we could call Deweyan, as expectations that tacitly structure social experience and which can only become explicit in problematic situations, and whose content can only be determined reflexively, as soon as these problematic situations must be addressed. The second thesis is that the normative stakes of social experience are richer than the available moral language is able to express. In Adornian terms, they constitute a "nonidentical" moment, given what the socially accepted moral language allows one to say. The general conclusion is that negative social experiences are also capable of furnishing a critical perspective on the socially accepted moral and political language, and that political philosophy must try to develop such critical perspectives instead of being content to make explicit moral common sense (according to the hermeneutic model) or to give it a noncontradictory formulation (according to the Rawlsian model of reflective equilibrium). More specifically, this implies that the normative content of recognitive expectations must be analyzed beginning with negative experiences of the denial of recognition rather than the ways in which principles of recognition are institutionalized.

At the methodological level, it further follows that the theory of recognition must be doubly oriented as a study of the structures of the experience of denial of recognition, and as a dialectical approach to normative questions. It must on the one hand orient itself along the path of a phenomenology of negative experiences, being careful to take account of the different dimensions of these experiences, by identifying the institutional structures and the social processes that explain the maladjustment of recognitive expectations with respect to context, as well as the intrasubjective processes that condition responses to this maladjustment. The development of such a phenomenology of negative experiences, supported by sociological and psychological or psychoanalytic insights, would comply with the Adornian demand for a combination of microscopic and macroscopic, of sociological and psychoanalytic, approaches to experience.[29]

Notably, such an approach allows us to account for the practical and cognitive significance of the experience of denial of recognition, by shining an original light upon the processes that lead from negative social experiences to political claims for justice. As soon as it is joined by a sense of injustice, the experience of denial of recognition becomes the source of specific demands, tied to the sorts of unsatisfied expectations and to the contexts in which these expectations are created and disappointed. This negative experience is equally at the origin of critical cognitive effects. In fact, the experience of injustice leads one to differently perceive the world naturalized by routine and habit, and it throws a new light upon the institutionalized principles of legitimation by showing their compatibility with injustice: it makes them appear in their untruth. It is certainly also true that while the experience of denial of recognition can orient social action toward the transformation of situations of injustice and domination, it can just as well produce an opposite result, in situations where social contempt is internalized instead of being experienced as intolerable, in situations where denial of recognition takes not the form of an experience of injustice but rather of social suffering (which will be an object of particular concern in *The Experience of Injustice*, but whose theorization is taken up elsewhere[30]).

Methodological negativism also raises questions like that of justice in a dialectical manner, we could say, insofar as it makes apparent that the normative demands that define justice are inseparable from a negation of negation—more precisely, a demand to negate this demonstrated negation which is the experience of denial of recognition. This approach to justice is thus dialectical in the sense of a negative dialectic that focuses on the moment of the negation of negation, and therefore concentrates on the abolitionist dimension[31] of the concept of social injustice, a concept that takes its political specificity precisely from the fact that it is defined by the demand to abolish injustice. The political concept of justice, which refers specifically to social justice, is differentiated from juridical and moral concepts of justice by this dialectical structure. The same holds, moreover, for all political concepts: equality in the political sense refers to a demand for the negation of social inequality, not to mathematical concepts of arithmetic or geometric equality; political liberty refers to a demand for the negation of oppression prior to any reference to moral or juridical ideas of self-legislation or to reciprocal limitations imposed by free arbitrators. Just as every concept is essentially abolitionist, so too every concept is essentially contested[32]—the political conflicts from which they are taken endow them with antagonistic meanings and values. As it is employed in *The Experience of Injustice*, this approach in terms of essentially contested concepts is intended to illuminate the effects of symbolic domination that accompany every attempt to make an indisputable use of a fundamental concept, and to justify a philosophical approach to political questions in partisan terms. It is on this last point that the problematics of essentially contested concepts and of abolitionist concepts are better articulated together. In conflicts concerning justice, for example, what is always at stake is the abolition of particular injustices, experienced by particular social groups but which other social groups refuse to consider as important. To understand justice by starting from the experience of injustice is thus to grasp the concept of justice in its essentially abolitionist dimension; but it also provides one with a method to participate in those struggles, by making apparent the type of legitimacy particular to the demands that emerge in one form or another from the experience of injustice. To start from the experience of injustice is, moreover, to adopt a critical perspective on the controversies about justice by interrogating the incapacity of certain socially institutionalized definitions of justice to account for certain experiences of injustice; that is to say, those definitions' inability to see these experiences as worthy of consideration within political deliberations and debates.

When *The Struggle for Recognition* was published and in the years that followed, Honneth's task was clearly to reformulate the Adornian privileging of experience through a pragmatist conception of social experience. At that time, he also intended to develop a critique of the main orientations of contemporary political philosophy, based upon Adornian negativism and a social theory that recognized the importance of social struggles and relations of domination in the social world. Later, these directions were no longer central. At the beginning of the 2000s, he himself acknowledged abandoning George Herbert Mead in favor of Durkheim in social theory: norms of recognition were no longer related back to tacit expectations animating social experience, but rather became institutional principles structuring modern societies and assuring "social integration."[33] And this abandonment of Mead for Durkheim was accompanied by a return to Habermas. In fact, at the same time as the centrality of domination and of struggles was fading, recognition was able to be thematized in terms of normative presuppositions of social life, on a Habermasian model of quasi-transcendental conditions for social integration. Negative social experiences ceased to function as the moment of non-identity that illuminates institutionalized normative principles' non-truth. The theory of recognition was recast as a theory of promises inscribed in the fundamental institutions of modernity,[34] on the model of the Habermasian theory of modernity as an incomplete project. At the methodological level, this rejection of social experience's priority was accompanied, on the one hand, by an abandonment of methodological negativism, and, on the other, by a shift from immanent critique to internal critique—immanent critique no longer functioned as an alternative to internal critique.[35] Social critique should no longer take the demands that arise from negative experiences as its guiding thread; rather, it should be founded upon the not yet realized promises inscribed within institutionalized normative principles.[36]

Honneth thought that this evolution was necessary to strengthen the initial project of his theory of recognition and to successfully answer the objections that it had elicited. But other reorientations were possible, and other paths have been explored, such as relational anthropology[37] and critical social ontology.[38] More than ten years after its initial publication, *The Experience of Injustice* will have accomplished its purpose if it shows us that the initial project was abandoned before all of its resources had been developed. For that initial program is what is developed here, albeit in a specific way that itself entails certain reorientations.

A first reorientation concerns the scope of applicability of an approach in terms of recognition. Whereas Honneth had tried (in the period that culminated in *Freedom's Right*) to give the widest possible scope to the paradigm of recognition and to minimize the importance of questions where it is most difficult to apply, it seemed to me to be necessary to delimit the specific scope of applicability for this paradigm, and to connect it with complementary theoretical perspectives. The principal thesis of *The Experience of Justice* is that the theory of recognition draws strength from its capacity to thematize the normative content of negative social *experiences* that can lead to an experience of injustice.

A second reorientation concerns the mobilization of complementary theoretical approaches. In proposing a dynamic conception of experience, and in understanding the concept of experience in Dewey's sense, that is, as the interaction between a subject and an environment, I was led to the idea that Honneth's approach should be completed as much by a social psychology (informed by psychoanalysis) that made explicit the subjective dynamics of experience as by a social theory (informed by sociology) that clarified the causes and contexts of the experience of injustice. The function of this social theory is to analyze the recognitive expectations that supply blood to social interactions, but also the effects of recognition (or recognitive effects) produced by institutions, the social relations of domination that traverse social situations, and the structural logics that govern institutional relations and transformations.[39] Later, in *Social Suffering*, I argued further that if the denial of recognition should be thematized as an experience capable of leading to several different outcomes (a point I had already stressed in *The Experience of Injustice*), it is just as important to complete the Meadian social psychology upon which Honneth had constructed his first model with psychodynamic approaches inspired by Sigmund Freud that are capable of accounting for the interconnections of the psychic and the social (as is the case in the psychosocial clinical study of exclusion and the psychodynamics of work).[40]

In a word, it was a matter of showing that the theory of recognition's domain of applicability was linked to its capacity to make explicit the implicit normative contents of particular negative social experiences and to analyze the cognitive and practical dynamics which result therefrom. The Honnethian approach gives us methods and concepts that are irreplaceable for an understanding of what is at stake in negative social experiences, but it must be completed by psychological models (in particular, by a theory of defenses against the suffering involved in negative social experiences) and sociological models (in particular, by a theory of habituation to domination and of the ways of expecting and giving recognition), if it will be able to account for the various dimensions of these experiences. It should, moreover, be articulated upon a social theory (on the four levels of interactions, institutions, social relations, and structural dynamics) in order to capture the ways in which social situations are liable to be transformed by the experience of denial of recognition.

A third reorientation concerns the question of identity. To distinguish his work from that of Charles Taylor and later Nancy Fraser, who associated recognition with the politics of identity, Honneth was not content to merely underscore that recognition is an element in all demands for social justice. He also refused to attribute a crucial role to the concept of identity in the sense of psychological, social, or cultural identity. He only took up identity in a limited sense that ultimately aimed to disconnect the question of recognition from that of the recognition of identities. The question of identity for Honneth is nothing more than that of the positive relation to oneself, intersubjectively constituted and intersubjectively vulnerable in relations of recognition. For Honneth, only a formal model of identity as a positive relation to oneself seemed compatible with the aspirations to universality that are associated with the idea of justice. It seemed to me that this approach to identity suffered for its abstraction and for its psychologically contestable character: how is a positive relation to oneself to be understood independent of the contents that give it its effectiveness and that refer, on the one hand, to the play of social identification, and on the other, to the underlying psychic processes? Another disadvantage of this approach, it seemed to me, was its inability to contribute to the analysis of processes of the politicization of identity across struggles as widely varied as those of minority groups and stigmatized peoples, from Chiapas to gay pride.[41] In an era like ours, marked by the extreme fragmentation of social struggles and by persistent prejudices against those struggles concerning identity, the paradigm of recognition, by making apparent the common stakes shared by social struggles as different as struggles over wages and struggles over devalued or stigmatized identities, offers invaluable resources for constructing the points of overlap without which every politics of social movements is doomed to remain impotent.

A fourth reorientation concerns the political dimension of the theory of recognition. In *The Struggle for Recognition*, Honneth presented his project as a social theory with a normative tenor and he took up the question of the political dimensions of his project in an ambiguous way. On one side, the idea of the "normative grammar of social conflicts" indicated an attempt to philosophize from the perspective of social movements and to philosophically justify their political importance. It thus demonstrated an engagement with the politics of self-emancipation and it approached politics *from below*, two elements of what could be called a popular politics. But on the other hand, the concern to ground social critique on universal principles led Honneth to attribute entirely formal normative demands, which he noted in the conclusion could be integrated into different political projects, to the three spheres of recognition (love, responsible for a positive relation to self as self-confidence; rights, responsible for a positive relation to self as self-respect; and recognition of the social value of our existence, responsible for a positive relation to self as self-esteem). *The Struggle for Recognition* was thus presented as a relatively neutral political theory, one that could be interpreted in liberal, republican, or communitarian ways. Moreover, it seemed to renew a traditional conception of politics as deliberation about the common good in the public sphere, while the model of social movements leaned rather toward models of radical democracy that foregrounded agonistic politics and the institutionalization of social conflict.[42] Finally, it seemed to presuppose a classical conception of political philosophy as a discourse furnishing universal principles for deliberations in the public sphere, a conception that the Marxian sources for the initial program of critical theory condemned.[43] Clearly, Honneth leaned toward a socialist interpretation of his theory, as he indicated in the debate with Nancy Fraser (and as his more recent works confirm), and it is true that we can distinguish between liberal, republican, and communitarian socialisms. But it nonetheless remains that the neutrality claimed in the conclusion contrasted with the paradigmatic promotion of social movements. Certainly, its criticisms of the Habermasian linguistic turn[ii]

---

ii. "Linguistic turn" is in English in the original.

and the role given to social conflicts proscribed in spirit any reduction of politics to the deliberative public sphere, but he didn't seem to draw out all of these implications at the level of legitimate methods in political philosophy.

Thenceforward, the question could be posed in the following form: How are we to make explicit the theory of recognition's politics? More fundamentally, which definitions of politics and of political philosophy are entailed by this theory? I have tried to show, with Jean-Philippe Deranty,[44] that the theory of recognition should be understood not so much as a method for intervening in the well-delineated field of philosophical reflection on the normative foundations of social critique, but rather as a proposal concerning the very practice of political philosophy and the meaning of the concept of politics. Whereas Honneth associates the normative content of the idea of a struggle for recognition with the ideal of a recognition that is ever more universal, founded upon a reconciliation rather than a simple consensus, and whereas he seems to assume the traditional definition of politics as a search for the common good, I have claimed that the theory of recognition assumes rather an agonistic conception of politics (which goes back to and revives the initial motivations for the theory of recognition, such as they were earlier formulated in *The Critique of Power* in 1985). It follows, in particular, that the theory of recognition should not be understood along the model of a political philosophy aimed at a universal agreement about the principles of social critique (à la Rawls), dismissing conflicts in the name of consensus; but it should instead adopt the model of joining with the collective efforts of the dominated and excluded, in order to understand the meaning of their social experience and to struggle against everything that dooms them to injustice and domination. To politicize the theory of recognition thus means to propose, on the one hand, that it intervene in the space of discursive confrontations structured by essentially contested concepts by methodologically assuming a partisan role on the side of those who are structurally subjected to different forms of denial of recognition (being made invisible, stigmatized, devalued); and, on the other hand, that it confront the problem of the limited legitimacy of struggles for recognition that are expressed within an antagonistic horizon.[45] Struggles *of* recognition, which are not struggles *for* recognition (in the sense that they do not have reconciliation as their telos) are not for all that stripped of all normative content. The political stakes of this thesis are particularly clear in cases of subalternity.

TOWARD A GLOBALIZED MODEL OF SOCIAL CRITIQUE

I began by recalling that *The Experience of Injustice* was situated within a specific political context, the development of the anti-global movement, which was simultaneously characterized by a great variety of demands and of forms of struggle and mobilization, and which saw the political emergence of new actors, belonging to subaltern populations (Dalits and landless peasants, for example). Even though the political and intellectual landscape is no longer the same today, it seems to me that the political aims as well as the approach of this book are still well calibrated to the political stakes of late. In fact, the crisis of neoliberalism has sparked a new revival of social movements (e.g., *Indignados*, Occupy Wall Street, the Chilean students' movement) and it has likewise sparked new challenges to a political philosophy ever more withdrawn into itself. It has been the occasion for an extreme diversification of forms of struggle and demands that call for particular efforts to participate in the construction of new convergences. An appropriate method will be able to bring together demands expressed in political languages that are apparently incompatible with the dynamics that lead to these demands. Moreover, the development of mass unemployment and the ongoing dismantling of welfare state social protections, in Europe and elsewhere, has entailed a diversification of the means of social exclusion and an increasing disconnect between forms of experiences of injustice and politically institutionalized languages that are increasingly subject to neoliberal norms. This has led to an increase in the populations, clearly marginalized outside the flow of global production, encountering even more difficulty than other groups in transforming their experiences of injustice into a political sort of collective demand, and that can be driven to a powerful resentment of institutionalized politics and social movements— all of which serves to support authoritarian populism, or else radically anti-political forms of protest, sometimes tragically illustrated in the form of a struggle against the experience of social contempt by means of a religious restoration of self-esteem. A response to these challenges presupposes the elaboration of models of social critique that would be able to describe the social injustices against which these social movements aim, as well as those that do not generally manage to achieve such political forms. Thus, our current situation seems to require a doubly globalized model of social critique: a language that contributes to the harmonizing of varied demands issued by social movements and that succeeds in filling out these demands from the perspective of a larger popular politics, a perspective that would be valuable as an alternative to authoritarian populism (or "counter-populism"[46]) and to antipolitical forms of rejecting social injustice. This is the challenge that this book works to take up through a reflection upon the forms of the experience of injustice.[47]

This reflection on the forms of the experience of injustice attempts to answer the following question: How can ordinary definitions of social justice be transformed so that they are able to give an account of the most common forms of social injustice today, while still being able to return to the discourse of current social struggles as well as the expectations of justice that structure experiences of injustice without taking an explicitly political form? To answer that, I propose to *re-elaborate* the ordinary definitions of justice by starting from the experience of injustice. This re-elaboration can take two logically distinct paths, depending on whether it is applied only to the form or also to the content of the usual definitions of social justice.

The first type of re-elaboration is a simple *reformulation*. It consists in accepting the meaning of the usual definitions of social justice and expressing them in a form that aims to account for, on the one hand, the characteristics of experiences of injustice that correspond to the situations that these definitions allow us to identify as injustices, and on the other, the demands that emerge therefrom. The advantage of an approach in terms of recognition stems from the fact that it allows us to inscribe the qualitative and referential dimension of the language of protest within these definitions of justice. This line of inquiry plays a central role in the first chapter; however, the rest of the book will undertake a re-elaboration of the definitions of social justice in another sense, that of a *recasting* of these definitions. It is thus a question of presenting a collection of phenomena as injustices—phenomena that spontaneously appear as injustices to those who experience them but are difficult to express in terms of the usual definitions of justice. For example, every individual victim of a mass layoff [*licenciement boursier*][iii] experiences an injustice without really having arguments available to assert that it really is one. Hence the need for a recasting, for a critical operation that is directed not only to the form but also the content of the usual definitions of justice. The aim is thus no longer merely to adapt the vocabulary of justice to the demands which it encompasses, but to those demands that it tends to exclude (read, deny) or to minimize by

iii. "Licenciement boursier" is a pejorative term referring in particular to layoffs intended to increase a company's stock price or shareholder value.

attaching them to subordinate rights. Recasting the definitions of social justice leads to a defense of the idea that social rights are not subordinate rights (a recasting of our *understanding* of the definitions) and that they should include a reference to identity and suffering (a recasting of the *extension* and *domain* of the definitions).

Just like a reformulation, a recasting does not propose a new definition of justice. It consists rather in showing that the spirit of the meanings usually associated with the idea of social justice authorizes or calls for the integration of new senses (social rights, rights of identity, rights of suffering). In reformulation, it is thus a question of starting from the experience of injustice in order to express and understand by other means what the current definitions of justice portray as social injustices. In recasting, the idea of the experience of injustice designates rather social injustices which are not included within current definitions of injustice. But in both cases, it is indeed a matter of starting with the concerns or stakes of these experiences for those who live them, stakes that the common meanings of the idea of social justice only explicates, but often in a deformed and limited way.

This simultaneously reconstructive and critical line of inquiry rests upon two complementary presuppositions. The first is that a specific philosophical approach is required to raise central political challenges such as the definition of social justice. The second is that, in a context marked by a divorce between political language and politically decisive social experiences, political philosophy cannot honor its normative ambitions without taking up a critique of politics and of everything within philosophy itself that reproduces this divorce. I have already indicated that the object of this inquiry is to elaborate a model of social critique adapted to the different faces of social injustice, and that demands that it commits to a double movement. The first, a task of political philosophy, is a normative reflection, in this case, upon the justification of the definition of social justice that is presupposed by this model. The second, a task of social philosophy, concerns the explication of the descriptive capacity of this model, that is, the verification of its capacity to effectively account for the different forms of social justice. To commit to this second path, we must adopt an interdisciplinary approach that will principally draw upon sociology and social psychology. For a model of social critique to be relevant, it is necessary and sufficient that it is capable of representing the objects that it claims to address—representing them (by accounting for their existence and certain of their characteristic traits) but, strictly speaking, offering neither a complete description of them (by displaying the various characteristic traits of different forms of social injustice) nor an explanation (by identifying all the causes of social injustice). When I draw upon the social and human sciences to characterize particular experiences of injustice, it is thus not a matter of offering descriptions or explanations of the experience of injustice as an alternative to those that political economy or sociology could produce, nor of offering explanations of the feeling of injustice as an alternative to what sociology or psychology could formulate. It is only a matter of proposing a model for interpreting the experience of injustice that would be sufficiently general to be able to take account of the variety of its different forms, sufficiently differentiated to be able to take account of the specificity of the descriptions and explanations offered by the social and psychological sciences, and sufficiently determinate to be able to take part in the conflicts about descriptive and explanatory models that traverse the social and psychological sciences.[48]

The aim is not to offer alternative descriptions but rather a model that allows us to forge a global picture of social injustice on the basis of those descriptions. In this global picture, the different forms of injustice will be interpreted as forms of denial of recognition. In fact, I rely upon the theory of recognition to ground a definition of justice and to create (by means of the theory of recognition's institutional effects) the intermediary concepts that will make it possible to connect the philosophical and social scientific discourses.

Finally, I should note that the reader will find here a version adapted for the American edition. Sections that were too closely tied to a French context of political discussion at the time have been removed and several arguments have been reformulated. The most significant modifications involve making the negativist and pragmatist orientations more explicit. The reorientations of Honneth's theory of recognition that have been outlined above were not yet entirely clear to me in 2004. That explains why only the first version of the theory of recognition was taken up (and criticized on certain points), while certain ideas characteristic of the reorientation of the 2000s—like the idea of "normative presuppositions of social life" and, more generally, the ideas defended in the 2003 debate with Nancy Fraser—were interpreted in light of the first model. This inconsistency has been removed.

I must also reiterate a debt of gratitude owed to those who generously read and discussed drafts of this book: Jean-Philippe Deranty, Yves Sintomer, Stéphane Haber, Christophe Hanna, Vincent Houillon, Fabien Jobard, Djemila Zeneidi, Bertrand Ogilvie, Marina Garcés, Christophe Fiat, Sandra Laugier, Claude Gautier, Sébastien Henry and Hugues Jallon. Thanks also to the members of the *Penser le Contemporain* group (especially to Étienne Balibar, Bertrand Binoche, Catherine Colliot-Thélène, Yves Duroux, Franck Fischbach, Stéphane Haber, and Jean-François Kervégan); to the members of l'ORSPERE [l'Observatoire Régional Rhône-Alpes sur la Souffrance Psychique en Rapport avec l'Exclusion] (especially to Jean-Furtos and Christian Laval); and to the Institut für Sozialforschung in Frankfurt (especially to Axel Honneth and Hermann Kocyba)—locations where the first fragments of this book were discussed.

Last but not least, I wish also to express my gratitude to Amy Allen, for having supported the project of an English translation of this book, and to Richard Lynch, for his careful translation and for having been so open to discussions concerning linguistic and conceptual issues.

THE EXPERIENCE OF INJUSTICE

INTRODUCTION

Political Philosophy and the Clinic of Injustice

One of the most striking phenomena within political thought in the last decades is very certainly the renewal of political philosophy as a specific style of discourse. Whereas the nineteenth century and a good portion of the twentieth saw political philosophy challenged both by the social sciences and by legal theory, the end of the last century saw various kinds of political philosophy reemerge, with each in its own way claiming to develop a theory of law and a normatively oriented social theory. At first glance, this seems entirely appropriate. Indeed, political discourse cannot do without normative claims (for example, to justice), and political philosophy appears well placed to solve the problems posed by these claims. However, many social critics on the left have felt a deep dissatisfaction with this renewal of normative political philosophy. There are many ways to explain this dissatisfaction. The most general is probably to note that most political philosophies are based upon an unclear conception of their object and of their political function.

Indeed, it can be observed that although normative political philosophies may take care to reflexively ground their concepts of society, of law, and of policy, they do not always sufficiently specify their conception of the political. Just as every philosophy of science (and every epistemology) presupposes a model of scientificity provided by the positive sciences, every political philosophy presupposes, on the one hand, a political model that crystallizes an ensemble of convictions connected to the relevant modes of political actions and, on the other hand, an image of the political effect of discourse, and of philosophical discourse in particular. Unthinkingly considered as personal or unprovable, these convictions and this image are rarely deemed worthy of a philosophical explication. But political philosophies require just such an elucidation if their value depends upon the fact that, for them, not only philosophy but also politics is at stake.

SEEKING CONSENSUS, OR TAKING SIDES?

Max Horkheimer argued, in 1937, that a philosophy that is self-aware must abandon the form of "traditional theory" in order to transform itself into a "critical theory" of society.[1] He thus meant to indicate that philosophy must recognize that every theoretical formulation is situated in a sociohistorical context that it unconsciously reflects and legitimizes so long as it fails to adopt a critical mode. Moreover, Horkheimer judges that philosophy's own ideal of rationality demands that philosophy take sides in favor of emancipation, by elaborating a social theory that is capable of embracing both the perspective and the hopes of those who have a stake in emancipation. The key elements of this line of argumentation are still relevant today, and ought to be mobilized in the normative interrogation of justice. A short discussion of the political presuppositions of political philosophy will bear this out.

This kind of philosophy elaborates certain theses that play out within a public space where different political discourses confront one another; it participates in this confrontation and thereby obtains a political dimension. Only two strategies are available for philosophy's reflection upon this dimension (and illustrations of both are easy to find within the principal orientations of contemporary political philosophy): the strategy of consensus and the strategy of taking sides. The first understands politics according to the model of a search for reasonable agreement among the greatest number, and has the philosopher play the role of a *mediator* whose statements should promote a search for consensus by facilitating the *translation* of diverse interests into a common language. This is par excellence the option adopted by John Rawls. For Rawls, constitutional democracies should offer their citizens a justification of the social and political institutions that would be acceptable to each, regardless of one's moral or religious commitments. These democracies should thus be based upon universally acceptable principles of justice and upon a principle of tolerance with respect to those conceptions of the good life that are compatible with these principles of justice. So political philosophy's assigned task can be understood as follows: In "avoiding deeper questions"[2] by "applying the principles of toleration to philosophy itself it is left to citizens individually to resolve for themselves the questions of religion, philosophy, and morals in accordance with the views they freely affirm."[3] In the context of such a conception, political philosophy appears as a theory of justification, and is reduced to a reflection upon the normative principles that allow philosophy to serve as a mediator/translator. What are the properties of different kinds of norms (different ways of expressing what ought to be)? What conditions give them legitimacy? When are they able to be the subject of a universal agreement? Such are the questions to be privileged. They are given almost exclusive attention. And yet, the theoretical problems encountered by normative philosophers are never only connected to the nature of norms. They are always just as much connected to the nature of concepts.

Of course, political discourses' confrontations in the public sphere are concerned with the norms that are able to legitimize a legal or social project, but these discourses are themselves structured by general concepts (freedom, equality, justice, security, etc.), and these general touchpoints are themselves traversed by political conflicts (between one or another definition of freedom, of equality, of justice, of security, etc.). Politics thus always has to deal with two kinds of discursive conflict: one proper to the confrontation of norms, the other to the tensions that traverse these concepts. But the controversies with respect to norms generally take on controversies relative to concepts. Debates about justice provide an illustration. It is in fact impossible to define principles of justice without confronting disputed questions concerning what constitutes a right, a liberty, and a good—in other words, without encountering conceptual problems that are just as much political problems. And what holds for political discourse is just as true for a philosophical discourse about politics. In fact, the philosophical description of the norms of political discourse is only possible in a philosophical discourse that, because it is itself political philosophy, is subject to the constraints of political discourse. Just like the political discourse on what ought to be, philosophical discourse about norms is not independent from the logical and political problems inscribed within the conceptual touchpoints of political discourse.

To clarify this point—crucial for the method employed in this book—
let's say that political concepts are "essentially contested concepts."[i] Walter
Bryce Gallie, best known for having formulated this expression, maintains
that political concepts, in particular, are characterized by the fact that our
use of them can be challenged by other uses, the legitimacy of which we can
challenge in turn.[4] This conflict is in fact about "essentially contested concepts" whose principal characteristics are as follows: (1) they are evaluative,
insofar as they are always tied to judgments concerning what ought to be;
(2) they are complex, inasmuch as the different meanings that they articulate can be organized in different ways; and (3) they can be formulated in
various ways that are in competition with each other, such that each use
of the concept is either aggressive or defensive and thus necessarily contested. These characteristic traits can be illustrated by the multiple meanings given to the term "democracy," or to "utopia," the uses of which even
more clearly show the vacillations of political meanings;[5] Gallie himself
defined "essentially contested concepts" with a sufficiently large number of
characteristics to allow for his methodological remarks to be put to divergent uses. I use it to underscore that the conceptual problems encountered
by political philosophy are inseparably both logical problems and political
problems. This entails, on the one hand, that no purely logical resolution of
these problems can be put forward (in the sense that a purely speculative
reduction of the aporias contained in the concepts of utopia or democracy,
for example, would be possible). It also entails, on the other hand, that it
is equally impossible to propose a purely political solution (by achieving a
consensus on the conceptual usage most favorable to the interests of all)
because the search for a consensus would presuppose agreement on the
legitimate uses of political vocabulary (i.e., the absence of essentially contested concepts).[6] An additional consequence can be immediately deduced:
in political philosophy, the strategy of consensus ultimately rests upon both
a naïve conception of political discourse (it underestimates the tensions
that traverse the communicative conditions of politics) and a concept of
politics that is too narrow to encompass the conflicts and indecisiveness
proper to politics, this "quandary proper to politics"[7] that shapes the discourse. Dependent upon inadequate presuppositions, the strategy of consensus necessarily leads to failure. If political philosophy wants to take on

---

i. In English in the original.

its political dimension, it must not try so much to avoid problems that cannot be hermetically sealed, as Rawls would like to do when he wishes to "avoid deeper questions," but rather to seek to open up political questions by elucidating the alternatives that have become settled in the vocabulary, through choices motivated by one or another political use of concepts.[8] It must adopt a different strategy, that of taking sides.

What constitutes "taking sides," or partiality, in philosophy? This, too, is an overlooked question (which must seem strange). Because political philosophy undergirds judgments about legal and social systems, mustn't we conclude that it always contributes to a process of social critique, that it gives support to those who struggle for the views it defends while opposing those who deny them? There is indeed a taking of sides, even if this partiality is rarely what philosophy identifies as its properly political dimension. From the essentially disputed aspect of political matters, it follows that side-taking is essential to the political dimension of a philosophy, but in general, the consensus model either bars philosophy from acknowledging its partiality, or it saddles philosophy with inadequate conceptions of partiality.

How do philosophies generally understand their own partiality? If we make reference to a rationalist model of social critique, political side-taking would be deduced from normative principles (as in theories of natural law), or from normative procedures (as in Rawls and Habermas) normatively grounded by the theory itself. The theory then claims its independence with respect to the particular sociohistorical contexts where its critical function is applied (this is the "traditional" form of theoretical activity, in Horkheimer's language), and it will present its own position as the result of a deduction rather than any partiality. The weakness of this first model is that a social critique is only politically effective when its discourse is consistent with that of individuals and groups who, living in a particular society, are interested in its transformation. If this condition is not fulfilled, the position held concerning the social order floats in an apolitical heaven; such is most likely the fate of any purely normative approach. Of course, the philosopher will always have the leisure to translate political conflicts into his own theoretical language, but he will not for all that connect with the political language of historical actors. The rationalist model of partiality fails to articulate the political dimension of political philosophy. To paraphrase John Dewey, the rationalist philosopher is content to translate human problems into philosophical problems instead of making philoso-phy a useful instrument for the resolution of people's problems.[9]

It may thus seem appropriate to turn to the model of hermeneutic cri-tique, developed in part precisely to respond to the kind of objection that has just been elaborated. We would then maintain that only the norms in force in a particular society can be intelligible to the individuals and groups affected by the critique of this society, and that these norms consequently constitute the only discursive instruments available to a social critique that is concerned with achieving its objectives.[10] However, in such a critical model, the espoused political options will not truly be able to be considered as par-tiality, because it is not so much a matter of deciding, for example, between different conceptions of justice to which all vaguely make reference—it is not so much a matter of taking sides as of arbitrating between them. In the end, all we have here is a refined version of the model based on consensus, in which the philosopher is no longer imagined as a mediator-translator but as a mediator-interpreter, and where philosophical mediation still pre-supposes a hidden agreement among all concerning certain fundamental intuitions while reducing the disagreements and the conceptual aporias to a superficial dross. The model of hermeneutic social critique presupposes a too-harmonious vision of cultures and customs, minimalizing the effects of divisions entailed by social domination and underestimating the violence of political conflicts that traverse symbolic spaces. Moreover, we might ask: Are the norms that are accepted within societies capable of adequately account-ing for the negative experiences of individuals who live in them?[11] In a world where the justifications themselves (even though socially accepted) display at least a certain degree of falsity insofar as they contribute to the justifica-tion of injustice, shouldn't political philosophy's task be as much to struggle against some of the shared forms of social justification as to better interpret them? Hermeneutic theories fail, as do constructivist theories, because of a deficit that is as much critical as political.

If political philosophy would take on its political dimension, what other solution is there except for it to understand itself as an instrument engaged in political struggles, as a discourse in the service of all those who, having experienced injustice, are interested in the transformation of an unjust social order? Taking sides thus means two things. On the one hand, at the level of reflection upon norms, it means defining modes of justification that are consistent with the political objectives sought by those experiencing social injustice, or, at least, modes of justification that would make it possible to reveal the fact of enduring injustice as an injustice. On the other hand, at the level of reflection on concepts, taking sides means defending conceptual alternatives that are able to take into account the claims of all those who endure injustice on a daily basis. This last demand is not at all incompatible with the earlier claim that politics deals with essentially contested concepts. The fact that conceptual aporias do not open up to exclusively logical or exclusively political solutions does not necessarily entail a skeptical position that would ascribe a purely relative value to all concepts. If political philosophy is to accept its political dimension as a form of side-taking, it must combine rational reflection upon logical aporias with an account of the political meaning of the various theoretically possible solutions. Conceptual problems being simultaneously logical and political, their resolution must also be both. Just as conceptual aporias emerge not only from logical problems but also from political problems, so too the resolution of these aporias will depend upon the elaboration of a logical solution in conformity with a political position, of a conjunction of logic and politics. We can thereby also address worries about normative political philosophy while still recognizing that normative political philosophy has its own legitimacy. Indeed, it is still up to political philosophy to determine the connection between logic and politics, using its own theoretical tools, even if the latter are applied to a political given whose irreducibility must be recognized—that is, to a political discourse that has itself created a kind of connection between logic and politics.

In the chapters that follow, my elaboration of concepts will thus attempt to incorporate both logical and political obligations. I will examine a certain number of essentially disputed ideas—justice, rights, institutions, identity, suffering, etc.—in an effort to recast and resituate classical debates of contemporary political philosophy: debates about theories of justice, about the relations between the just and the good, the connections between norms and institutions, the politics of identity, the relations between justice and care.[ii] For the most part, I will start with classical formulations presented by authors like John Rawls and Jürgen Habermas—or, to a lesser extent, Michael Walzer and Charles Taylor; Michel Foucault and Antonio Negri; and Pierre Bourdieu, Robert Castel, and Luc Boltanski—because they are the ones who have defined the terms of debate today, and because it is

---

ii. "Care" in English in the original.

politically and theoretically unproductive to neglect the ways in which problems are most often posed, even while maintaining the right to address only "real problems." To claim that the only politically relevant opposition is a rejection of the terms of the debate is to assume that withdrawal is a precondition for any hope of influencing these debates. This position has trapped most intellectuals of the radical left in the 1980s and 1990s, whether they were deconstructing, advocating "becoming minorities," or merely responding to criticisms of Marx. This approach, which probably emerged from the political defeats of the 1970s, was once a source of resistance, but now seems to be no more than an excuse for well-worn radicalism. Each chapter will start from the current state of these debates, not in order to invalidate them, but so that I can put forth a critique in the form of a displacement. I will seek to move them toward what can be called "the experience of injustice," by which I mean not only the experience of being subjected to injustice, but also a related set of politically crucial questions that previous debates have failed to truly take into account. The method I employ could be characterized as constituting a *clinic of injustice*, in two senses: on the one hand, in an Adornian sense,[12] because it begins with an interpretation (*Deutung*) of the uniqueness of negative experiences in order to draw out the physiognomy of the social world from them and to develop an appropriate normative language; on the other hand, in the sense of the "clinical method,"[13] because it takes as its starting point the vague definition of injustice (as socially created inequality) that accompanies the feeling of injustice experienced by those who are subjected to the social order and then, standing at their bedside, attempts to rearticulate the standard conceptions of justice through a study of their complaints and their responses. The clinic of injustice will treat these complaints and behaviors as indices or symptoms: it will investigate them for the specific characteristics of the injustices endured. These complaints and responses can be interpreted merely as indices or symptoms of injustice insofar as they only constitute accidental elements of injustice—that is to say, effects (since it is social situations that are just or unjust, and not the experience of those situations)—and effects that are not necessary (since an unjust situation does not have the same effect upon everyone, and is not necessarily experienced as unjust). These characteristics are not posited as indices or symptoms of injustice from the standpoint of an exterior authority on the experience of injustice, because more often than not the experience of injustice is accompanied by a feeling of injustice, and is so interpreted by those who live through it. Hence, my thinking about the experience of injustice is but an extension of a reflection born from the experience itself. Nor will it be possible to adopt an external standpoint in order to change socially accepted normative language in light of this experience. In fact, in the feeling of injustice, and in many of the denunciations of injustice, the term "justice" is invoked even when the use that is made of it is partially inadequate or approximate. We should begin from this kind of usage of the vocabulary of justice and injustice in order to identify unjust situations, and in order to elaborate those claims capable of giving an adequate account of unjust situations and guiding practical efforts intended to transform them.

In what follows, I will thus try to describe the experience of injustice in order to develop a model of social critique motivated by a taking of sides in favor of those who endure social injustice. If a description of injustice—or more precisely a characterization (a model description reproducing the typical characteristics)—can be united with such an objective, it is most likely because a general connection exists between description and justification of the social order. In the same way that a particular sort of justification presupposes a particular kind of description of the objects justified, a particular kind of description always presupposes value judgments about the objects worthy of being described.[14] To describe the experience of injustice by capturing its typical characteristics is to simultaneously attempt to invalidate both the socially established modes of justification and the socially established modes of description, by starting with what is able to escape from both. This will yield characterizations that are incompatible with socially established modes of justification and will demand a reformulation of normative principles from which we will describe the value of institutions and social relations. This process will begin with the behaviors and claims of those who endure injustice, not in order to legitimate them by translating them into the normative language of modern constitutional democracies, nor to interpret them in terms of principles of justification in force in the various social spaces,[15] nor even to articulate the forces that aspire to change in the language of what already is, but on the contrary, to demonstrate the simple fact that these behaviors and claims cannot be articulated in the established normative lexicon and to demand its transformation. Should we interpret the world or change it? It may be that we still face this Marxian choice.

It is rare for social critique to undertake to destabilize discourses of legitimation not through a critique of their foundations or contradictions, but rather through a critique of the procedures that construct the object that these discourses attempt to legitimize. Here again, Adorno is an anomalous case. At the very time when, with Husserl and Wittgenstein, philosophy placed the question of description at the heart of these investigations, Adorno undertook an unprecedented critical intervention: neither a definition of meanings through the description of a term's uses, nor a description of the world such as it is given to consciousness; but rather a description of the world as it is not generally perceived, such that it cannot be truly signified in language games structured by defenses against suffering, collective denial in the face of disturbances, and the process by which domination is legitimated. In what follows, we will not find a simple description of consciousness of the world, nor a simple description of uses associated with language games, but rather an approach that begins from the characterization of (psychological, moral and social) facts that consciousness does not want to see and that socially accepted normative principles make it difficult to express.

At a time when justifications take the overall form of media descriptions of the world (aiming to satisfy consumers with images and words, to foster identification with the described reality, to downplay or entirely erase social suffering and the effects of injustice and domination), at a time when powerful discourses of legitimization seem to be in retreat, except in the form of xenophobic populism and fundamentalisms of every stripe, the Adornian idea that ideology has become the form in which society appears to individuals (an idea inspired by a reformulation of the problem of commodity fetishism) seems to regain a new relevance.[16] It raises a specific challenge to social critique, one that a clinic of injustice attempts to take up. It is not so much a question of measuring the disparity and incompatibility between normative principles and the situations to which they are supposed to apply, as of interrogating the modes of describing social reality that are associated with these principles, and of setting certain characterizations (model counterdescriptions) against them to argue for a modification of the meaning of these principles. Such an approach does not at all claim to gain access to a pure reality independent of any theoretical framework or shared vocabulary, nor to a true description that would allow us to determine the value of all other related descriptions and discourses.[17] Our descriptions are always permeated by socially accepted cognitive and evaluative frameworks. It is nevertheless the case that individuals' ordinary knowledge of the injustices that they suffer and the social contexts that produce them are able to ground alternative social descriptions. In general, situated knowledge, while partial (read: disabled) and rudimentary (read: incoherent), is richer than the generalizations by which the social is automatically grasped and more enlightening than scholarly discussion sometimes admits. Moreover, the dominated and the deprived[iii] have knowledge that opens up the possibility of a subversion of socially accepted normative principles when the latter are wrongly applied to the situations that they experience. If we articulate this ordinary knowledge, if we go along with the reflexive dynamics by which individuals explain it, and if we extend it by mobilizing the resources of social science and philosophy, then we have an opportunity to alter the landscape. It would become possible to bring out those elements of social experience that destabilize the socially dominant representations and the debates that rest on them.

But the experience of injustice holds the capacity for a potential critique, not only as a describable object, but also in itself. If starting from a description of *experiences* is of interest, this is also because certain negative experiences suggest that what is at stake in our experiences exceeds what we are able to express in normative language games.[18] To be sure, the meaning of normative language is performed within the forms of life to which it is connected, as Wittgenstein has pointed out, but it is also enacted in these negative experiences where the intolerable character of particular uses is felt, in the experiences that bring out the socially pathological character of our forms of life.[19] These experiences are not merely the site where the meaning of this language and the limits of its use are defined—they are just as much the place where the necessity of its transformation is demonstrated.

And so in what follows, with the phrase "the experience of injustice," I will mean an ensemble of characteristics that should be considered as indices or symptoms of the injustice of situations, but I will also mean the processes triggered by *normative expectations* (in the sense that they focus on what should be, in contrast to factual expectations that are concerned with what will happen) that constitute the concerns about which various definitions of justice are a more or less appropriate explanation. To characterize the experience of injustice is thus more than merely specifying

---

iii. See the translator's note for a discussion of these two terms.

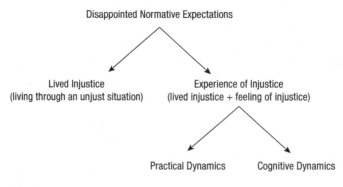

FIGURE 1

injustice beginning from indices or symptoms; it is to recontextualize the language games of justice and injustice by connecting them to these normative expectations and to the *practical and cognitive dynamics* that arise from the disappointment of these expectations. (See figure 1.)

THE CONCEPT OF THE EXPERIENCE OF INJUSTICE

The need for a philosophical reflection specifically bearing upon the experience of injustice has already been noted by Judith Shklar, who was astonished, in *The Faces of Injustice*, by how little attention political philosophy has generally given to injustice. Inspired by a Wittgensteinian approach, she found it deplorable that the unjust would merely be considered as the absence of justice, or as the opposite that allows it to be defined. She asks, "Why then do most philosophers refuse to think about injustice as deeply or as subtly as they do about justice?"[20] In fact, experiences of injustice ought to be considered as sui generis phenomena that offer a critical perspective on definitions of justice. However, the approach taken in what follows here is not at all the same as Shklar's. While she is principally interested in individuals' perceptions of the injustice of their situations, what is meant here by the experience of injustice is the manner in which it affects the lives of those who endure it and inaugurates dynamics that will develop demands [*dynamiques revendicatives*][iv]—one of the aims of this book is precisely to

iv. See the translator's note for a discussion of this phrase.

question the purposes of political philosophy, starting from the specific type of normativity that emerges in these dynamics. While Shklar theorizes the experience of injustice from within a skeptical perspective, questioning whether the discourse on injustice can overcome the aporias that run through our feelings regarding justice and injustice, my critical perspective envisions shifting the debates and re-elaborating the definitions. According to Shklar, the fact that the application of principles of justice in democratic societies is compatible with the emergence of a generalized social injustice could only lead to doubt about the value of principles of justice, but not to the possibility of replacing those principles with new ones. Common sense has access to a sufficiently clear notion of injustice to identify its different forms, but it remains incapable of articulating effective solutions—one usually experiences injustice without access to an experience of justice that could answer it.[21] From the compatibility of an unbridled social injustice with a legal and social order that conforms to the best-established principles of justice, Shklar deduces neither the necessity of changing the definitions of justice nor the necessity of transforming the social order. On the contrary, I conclude therefrom, on the one hand, that we must re-elaborate the principles of justice in light of the *normative expectations* that define the stakes of the experience of injustice, and, on the other, that we must seek out both the possibility for and the nature of a legitimate transformation of the existing legal and social order within these *dynamics* that are born from the experience of injustice.

By "experience of injustice," I will mean on the one hand a *feeling* of injustice resulting from the nonsatisfaction of the normative expectations of those who undergo injustice, and on the other hand, an ensemble of *practical orientations* (reactions including the rejection of unjust situations, or flight from or struggle against them) and of *cognitive* processes (the passage of unsatisfied expectations from a tacit to an explicit stage, reflection upon the injustice of a situation, research into the best responses given the available resources, etc.)—practical orientations and cognitive processes that are able to come together in the form of *demands*. The concept of the experience of injustice thus designates the injustice lived in its practical and cognitive dimensions of a potentially transformative action guided by a feeling; it designates living through unjust situations (lived injustice) accompanied by an at least inchoate consciousness of injustice (a feeling of injustice).

Injustice does not necessarily produce either a feeling of injustice or action in protest.[v] It is entirely possible that the nonsatisfaction of normative expectations, however fundamental, never attains the form of a feeling of injustice, that it simply leads to forms of dissatisfaction and suffering that individuals do not grasp as injustices. We can speak in this case of a *lived injustice* (and then, it is only *for us* that this lived experience is one of injustice) *that is not lived as* an injustice or that does not get so far as to transform itself into an *experience of injustice* (one of the tasks of social critique is to articulate a normative framework that would allow this transformation). This kind of lived injustice will be illustrated in situations sometimes characterized by the term "social suffering" (chapter 6). Moreover, lived injustice can provoke psychological dynamics that even undermine the normative expectations that allow us to speak of a lived injustice—this is the case of "psychic suffering" in the strict sense of the term, at the very limit of the experience of injustice, of lived injustice, and the very problem of injustice (chapter 7). It is only when the living through of an unjust situation is accompanied by a feeling of injustice that it can lead to practical activity directed towards the transformation of a context presented as unjust (one of the tasks of social critique is to begin with the movements demanding such transformative actions and to demonstrate their legitimacy). But it is also possible that the feeling of injustice merely leads to a desire for symbolic compensation for injustice, or to vengeance, or even to a self-destructive activity—that is, to an activity directed against a particular individual (as, for example, when injustice is considered as an irreparable humiliation), instead of leading to an action oriented toward political demands.

To begin with the experience of injustice is to adopt the perspective of movements that lead from a negative experience to the possibility of a protest action directed against the conditions of this negative experience, in order to elaborate a model of social critique whose principle is defined by the resources and motivations of struggles against social injustice in general. But this model must also account for the difficulty of transforming injustice into a struggle against injustice. As I suggested in the Preface, we must at least qualify the thesis expressed by Hans Joas[22] (and largely presupposed by Michel Foucault and Jacques Rancière) that social struggles constitute

---

v. See the translator's note for a discussion of this phrase.

the primary means by which societies can correct their pathologies and orient themselves on the path of democratization of democracy. In a way, it is only the luckiest of injustice's victims who have the opportunity to make the conditions of their lives the object of political demands in the form of social struggles and to thus bring disputes and disagreements into the public sphere. For social critique, the perspective of social movements remains too narrow, and from this statement it is tempting to declare relevant the prioritarian thesis that social justice should be conceived by beginning with the worst injustices, those that do not give rise to social struggles. However, the aporias of prioritarianism are too numerous for it to be maintained (a point to which we will return). Social critique must indeed address itself to the entire spectrum of injustices that are endured. It must, first of all, endeavor to make explicit the normative potential of social struggles, thus acknowledging the rationality of disagreement.[23] Next, it must endeavor to articulate the frameworks that enable lived injustices to transform into experiences of injustice that are capable of opening up into social movements, thus contributing to "the insurrection of subjugated knowledges."[24] Finally, it must try to produce a definition applicable even to injustices whose effects are too deep to be able to be lived as injustices. It must produce a model that simultaneously applies to the diurnal politics of public demands and to the "nocturnal politics" which wrestles against those elements constituting stumbling blocks that prevent routinized dominations and ordinary exclusions from becoming the objects of publicly established political struggles.[25]

Various objections immediately spring forth to challenge the interest of such a shift in the terrain of the experience of injustice. A first kind of objection consists in condemning, from a logical point of view, the circular character of an approach that begins from injustice in order to define justice. If the concept of injustice presupposes the concept of justice, doesn't the attempt to define justice starting from injustice conceal a fallacious assumption of the conclusion (the presupposition of a definition of justice in our description of injustice)? And how could it then claim to justify a definition of justice? As to whether it actually assumes the conclusion, it certainly does, if we understand that to mean that adopting the perspective of the experience of injustice comes down to taking sides against unjust situations and for attempts aiming to transform them. But insofar as the principles of political philosophy are always linked to partiality (because its concepts are always essentially contested), this fails to constitute any kind of serious objection to the approach undertaken here. As to whether it is actually circular, that too is undeniable, but not in the sense that one merely deduces as a conclusion what was initially a given. On the contrary, this approach consists rather in showing that the meanings of what is commonly called "justice" elaborate the stakes that exceed what is expressed by the usual definitions of justice, so that we are justified in undertaking a re-elaboration of the definitions of justice.

A second series of objections consists in underlining, from a sociological point of view, that the feeling of injustice varies depending upon the social environment as a function of various socially accepted principles of justice, such that it would be impossible to bring the experience of injustice into play against principles of justice and to arrive at a general definition of social justice.[26] These objections do not seem to be any more convincing. Certain experiences of injustice effectively correspond to situations that, within a given social space, violate the accepted principles of justification. This is the case, for example, when the stipulations of a worker's employment contract are not honored. In such a case, it is undeniable that the victims of injustice presuppose a socially accepted representation of justice, and that they are only demanding that it be applied. But there are other sorts of situations in which the experience of injustice has the capacity to alter the victims of injustice's ideas of justice. Regarding injustice, our consciousness is not only capable of issuing judgments with the help of a pre-established principle, valid within the social space in which we are situated; we can also experience the inability to adequately formulate a feeling of injustice with the help of the socially available ideas of justice.

To clarify this point, it can be useful to recall the meanings that Jean-François Lyotard gave to the concepts of "differend" and "wrong." For Lyotard, the differend, in contrast to litigation, designates a conflict that cannot be solved by means of an available rule; and a wrong results from the injustice borne by a party from the application of a rule that does not acknowledge that party's claims.[27] Litigation thus defines those plaintiffs who are privileged with the power to demand reparation for injustice that they have experienced, in stating the rule that has been violated. Violations of employment law are an illustration. Conversely, a wrong defines victims who are deprived of the means to give evidence of the injustice that they have suffered.[28] Employment situations also illustrate this, but this time in a case where the experience of injustice is due to the execution of an employment contract in conformity with labor laws. In making reference to the Marxian conception of exploitation as extortion of surplus labor, Lyotard takes the example of wage labor in which the symmetry of the labor contract (a contract between two legal persons endowed with equal rights) forbids the employee from presenting what he has experienced (the surplus-labor extracted by the employer and all the domination and suffering that goes along with it) as an injustice, at the risk of invalidating himself as a legal subject who freely contracted with his employer.[29] In such a case, the employee experiencing (more precisely, "living") the exploitation as an injustice is deprived of the normative language that would allow him to describe it as an injustice. For Lyotard, the experience of a wrong is unproductive by itself, and it falls to the philosopher, the poet, or the political theoretician to create the language that will allow those who suffer to escape their silence: "What is at stake in a literature, in a philosophy, in a politics perhaps, is to bear witness to differends by finding idioms for them."[30]

The thesis defended in what follows is, on the contrary, that the experience of injustice brings with it a specific productivity. It sparks a cognitive shift when it takes the form of a wrong: it makes one see the principles differently. In this sort of negative experience, the very consciousness of justice finds itself altered because the principles that had been hitherto judged legitimate (for example, the principles of employment law) can no longer claim a complete legitimacy. We could say that this negative experience takes the form of an experience of consciousness in the Hegelian sense of the term.[31] The experience of the unsuitability of our knowledge (as it happens, of our normative knowledge) for the objects to which it applies compels a recasting of this knowledge and this recasting changes our vision of the world. The crucial point is most likely that the experience of injustice is not simply the disqualification of normative knowledge, but that it is equally a call for a recasting of this normative knowledge—as it happens, a transformation in one's acceptance of the socially established principles of justice. This recasting can itself take two forms: one of *extension*, when the cognitive content of the experience of injustice is linked with the realization of an illegitimate restriction, that is to say, to a quantitative unsuitability; and one of *transformation*, when the cognitive content of the experience of injustice is linked with the realization of the qualitative unsuitability of a principle.

The recasting can thus, first of all, take the form of a simple extension of the meaning of the principles of justice, when an injustice is due to the fact that a normative principle is established under restrictive conditions of application—this is the case, for example, of various restrictions that have impacted political rights and especially the right to vote (active and passive citizens, men and women, citizens and foreigners). The injustice can thus give rise to a "disagreement"[32] in Rancière's sense: the parties in litigation do not manage to understand each other because they have two different understandings (as it happens, two different extensions) of the principles that are in dispute, but they can and do discuss them by invoking the established principles of justice. When they discuss them, the victims of injustice articulate the insufficiency of the restrictive interpretation of the principle and demand the broadening of this interpretation (as in the case these days of undocumented workers' demands).

The recasting could also take the form of a more radical modification of the principles of justice, when there is no understanding of the established normative principles that would allow a lived situation to be described as unjust. The victims of injustice can demand the transformation of the social conditions behind this kind of injustice, but this demand no longer implies the merely unrestricted use of the applicable principles of justification. An adequate expression of the injustice implies that other pertinent criteria are taken into account in the definition of justice. Such is the case for the feminist movement, whose political demands have been quite explicitly accompanied by a call for the transformation of definitions of justice, so that the voices of the dominated may be fully heard;[33] but we will see later that such transformations of the principles of justification were already at the heart of the socialist and communitarian critiques of liberalism, and that these transformations are also called for by forms of social injustice linked to the denial of identity and to social suffering. In such situations, those who suffer injustice can thus fail to express it,[34] but this failure is not the rule, because the experience of injustice prompts one to question the validity of the principles that prevent this experience from being articulated, and thus motivates a demand for the transformation of principles of justice rather than silent acceptance.

If the experience of a wrong is the experience of the failure of our normative knowledge, it means that something is happening in the experience of injustice that does not exclusively depend upon our normative knowledge, and it means that what is at play within the experience exceeds what can be said about it. The experience of injustice is always the experience of the failure of an ensemble of fundamental normative expectations, and its expression is always conditioned by an ensemble of socially available normative ideas. It is these normative expectations that, in the eyes of those who endure injustice, are liable to withdraw their authority from the socially available ideas of justice. It is thus these normative expectations that could lead to efforts to extend or transform the definitions of justice. The fact that different social spaces make reference to different principles of justice does not constitute an objection to this claim, as soon as we acknowledge that the experience of justice does not exclusively depend upon a judgment applying a valid norm within a particular social space. We must admit that the principles of justice in effect do not provide any general definition of social justice because they vary in different social spaces,[35] but we must also add that the experience of injustice can lead to a general definition of social justice because it is in that experience that the general possibility appears of an incompatibility between these particular principles of justice and the general normative expectations that govern our relationship with the entire social world.

A third series of objections consists in underlining, from a philosophical point of view, that the feeling of injustice is vague and imprecise, not only because it varies among individuals and social groups, but above all because it clearly goes beyond the domain of questions relevant to justice. Thus one can observe that, often, the victims of misfortune (of naturally occurring hardships, such as weather-related disasters) try to illegitimately present themselves as the victims of injustices (hardships for which other people or society is responsible).[36] The feeling of injustice thus leads to a conflation of problems. It is undeniable that the feeling of injustice is variable and sometimes confused, and that reflection on justice always brings about a better understanding as to the nature of justice and injustice than a simple feeling. All these observations serve to underscore that the feeling of injustice can at most be considered as an indication or a symptom. But the problem is precisely to know what status is to be granted to such indications and symptoms in a reflection upon justice. The whole question is, indeed, to determine whether reflection upon justice should start from a rational construction or an interpretation of the norms of justice, or rather, on the contrary, from a description of injustice guided by the words and behavior of those who suffer it.

Two arguments militate for the latter option. Remember first of all that the perspective of those who suffer injustice is always different from that of those who observe it at a distance, and it is a safe bet that those who suffer injustice are more likely to have an adequate understanding than those who merely observe it. It is enough, here too, to mention Shklar and the example of natural disasters: those who are spared tend to see it as a simple misfortune and not an injustice, whereas the hardest-hit victims more easily perceive the social dysfunctions that magnified its consequences.[37] Our perception of the world depends upon our social position, our practical dispositions, and the social knowledge that goes along with them. This is also true for our perceptions of justice and injustice, as has been underscored by feminist standpoint epistemologists.[38] Marx had already noted this, when he underlined the critical perspectives contained in the standpoint of the dominated and deprived, regardless of whether it was a question of their position in the factory[39] or their position in society.[40] To approach social justice from the perspective of the experience of injustice also means trying to make the most of the resources of the social vision of the dominated and deprived, without any illusions as to the purity and the truth of this social vision: by itself, the experience of injustice does not deliver an understanding of justice; it only defines a critical perspective and some demands. Must we add that, particularly concerning political philosophy, victims' perspectives on the social order could provide a valuable service by bringing a corrective to the academic bias (belonging to a social position that is both detached and overdetermined by the internal stakes of the academic world) of the professionals of normative reflection?

Recall, in the second place, that political concepts draw their specificity not only from their essentially contested character, but also from their incorporation of a very particular kind of practical concept. Concepts such as equality, freedom, or even justice have an essentially abolitionist insofar as their principal function is to struggle against inequality, domination, and injustice.[41] They thus have a practical dimension that is different from what is characteristic of moral concepts. If the latter are all also concerned with action, it is insofar as they provide the elements for decisions to act in controversial situations and as they enable judgments about past or anticipated actions. They are only practical insofar as they are related to a decision or a judgment. Political concepts, too, are concerned with decisions and judgments, but they also comprise a supplementary dimension that is aimed towards transformation of the social world. The meaning of the concept of justice is specifically concerned with the transformation of unjust situations, and this is why it must be recontextualized not only in light of the normative expectations that define the stakes that are explicated in the definitions of justice, but also in light of the dissenting movements that are born from the nonsatisfaction of these expectations.

In other words, the domain of political questions is distinct from that of moral questions because politics is not merely a discursive exchange of reasons for action and of evaluative judgments, but is also action oriented towards social transformation. More precisely, political action draws its specificity from the fact that it begins in the refusal of certain social situations (which always have to do with particular social inequalities, of which certain groups are victims), that it develops within a struggle against social groups interested in maintaining these situations, and that it aims for a more egalitarian social situation. To speak of a struggle implies an orientation opposed to the action. Indeed, political action can thus aim at a simple defense, that is to say, a reinforcement, of inequalities, but in this conservative or reactionary form, it still presupposes the kind of political action oriented toward the transformation of unequal situations against which it struggles or whose emergence it anticipates. Political action thus draws its specificity from its connection to the experience of socially produced inequalities, that is to say, with the experience of injustice—a specificity that the traditional approaches to justice are quite unable to take into account. Ultimately, if we want to think politically about justice, it would even be wise to set the perspective of justice (that of judgments starting from principles of justice) against that of the experience of injustice. In order to more precisely spell out this thesis, I will speak of a triple connection between the experience of injustice and political action.

First characteristic: The experience of justice is a qualitative experience that implies a qualitative demand (the abolition of injustice), whereas the grammar of language games treats justice as a quantitative shift (the principles of justice most often reduce the just to a proportion and, in the same way, to the *more or less* just). If we accept social psychological approaches like those of John Stacy Adams,[42] the feeling of injustice is carried out in the form of a comparison, such that there would never be an occasion to oppose (as we have just done) the qualitative dimension of the experience of justice and the quantitative grammar of language games describing justice and injustice. The feeling of injustice in working conditions, for example, is often grounded in a comparison between different levels of remuneration as a function of the social utility and the assessed onerousness of the work.[43] The feeling of injustice seems here to be due to the application of a socially accepted (and quantitative) principle of justice, according to which one's salary ought to be proportional to the work's difficulty and value, and it seems to assume a comparison (a quantitative assessment) of the work's onerousness. The argument doesn't appear convincing, insofar as it fails to distinguish between the dynamic leading to demands for justice, i.e., political demands (the factors that give experience the form of an experience of injustice and lead one to make demands), and the logic of the *public justification* of those demands. The feeling of injustice in a work situation offers one of the best illustrations of why this distinction is necessary. Demands for pay raises never depend in the first instance on a comparison of different professions, but rather the feeling that the salary does not show evidence of an acknowledgment of the onerousness or social value of the work, a feeling that the salary expresses a kind of contempt for the people who do the work. Now, one never wants to be a little less disrespected; either one refuses to be disrespected, or one accepts it. It is only at a later time, when reflecting upon the best means for a demand to succeed, that the public defense of the legitimacy of the demand will lead one to present the qualitative demand for a recognition of one's work in the quantitative language game of the virtues and specific challenges of different occupations.

Second characteristic: The experience of injustice is referential, in the sense that it is always the experience of a particular injustice produced by a particular situation, whereas in reducing injustice to the simple violation of a principle of justice, the problematic of justice makes it possible to consider injustice in general, independent of the social contexts that give rise to it. The feeling is certainly not liable to furnish on its own an adequate description of the processes that led this or that injustice to be produced in one social situation or another, but it nevertheless carries within itself the demand that the felt injustice correspond to a specific social situation, along with a demand for the social transformation of that situation.

Third characteristic: The experience of injustice is affective, insofar as it is defined by the feeling and the practical dynamics that inaugurate the struggle against an unjust situation. Certainly, it cannot be a question of leaving politics to the dynamism of affects that, by themselves, make possible neither an identification of injustices nor a definition of the relevant forms of struggle against them. But the claim that we should begin from the experience of injustice does not at all imply that all of its results will be good: it only defines a point of view from which the value of struggles against injustice can be interpreted. Nor does the claim to begin from the experience of injustice take as its objective the avoidance of the question of what criteria legitimate struggles against injustice. Its only function is to ask the question in light of a specifically political normativity, instead of seeking them quite simply in moral or legal norms (respect for liberties or dignity), or in moral or legal conceptions of politics (politics as applied ethics or submission of the collective will to rules of law).

In an earlier work, I based the adoption of the point of view of injustice on a moral argument: in a generally unjust society, the only way to escape the moral hypocrisy that consists in trying to live a moral or good life while passively participating in injustice is to struggle against injustice.[44] In the pages that follow, the concept of the experience of injustice is more specifically joined with a tripartite methodological intent: (1) to take account of the properly political dimension of the concept of justice by linking it to the practical dynamics of resistance that make it an abolitionist concept; (2) to define a critical point of view on the logical and political tensions that belong to essentially contested conceptions of justice, by starting from the normative expectations that, on the one hand, underpin the socially accepted conceptions of justice and, on the other, are liable to withdraw all their normative force from these conceptions; and (3) to reformulate, enlarge, and transform the usual definitions of justice by starting from the experience of justice as a negative experience endowed with its own cognitive resources.[45]

THE PARADIGM OF RECOGNITION

The model of social critique that I am trying to elaborate takes the theoretical concept of *recognition* as its principal theoretical engine. To achieve this goal, we do not need to undertake an exhaustive study of all the meanings that can be assigned to the term "recognition," as Paul Ricoeur has done in *The Course of Recognition*. Generally, it is unlikely that a survey of the various accepted uses attributed to a term in a dictionary would hold real philosophical interest. And despite the high regard that we hold for a thinker like Ricoeur, it is somewhat surprising in political philosophy that dictionaries would hold so much authority as to put one "on guard against any reduction to one particular sense, so frequent among contemporary thinkers—for example, the recognition of individuals in situations of discrimination against them."[46] The motivation for a survey of the meanings of the term "recognition" is of course to spell out its cognitive aspects (recognition as a form of knowledge of the other) and practical aspects (recognition as conduct with respect to the other), but as Ricoeur himself admits, as soon as recognition is interpreted within the Hegelian landscape of mutual recognition, as in this work, the cognitive aspect of recognition (representation of the specific characteristics and value of an individual or group) no longer has much to do with recognition in the theoretical sense of the term (recognition in the sense of *re-cognition*: recognition of an object or individual, recognition that two phenomena belong to a single entity, etc.). For our purposes here, it will thus suffice to describe for ourselves the various characteristic traits of mutual recognition.

Hegel tried to articulate the logic of mutual recognition in the famous chapter 4-A of the *Phenomenology of Spirit*, whose argument we should briefly recall.[47] Given that I apprehend who I am through the intermediary of an other's acts towards me, through his speech and his behavior, I must attempt to demonstrate my value to him through my acts, in order to maintain a positive awareness of myself. Recognition thus intervenes as a condition for self-consciousness and as the object of a demand for which my own acts serve as the carrier. But in order that the other could be the object of such a practical demand (practical in the sense that it concerns the other's act toward me, and that it is mediated by my own acts), I must first recognize the value of his judgment. In this way, the practical demand for recognition presupposes in its turn a twofold cognitive recognition: an identification of the other as a recognizer (the recognition of the other as a valued being whose judgment, for this very reason, matters to me) that anticipates an identification of the valuation expressed in his behavior (a recognition of his behavior as testifying to a favorable or unfavorable evaluation of my own value). In what follows, it will indeed be a matter of recognition in these senses: of recognition (1) as identification of the other (as one of those I identify as my enemy—for example in a context of social conflict—and whose judgment thus matters little to me; or, on the contrary, as one of those I identify as my peer—for example, in a work situation—and from whom I obtain an image of my own value); (2) as identification of his behavior with respect to me (as a behavior expressing an evaluation of my person or my acts); and (3) as an evaluation by the other of my acts or my person (of the value of my work or my culture, for example).

In what follows, I will also not undertake a historical investigation of the philosophical constructions of recognition. The task is rather to show that the concept of recognition can contribute to the elaboration of a critical theory that would evaluate the political and social problems of our time. To ascribe these tasks to the theory of recognition entails situating oneself within a tradition that goes back to Hegel and even to Johann Fichte, whose principal figures include Karl Marx, Alexandre Kojève, Jean-Paul Sartre, Simone de Beauvoir, Frantz Fanon, Jürgen Habermas, and Axel Honneth.[48] Honneth, who was initially a student of Habermas, took from the latter the idea of a critical theory of society founded upon the analysis of the normative content of social life. For Habermas, the concept of communicative action served to underscore that social interaction presupposes forms of linguistic agreement between individuals and, in the same way, that normative demands structure social life from within even as they go beyond it with their validity claims. Honneth acknowledges that such a theory of the communicative presuppositions of social life provides a critical vantage point that is relevant for a society in which the social spheres that affirm collective deliberation and the demand for a free agreement among all are becoming ever narrower and narrower. But he maintains that it is still insufficient, in two respects: on the one hand, because it does not really take account of social struggles' active contribution to social evolution and the democratization of democracy;[49] on the other hand, because it does not truly manage to bring the motivations of those who are practically engaged in struggles against social injustice into its theoretical framework.[50] Honneth's approach thus consists in elaborating a hermeneutics of social life, on the basis of a phenomenology of the experiences of injustice, in order to account for the specific normative content of social struggles. In *The Struggle for Recognition: The Moral Grammar of Social Conflicts*,[51] he adopts the thesis that social critique must take the ways in which society's *communicative expectations* are not respected as its guiding thread. But he adds that the perspective that reduces the communicative element to a linguistic element is too narrow, because experiences of injustice are based upon injuries to both the linguistic and *nonlinguistic* communicative presuppositions that the concept of recognition identifies. In fact, the expectation of recognition is a communicative normative expectation that can be satisfied either through modes of linguistic communication or through nonlinguistic modes of communication (such as the modes of self-presentation in interactions). These recognitive expectations constitute, so to speak, the normative context for various forms of linguistic communication, in such a way that they could cause the latter to lose all their validity as forms of communication by making them appear empty (when, in linguistic communication, the other seems only to want to extract recognition from us, by speaking through us rather that to us),[52] or distorted (when the recognitive effects that communication tends to produce seem incompatible with our expectations for recognition).[53]

To put the linguistic moment into proper perspective, Honneth explains that the interaction is not only structured by the presupposition that one can try to resolve disagreements within linguistic means, but also by the recognitive expectations that are anchored in the intersubjective constitution of individuality and which are expressed through both linguistic and nonlinguistic means. Insofar as individuation is a result of socialization, individuality is intersubjectively constituted and this entails that it is intersubjectively vulnerable: because the individual's moral integrity depends upon recognition by the other, the moral injuries of a denial of recognition are critical events. Only an enlargement of the communicative paradigm toward nonlinguistic communicative forms is likely to lead to the "moral grammar of social conflicts" that is required by critical theory. In fact, the actual motivations behind social movements come under the aegis of different forms of the feeling of injustice, which themselves must be interpreted as subjective experiences of the denial of recognition—they are explained as different forms of social disrespect or of the denial of socially established recognition.

According to Honneth, who for his part takes up a typology articulated in Hegel's early work, we should distinguish three kinds of recognition. The first sphere of recognition is the sphere of intimacy, where the subject finds the satisfaction of its fundamental emotional needs. Recognition's vector here is love, which facilitates the establishment of a positive relation to oneself that takes the form of *self-confidence*, that is, belief in the value of one's psychophysical existence. The second sphere is recognition of the equal value of persons. The vector for recognition here is the law (rights), which makes possible the establishment of a positive relation to oneself that takes the form of *self-respect*, that is, certainty in the value of one's freedom. The third sphere is recognition of one's contributions to society. Recognition's subject is thus work, and the vector includes various forms of wages, direct and indirect, and social solidarity. Here, the positive relation to oneself takes the form of *self-esteem*, that is, belief in the social value of one's activities. This positive relation to oneself, intersubjectively constituted in these three distinct social spheres, is intersubjectively vulnerable in such a way that it is always inseparable from a need for others' confirmation; it is in this way that the need for recognition designates an ensemble of *normative* (in the sense that they are not merely desires but rather requirements) and *fundamental* (in the sense that they define the decisive stakes for us) expectations.

Thus understood, the concept of recognition simultaneously makes reference to the expectations that are the blood supply for all social relations and that can be satisfied or not (recognition or nonrecognition). Tacit expectations supply lifeblood to interactions (we are not aware that we expect recognition in our ordinary interactions), but they can become conscious in situations where recognition is denied, or can even be transformed into demands for *recognition*. The critical function of the concept of recognition emerges, first of all, because it has a normative side (it designates a set of expectations concerning the behavior of others, or the responses of institutions) and a factual side (de facto recognition or nonrecognition, that is, the satisfaction or nonsatisfaction of recognitive expectations). It is due to this conjunction that the theory of recognition can take the form of a critical theory of society—a theory lofty enough to encompass normative reflection on the principles of social justice, while still rooted in the description of various institutions and social relations, even including singular interactions that give rise to injustice. The critical function of the concept of recognition emerges, secondly, because the passage from tacit *expectations* of recognition to a *demand* for recognition provides a model for analyzing how negative social experiences can produce reflexive dynamics about what is at play within them and about how to offer solutions through dissent. To clarify the relationship between the approach developed in these pages and Honneth's, I must add a general remark about the relation between recognition and justice.

For Honneth, the connection between recognition and justice is primarily empirical and logical. The empirical connection is psychological in nature: the different forms of the feeling of justice always seem to presuppose a feeling of disrespect or of the denial of recognition. The logical connection is a function of the fact that justice and recognition are coextensive. It reflects the possibility of subsuming our various intuitions of justice under the concept of recognition: the space of intuitions about justice is entirely encompassed within the domain circumscribed by the three spheres of recognition. I do not wish to dispute these two arguments, but rather to add that if it is legitimate to study justice and injustice in terms of recognition, this is also because the concept of justice presupposes the concept of recognition. In other words, the connection between justice and recognition is not only based upon a psychological relation and their coextensive domains, but also upon the very meaning of the idea of justice. It is clear, in fact, that the demand for justice is not merely a demand for equality or for the absence of illegitimate inequality, but also a demand for action that puts an evaluation into practice. This is exactly the meaning of the broadest possible definition of justice that could be given: let each receive what is his due as a function of his acts. An act of justice with regard to the other thus presupposes a double act of recognition: a cognitive recognition of his value (of his person or of his acts), and an action that practically expresses this recognition (a practical recognition of his value). If we now understand the concept of justice as no longer a descriptive concept (describing what is characteristic of just actions) but as a normative concept (expressing a demand), connections between justice and recognition once again emerge. The demand for justice implies a complex relation between a *self-consciousness* (the awareness an individual has of his own value or that of his acts) and a *practical effort* (the attempt to assert the value of one's person or act for the other) consisting in a demand that is itself twofold, because it expects of the other that he will evaluate things appropriately (cognitive recognition, in the sense of identifying a person as a person worthy of being respected or an act as one that has value) and that he will put this evaluation into practice (practical recognition). Hence, the idea of justice implies a certain kind of connection on the one hand between cognitive recognition and practical recognition, and on the other hand between the demand for recognition and the possibility that this demand could be satisfied. And this kind of connection is at the heart of the Hegelian concept of mutual recognition.

By interpreting the connection between recognition and justice as an analytic connection, and not merely as an empirical and logical connection, I believe I can make an argument to justify the idea that the theory of recognition is not only the instrument of a reformulation of the intuitions of justice, but also the instrument for a recasting of the definitions of justice. This argument is pragmatic in character; it starts from the principle that normative concepts are tools intended to express and make explicit those aspects of our experience that are dependent on normative expectations. This argument will lead us to think of conceptions of justice as ways to formulate the specific characteristics of a certain number of specific normative expectations, as well as the experiences in which these expectations remain unsatisfied. The idea of an analytic connection between recognition and justice provides additional grounds for the description of these expectations as expectations for recognition. It allows us to take seriously the fact that when individuals face the difficulties they have in expressing their sense of injustice by means of the established conceptions of justice, they can have recourse to a vocabulary of recognition (in asserting that they refuse to be disrespected or humiliated). In the same way, it grounds the approach comprised of a *re-elaboration* of the meaning of the *definitions* of justice in light of a *description* of what is at stake in an experience of injustice *in terms of recognition.*

PART I

Injustice and the Denial of Recognition

Chapter One

SOCIAL MOVEMENTS AND CRITIQUE OF POLITICS

It would be meaningless to speak of any consensus in contemporary political philosophy, since so many theoretical and political disputes run through it. On the other hand, we can ask whether the most widely practiced styles of political philosophy do not all share the same inability to respond to the political disaffection that is contemporary with the revival of normative political philosophy. Jacques Rancière has underscored this paradoxical conjunction between the ongoing disappearance of politics and the revival of political philosophy, noting that "The resurrection of political philosophy thus simultaneously declares itself to be the evacuation of the political by its official representatives."[1] Must we see this, as Rancière does, as the illustration of an incompatibility between philosophy and politics, or rather of the necessity for philosophy to take up the challenge of a critique of politics? This question stands in a twofold relation with the experience of injustice. On the one hand, disaffection with politics seems to be the result, at least in part, of a narrowing and closure of the space of institutionalized politics which renders politically inexpressible a number of demands by those who suffer injustice, demands that together produce the feeling that political issues no longer have anything to do with real social problems.[2] On the other hand, by remaining silent about the social disrespect that victims of injustice endure, established politics reinforces the feeling of being disrespected by institutions and produces a social disrespect which is, so to speak, raised to a second power: the experience of a particular social injustice is reinforced by the feeling that those who suffer it do not deserve to be politically accounted for. The question thus arises whether contemporary political philosophies only reproduce the symbolic violence of a public space implicitly declaring that what these individuals suffer in society does not deserve to be taken seriously, or whether, on the contrary, they are able to contribute to shifting political debates that would pay heed to the various contemporary forms of injustice. This amounts to asking how political philosophy can internalize the standpoint of the experience of injustice.

Such an internalization would entail developing a critique of those political forms that serve to hide or make invisible certain kinds of injustice. It would thus entail a broader critique of politics. But clearly this political critique cannot be treated as merely a theoretical question because it also contains a practical dimension—that of social movements. The latter can be considered as a "space of appeals," in the senses both of a request for answers to social problems and an appeal (in the legal sense) stemming either from the failure to take a demand into account or from the refusal to hear a request in the classical institutional arenas.[3] Social movements are able to bring issues into the political public sphere that would otherwise have been left unmentioned.[4] They appear to be one of the only forces liable to deform the logic of institutionalized politics by breaking down the walls that mark its limits. Are contemporary political philosophies able to take account of this important contribution to the democratization of democracy? This question cannot be dismissed, especially as some on the left defend a strategy to "change the world without taking power,"[5] no longer hoping to achieve democratization by any other means than through social movements' laying siege to political institutions. It is not necessary to go as far as that in order to recognize that the political importance of social movements requires that philosophy take account of their particular resources.

CRITIQUE OF POLITICS OR CRITIQUE OF PHILOSOPHY

It could be thought that the success of Rawls's and Habermas's political philosophies stems from their desire to struggle against an orientation that reduces the political public sphere to purely technical and administrative questions of territorial management, its security, and economic activity. It is with this end in mind, in fact, that they stress that a democratic life maintains an essential connection to collective deliberation about social justice.[6] But are their political philosophies able to take in and address injustices about which the established politics is silent? Can they include within their concepts, arguments, and claims the point of view on social injustice adopted by the politically excluded? This question can be understood in a strong sense or a weak one. In a weak sense, it merely urges that the demands of those who suffer injustice in the real world be taken into account. In a strong sense, it demands moreover that political philosophy welcome within itself the ways in which they articulate their demands—in other words, that they take into account the political language of political actors. Political philosophy must meet this twofold challenge, for political disaffection can be the result of a twofold cause. It can be explained either through the absence of a political accounting of certain demands, or through an accounting that renders them unrecognizable by those who articulate them, taken up in a language where the dominated and the deprived can no longer recognize their own aspirations.

We probably ought to credit Rawls and Habermas with trying seriously to take up the more demanding of these two challenges. In fact, they both try to adopt the viewpoint of the socially disadvantaged in order to define the nature of a more just world. Rawls maintains that social and economic inequalities are only justifiable if "they are to be to the greatest benefit of the least advantaged members of society."[7] As for Habermas, he posits in principle that political philosophy must take account of "the problems that objectively impose themselves on participants," and maintains that "[a] social theory claiming to be 'critical' cannot restrict itself to describing the relation between norm and reality from the perspective of an observer."[8] From this point of view, their approaches are radically different from that of the various forms of contemporary neorepublicanism that criticize social problems, either because they constitute obstacles to full political participation, or because they are likely to lead to the development of the sorts of domination that political participation is intended to abolish. In both cases, the problems suffered by society's least advantaged are critiqued from a viewpoint that is clearly external to their concerns. When they have an experience of injustice, those least advantaged do not find it intolerable because it might deprive them of full political participation or it might lead them towards new forms of domination. To understand how the dominated and the deprived express their demands, the problematic of justice seems undeniably more pertinent than that of republicanism, and Habermas's and Rawls's theories have this advantage. Nonetheless, with both theories, the challenge offered by the language of protest is only partially addressed. In fact, when Rawls claims to adopt the viewpoint of the "least advantaged" and when Habermas proclaims that he starts from "the problems that objectively impose themselves on participants," they actually describe only the methodological rules to be followed in order to define the principles that a just society must satisfy, not the rules determining the point of view from which these principles must be formulated.

What is justice? Rawls and Habermas answer this question differently, but they both seek the answer within the resources of practical reason. It is in fact citizens' capacity to be reasonable and rational that allows them, in the circumstances of the original position described by Rawls, to agree upon the principles of justice and to thus assert their fundamental equality. Likewise, for Habermas, it is the moral use of practical reason that provides the ultimate basis for democratic debates and allows one to define the contents of legitimate law.[9] For both, the structure of principles of justice and fundamental rights is constructed upon the moral capacity to adopt a universal point of view; these principles and rights thus embody, so to speak, the normative potential of practical reason. But this reveals the limits of their theoretico-political project, because it is clear that the political demands of those who suffer injustice are not expressed in the language of the requirements of universality proper to practical reason. We have already said this: most often, experiences of injustice stem from the feeling that one's life circumstances are unbearable or too degrading, rather than from the consciousness that they violate explicitly formulated principles of justice or fundamental rights, and even less from the conviction that these rights are fundamental because their validity can be rationally demonstrated.

Rawls's and Habermas's political philosophies thus fail to completely meet the conditions for the strong version of critique of politics: they do not recognize political demands as they are expressed by those who suffer injustice. On the other hand, they do seem to satisfy the weaker version of critique of politics. To reformulate the demands of those excluded from politics within the language of practical reason indeed seems to be one of their objectives. If the most deprived among us do not interpret the social failings that they experience as a situation's misalignment with rational principles, this does not for all that mean that these social failings could not be characterized by such misalignment. Would a description in terms of misalignment be able to account for the properly political demands contained within the experiences of injustice that are excluded from the political sphere? Would such a description be the only critique of politics for which philosophy as political philosophy could truly take responsibility? It seems not. These experiences of injustice are the carriers of other political demands, and they define other ways of envisioning the critique of politics.

We should probably begin by noting on this point that the experience of injustice is not so much the experience of an injustice in the sense of a contradiction with an explicit definition of justice, but rather the experience of a *relation* and a *situation*. We have already seen that experiences of injustice should be interpreted as experiences of an injury to one's personal integrity in the sense that they are rooted in the feeling that an essential aspect of one's dignity is tarnished, a feeling of something intolerable.[10] In its affective aspect, an experience of injustice is an experience of the unbearable, and as an experience of the intolerable, it transforms one's pre-reflective experience of oneself and the social environment. When I am the object of an unjust judgment, my own existence becomes a problem for me: I refuse to be what I am recognized to be. Through the intermediary of an other's recognition, I become other than myself (*self-alienation*).[11] At the same time, the social environment ceases to be self-evident: it appears to me as that which blocks my attempts at recognition; it appears to me as a foreign and hostile world, or as an "alienated" or "estranged" world (*world-alienation*).[12]

The experience of injustice is one of alienation; it is, moreover, one of an unjust *situation*. In fact, individuals always associate their feeling of injustice with particular social interactions or contexts, and it is likewise always against the latter that they direct their complaints concerning justice. To be sure, one can have a diffuse intuition of a structural injustice (for example, of the universally unjust character of a structurally inegalitarian society), but the crystallization of such an intuition into a feeling of injustice is always occasioned by a situated injustice, and it is beginning with such feelings that the consciousness of structural components of injustice can then be reflectively articulated. When a denial of recognition is lived as an injustice, one's attention is directed toward the different means of denying recognition and toward their various justifications.

When individuals suffer social injustice, the specifically political dimension of the experience of injustice is directly tied to this twofold element of alienation—as experience of an alienation and of a situation—as well as to the process of refusal that occurs within this experience. Before being formulated in a political public space, the experience of injustice is political, first as a *process* inscribed in the qualitative experience of a refusal to accept the intolerable, and as a *situated* refusal. A first problem is linked to the fact that the point of view most commonly adopted by theories of justice does not allow them to take account of these qualitative and situational components of the experience of justice. A second problem is linked to the fact that their point of view is barely able to account for the dynamics of politicization to which the experience of injustice gives rise, and more generally, to the role that the experience of injustice can play in processes that could contribute to the democratization of democracy.

The contemporary understanding of principles of justice ordinarily leads to an approach to justice that can be called *quantitative* insofar as it makes justice a question of degrees. Most commonly, it is held that actual social situations can only be more or less in conformity with abstract principles of justice. But what is unbearable is not more or less unbearable, it is simply unbearable. More generally, the confrontation between a situation and principles of justice does not make it possible to take account of the qualitative dimension of the unbearable: one lives with the unbearable; one doesn't measure it. In the same way, the framework of theories of justice forbids them from accounting for the *situational* dimension of the experience of injustice. In fact, such theories rest upon the presupposition that it is possible to think about justice as such, abstracted from any diagnosis of the concrete situations that produce injustice. This presupposition leads to the removal of any reference to specific unbearable characteristics from the experience of injustice and, in the same way, to the loss of an abolitionist dimension of the concept of justice. This presupposition leads, moreover, to a static definition of social justice (to a definition of justice as a society's *state*), whereas for those who suffer injustice, the primary function of a demand for justice is to guide their efforts in order to transform unjust situations. As described by a theory of justice, injustice is presented not only in another language, but also according to a different logic than that which permeates the experience of injustice. It is always on the verge of losing the essential meanings that it takes on for those who experience it, so that it is the very content of demands for justice, and not only their form, that is thus radically altered. In Rawls's and Habermas's theories, this general problem manifests as difficulties (idiosyncratic, to be sure) that are not politically trivial.

We can begin by noting that the quantitative point of view of theories of justice is particularly inadequate when it is a matter of elements as fundamental as personal integrity and self-respect. We know that, for Rawls, justice is defined as the equitable distribution of primary goods, understood as "things that every rational man is presumed to want."[13] A Theory of Justice can then present the general conception of justice in the following terms: "All social values—liberty and opportunity, income and wealth, and the bases of self-respect—are to be distributed equally unless an unequal distribution of any, or all of these values is to everyone's advantage."[14] It is already curious that self-respect and liberty would be considered as goods that are liable to be distributed in the same way as wealth. Political problems take shape behind this conceptual problem, political problems that clearly appear in the articulation of the two principles of A Theory of Justice.

Rawls formulates them, for instance, in the following manner:

First: each person is to have an equal right to the most extensive basic liberty compatible with a similar liberty for others.

Second, social and economic inequalities are to be arranged so that they are both (a) reasonably expected to be to everyone's advantage, and (b) attached to positions and offices open to all.[15]

The social bases of self-respect are arranged (just like wealth) among the advantages of social cooperation that, along with equality of opportunity, constitute the subject of the second principle. Rawls thus affirms that a just society is not only defined by an equitable distribution of opportunities and wealth, but also by an equitable distribution of self-respect. This seems to mean the following: just like wealth, social disrespect could be unequally distributed among social groups in a just society, as long as it were compensated by better access to social positions or by greater wealth. To those for whom social disrespect is an unbearable experience, such compensation would probably be difficult to accept.

It is probably in order to avert this disastrous conclusion that Rawls distinguishes between self-respect and integrity of the person, while identifying integrity of the person as one of the fundamental liberties guaranteed by the first principle of justice. In *Political Liberalism*, the first principle is reformulated thus: "Each person has an equal right to a fully adequate scheme of equal basic liberties which is compatible with a similar scheme of liberties for all." And these basic liberties are defined by the following list: "freedom of thought and liberty of conscience; the political liberties and freedom of association, as well as the freedoms specified by the liberty and integrity of the person; and finally, the rights and liberties covered by the rule of law."[16] Rawls maintains, moreover, that these liberties can enter into conflict with each other and thus should be limited in order to fit within a coherent system,[17] and that they "can be made compatible with one another, at least within their central range of application."[18] It is already difficult to understand in what sense the integrity of the person can be considered as a liberty; it is even more difficult to determine what its "central range of application" is. And how are we to concede that a restriction of this liberty could be just? In what form is it legitimate to limit protections with respect to physical or psychological aggressions? In total, could such quantitative restrictions on self-respect and the integrity of one's person be lived as anything other than a qualitative violation of the integrity of one's person, a violation that falls directly within the scope of the experience of the unbearable? Rawls's conceptual equipment seems quite unable to account for some of the essential dimensions of the experience of injustice.

One could reply that in *A Theory of Justice*, "self-respect" is considered the most important primary good,[19] and that Rawls's political objective is to justify the social modification that would allow a better distribution of social recognition.[20] But the claim that self-respect is the most important primary good is in contradiction with its being located in the second principle. Rawls explains that it is the good without which life is no longer worth living and without which all other goods lose their value, so that it seems to be given the priority that appertains to the set of primary goods. However, self-respect is still understood as one of the advantages of social cooperation whose equitable distribution depends upon the second principle, such that defending fundamental liberties takes priority over it. Finally, the demand for a just distribution of the social bases of self-respect remains a secondary demand, and if it is only secondary despite the importance that is explicitly attributed to it, that is because, in the end, it does not really constitute a social problem for Rawls. In fact, self-respect depends, on the one hand, on our capacity to demonstrate our own varied abilities and talents, and, on the other, on recognition of the value of our person and our actions. This is why the idea of justice assumes on this point, on the one hand, an equal distribution of opportunities to demonstrate our abilities, and on the other, a recognition of our activities' value, the latter implying that "there should be for each person at least one community of shared interests to which he belongs and where he finds his endeavors confirmed by his associates."[21] If Rawls is satisfied with such a formal definition of social recognition,[22] so empty from a sociological perspective, so unable to account for the complex machinery of social disrespect, that is because in the end he believes that it is the public recognition of the value of our liberties by just political institutions that constitutes the most stable guarantee of self-respect.[23] Civil recognition would thus ground social recognition. That civil recognition could allow the proliferation of a social disrespect destructive to self-respect—that, in particular, it could lead to a profound disgust with politics—these are things Rawls doesn't consider. Here again, constructivism ends in a critical deficit.

Habermas's theory appears to avoid the preceding difficulties, in particular because it avoids getting entangled in the description of determinate principles of justice. By justice, Habermas understands that which falls under the application of the rule of universalization within the framework of public deliberation.[24] He proceeds, like Rawls, to study the conditions of a just society by taking the demands for universality inherent in practical reason as his guiding thread. But he reproaches Rawls for obscuring foundational questions by wanting to deduce determinate principles of justice: "The principle of discourse ethics prohibits singling out with philosophical authority any specific normative contents (as, for example, certain principles of distributive justice) . . ."[25] According to Habermas, the principle of universalization defines an evaluative procedure rather than a deductive method; it makes it possible to define the forms that discussions about justice should take, not to deduce their conclusions. In *Between Facts and Norms*, he makes it possible to formulate a "legal code" stating the ensemble of fundamental rights, among which is counted respect. The legal code is comprised of three kinds of rights: rights of private autonomy (pertaining to subjective liberties of action), rights of public autonomy (pertaining to the processes that constitute the public will), and social rights that are introduced as rights serving to ensure the use of the first two kinds of rights.[26] To the extent that the social conditions of autonomy (of which the social conditions of personal integrity are clearly a part) appear as rights, it seems that this theory of justice grants its full significance to injuries to personal integrity. Nevertheless, we must investigate the political significance of the claim that the third category of rights "can only be justified in relative terms."[27] We can note, by the way, that this claim leads Habermas to pay only scant attention to these rights, and to thus reproduce within his own discussion the silence of established politics regarding the moral experiences of the dominated and deprived, those whose social rights have been denied or only granted in ways that render them valueless.

It is also permissible to investigate the political orientations that would follow from democratic deliberation within the framework of such a legal code. Habermas relies upon the dynamics of dialogue in order to get beyond the exclusive perspective of participants' particular interests and to achieve consensus. Yet for the discussion to attain a true universality, the actual participation of all concerned persons is required. To begin, shouldn't we worry that nonparticipation of those among the dominated and deprived who have already been crushed by social disrespect and its political redoubling would have major effects upon the interpretation of what is right? Moreover, if—as the feminist critique of justice suggests[28]—the established normative vocabulary implies a structural disqualification of the demands linked to subaltern activities, shouldn't we worry that the political discussion would be structurally diverted away from a true universal? And consequently, how can we accept that the democratic principle thus conceived is the source for a truly legitimate law?[29] Here again, we can worry that the proposed theoretical framework will prove incapable of accounting for the legitimacy of demands excluded by politics.

Determinate principles of justice, or a legal code? Rawls or Habermas? This alternative encompasses a divergence concerning the relationship between the definition of justice and social reality. For Rawls, the definition of justice is clearly static, insofar as the two principles of justice measure the value of the institutional structure of societies. But he must also assume the fact that actual social situations can only be more or less in conformity with abstract principles of justice, and when the two principles are no longer merely considered as elements of a definition but also as criteria, their operative value seems to depend upon a comparative and dynamic approach. *A Theory of Justice* addresses the question of criteria for justice by asking whether this or that institutional transformation is to the benefit of the least advantaged, and it thus seems to make space for a perspective that would be typical of the experience of injustice. However, *A Theory of Justice* only accords this perspective a limited right, insofar as it is restricted to questions of application of a definition that is in itself static, and it only gives this perspective a limited interpretation, insofar as the problem of the transformation of injustice is reduced to the quantitative problem of its reduction. For Rawls, the challenge has clearly to do with the improvement of a social order whose overall structures are already rational. The first principle defines the structural conditions of a generally just society: different individuals should have access to the same system of liberties corresponding to the most basic liberties, those that are generally recognized as rights in modern constitutional democracies. The second principle defines the dynamic conditions for a transformation of residual injustices: restrictions upon the most basic liberties "must strengthen the total system of liberty shared by all," or "must be acceptable to those citizens with the lesser liberty."[30] Such a perspective clearly prohibits a recovery of the point of view of those who, suffering injustice in a particular institutional context, perceive those institutions as profoundly unjust and thus conceive the demand for justice as that of a qualitative transformation. Dependent upon the progressive vision of social history that characterized the post-World War II economic boom, this perspective comes with the conviction that a "property-owning democracy," even a "liberal socialism," would be more in conformity with the principles of justice than a "welfare-state capitalism."[31] This does indeed require radical social transformations, but they are only envisioned as better applications of an already-established normative framework.

Habermas brings together the questions of justice and of social transformation differently. The legal code only articulates a definition of justice that concerns the modes of regulating conflicts within the horizon of possible social transformations. It would thus probably become possible to justify transformations that impact structures in the real social order. However, in order for this possibility to be imaginable, those who suffer the worst injustices produced by the social order must be able to participate in the discussion, which remains problematic. By referring the application of criteria of justice only to the dynamics of the political public space, Habermas actually excludes the most radical demands and thus reduces the relevance of his model to the political context of a struggle against the residual injustices of a generally just world, in conformity with his general interpretation of modernity as a process of rationalization.

In order to integrate the possibility of more radical social transformations into the theoretical framework of theories of justice, a Rawlsian correction of Habermas has been proposed, suggesting that the Habermasian principles should be applied in conformity with the Rawlsian prioritarianism: those who suffer the social order's injustices should be given priority in the public sphere.[32] But are we satisfied with such a displacement of the problem? In fact, the Rawlsian prioritarianism is not really one. It claims to give priority to the poorest, but in fact its theoretical equipment excludes those who suffer anything other than residual injustices. Should we then reformulate the Rawlsian prioritarianism of the least liberty into a prioritarianism of "those who have no part"?[33] Then we would run up against a more general problem: a prioritizing definition of justice stands in the way of a consideration of the variety of experiences of injustice.

Consider, for example, the way in which injustices suffered by employees in a neoliberal company can be integrated into a global social critique. As long as the problem is posed within the framework of a theory of equal liberties, we probably have to conclude that the inequalities to which the employees are subject are less than that those suffered by the unemployed. The risk is thus of portraying everything that employees experience in their work as unbearable (whether it concerns evaluations of individual performance that are more and more detached from the realities of the work, arbitrary exercises of power that expand with the increasing precariousness and flexibility of the work, the unlimited intensification of work and the worsening of working conditions, etc.) as a merely relative injustice, even though all this is experienced as more than a "relative injustice." The fact is that in recent decades, in the political public space (just as in trade unions' collective actions, which focused on employment rather than on working conditions and wages), workers have often been considered as privileged with respect to the unemployed, and so workers have thus seen their own feelings of injustice portrayed as illegitimate. According to Christophe Dejours, this has led to disaffection for politics and union action, and more generally, to the banalization of social injustice for those who see their experiences of injustice deemed unworthy of consideration in comparison with others.[34] Quite far from being an effective form for the democratization of democracy, prioritarianism is one of the principal vehicles for disaffection with politics.

The Habermasian definition is no more able to correct the Rawlsian definition than the inverse, for their shortcomings demark the general limits of the problem of theories of justice. They are the very limits that render the normative political philosophies of a Rawls or a Habermas ill-suited for taking up the challenge of the critique of politics. They posit in principle that, since social experience is always structured by principles of public justification, political theory must start with an analysis of the forms of this justification, and only those social demands that manage to get past the filter of public justification can claim political value.[35] It is true that the experience of injustice is always conditioned by representations of justice and by forms of public justification. But the latter are not, for all that, perfectly compatible with these experiences that can initiate processes of recasting. On the one hand, the experience of injustice can contribute to enlarging the meaning of principles of public justification, as when "those who have no part" [*les "sans-part"*] assert that they are not entitled to rights that are supposed to hold for everyone (the right to vote; the right to work, to health, to housing, etc.). On the other hand, the experience of injustice could just as much be born from situations in which lived injustice is quite simply inexpressible by the principles that regulate public justification—situations that then call not so much for an extension but rather a transformation of the definitions of justice. In such situations, it is the very content of public justification that is in question, so that the filter of public justification totally changes its meaning.

As was already indicated in the introduction, the experience of injustice can take three different forms. A feeling of injustice could be based upon an assessment that the principles of justice established in the political public sphere or in particular institutional arenas have been violated. It could also be based upon the feeling that these principles are understood in a too-restrictive sense, because their interpretation in fact excludes groups of individuals from the rights that they define. Finally, it could be based upon the feeling that these principles are false because they are consistent with injustices that are as grave as they are inexpressible in the established normative language. Theories of justice can only adequately account for the first type of experience of injustice. In the other cases, the experiences of injustice call for processes of reciprocal adjustment between experience and principles of justifications, between a process of politicizing experience and a process of transforming the principles of justification. During such processes of the politicization of experience accompanied by such a normative dynamic, the principles of public justification can be facilitating elements (in the second case), but also inhibiting elements (in the third case).

Hence the value of the approach in terms of the experience of injustice: not only does it offer a perspective on politics that accounts for the qualitative, referential, and dynamic (aimed towards the abolition of an unbearable situation) dimensions of political demands, but it defines a point of view critical of the normative language games that stand in the way of demands aimed against the injustice of situations. And hence the value of the paradigm of recognition, which makes it possible to take account of the experience of injustice in its *affective dimension* (by taking seriously the feelings provoked by the nonsatisfaction of recognitive expectations), in its *alienating dimension* (an experience that makes a positive self-relation problematical, or goes so far as to turn it into a negative self-relation, or even to break it), in its *dynamic dimension* of struggle against the denial of recognition, and in its *dimension of possible discord* between fundamental recognitive expectations and the social grammar of recognition.

However, the necessity of a critique of politics does not only raise a theoretical problem. It also poses the practical problem of actual processes that can challenge the dynamics that tend to limit the scope of legitimate political discussions and to disconnect the political public sphere from social experience. Social movements, as they are motivated by a specific dynamic of articulating demands, have the capacity to deform the logic of established politics. They constitute the vehicle for an actual critique of politics. If normative political philosophy wants to rise to the challenge of the critique of politics, it must also take account of the normative potential of this critique. This is why we must now ascertain how a political philosophy with normative import can accept this actual critique of politics within its theoretical framework.

To clarify the status of such an investigation, note that in the pages that follow I will only be concerned with social movements *in general,* and principally with their normative motivations—the norms and values presupposed by the pursuit of their aims. I will not address the ways they are mobilized or organized, or their repertory of actions. The aim here is not to provide an account of all the features that define social movements as specific *social phenomena*, but rather to account for them as specific *political phenomena*. Thus, this project does not aim to vie with a sociological description of social movements, but rather seeks to introduce a way to interconnect the self-understanding of the actors in these movements with a sociological analysis, and a philosophical consideration.

Social movements in general will be understood as a type of collective action characterized by an aspect of protest, that is, by a kind of conflict that challenges either the general organization of society or some particular institution.[36] We should distinguish between different kinds of protest actions: mob actions (such as riots), social movements, and political movements. Social movements can be distinguished from mob actions by their organization. They are distinguished from political movements by their modes of actions (which cannot be reduced to interventions within the political public sphere), by the objectives they seek (institutional transformations as opposed to the conquest of political power), and by the discourse that they articulate (a justification for particular objectives, not for a general social project). In what follows, I will discuss social movements generally—an approach that seems simultaneously both legitimate and necessary; on the one hand, because the different kinds of social movements seem to be comprised of comparable motivational components and these motivational components suggest analogous normative dynamics; on the other hand, because only an account of these normative dynamics will make it possible to account for the continuum of protest actions (riots can be transformed into social movements, and social movements can combine with or end up as political movements).

Employing the criteria of engaged social groups and the definitions of justice that their objectives presuppose, we can identify three "ideal types" of social movements: social struggles, identity struggles, and the struggles of the deprived [*luttes des "sans"*].[i] "Social struggles" designates those social movements concerned with social groups that are constituted as "social classes," and whose principal objectives are linked to the redistribution of wealth. The term "identity struggles" encompasses social movements concerned with social groups that are formed as "status groups," and whose principal objectives are linked to the recognition of identities (the struggles of cultural minorities, for example)[37] or the struggle against a negative

---

i. See the translator's note for a discussion of *les "sans"* and *luttes des "sans."*

TABLE 1.1

Types of social movements	Social struggles	Identity struggles	Struggles of the deprived
Objectives	Equitable distribution of wealth	Equitable recognition of identities	Integration within stable and rewarding social relations
Social basis	Classes	Status groups	*Absent (or to be established)*

identity (the Dalits or Untouchables movement in India, for example). "Struggles of the deprived" are social movements without a social base, whose objectives are aimed at reinsertion into stable and rewarding social and political relations (for example, movements of the unemployed, of undocumented immigrants, and of the homeless). The first two types of social movement emerge out of situations that are characterized by demeaning social relations, and it is in this sense that they originate in the denial of recognition and take recognition as their goal. The third type of social movement emerges out of situations that tend to exclude individuals from either rewarding or demeaning social relations, and so it is in a different sense that they originate in the denial of recognition and take recognition as their goal. But in all three cases, the normative component of their motivations is tied to recognition, and this simple observation suffices to justify a general approach to the normative components of social movements within the framework of a theory of recognition. A more precise analysis of the specific motivations and objectives of social struggles (labor and wages), of identity struggles (positive identity), and of struggles of the deprived (social reintegration) will be taken up in chapters 3, 5 and 6.

THE NORMATIVE CONTENT OF SOCIAL CONFLICTS

As early as the 1988 "Afterword" to *The Critique of Power*, Honneth insisted that "the conceptual framework of an analysis has to be laid out so that it is able to comprehend both the structures of social domination *and* the social resources for its practical overcoming."[38] This is the project that he undertakes in *The Struggle for Recognition: The Moral Grammar of Social Conflicts*. The idea of a moral grammar sounds strange, given that the most recent sociological analyses of social movements assign no decisive function to normative elements. Whether within the frameworks of theories of collective behavior or those of rational action, whether within approaches in terms of opportunities or of the analysis of mobilizing structures, it has in effect been agreed upon that the normative elements of social movements have no decisive function.

If we accept theories of collective behavior, like that of Ted Gurr, the intensity of social frustrations constitutes the triggering factor. If we accept theories of rational action, like that of Mancur Olson, the decisive element is the superiority of the gains envisioned with respect to the costs of mobilization borne by individuals.[39] However, Gurr reveals that these frustrations can fail to lead to collective mobilization, and that a project of legitimization and of ascription of responsibility undeniably figures among the symbolic conditions that make mobilization possible. Ought we not conclude that the transformation into a demand immediately supposes that a representation of how things ought to be must be added to the frustration?

As for answering theories of rational action, it suffices to take the example that seems to best support them: social struggles for wage increases or against massive layoffs. It is clear that, in such cases, cost-benefit analysis is taken into account, as evidenced by strikers' justifications, which often underscore the moral (wearying and discouraging) and financial (loss of wages) hardships of the collective action in which they are engaged: "Do you really believe that we enjoy going on strike, with all the costs that we bear?" But is equally clear that a higher salary or the preservation of a job represents more to the workers than a set of material advantages: these things constitute the medium for a recognition that their existence has value, as indicated, for example, by discourses that lash out at "starvation wages," at businesses that reduce their workers to "disposable labor," or at a simple variable of financial adjustments that effectively treats individuals "like dogs." In order for an institutional decision to lead individuals to take part in a collective struggle that is always expensive in terms of time and energy (sometimes also financially) and rarely completely victorious, a qualitative (the crystallization of a deep and lasting unease into a state of being fed up [*ras-le-bol*][40]) and normative element must be added to the frustrations and the costs of inaction: the feeling of having one's integrity and one's dignity trampled upon.[41]

So too, analyses of opportunity and of mobilization networks have led to an underestimation of the role of normative elements in social movements by attributing a preponderant role to the movements' structural conditions and by conceptualizing their motivations as variable and contingent factors susceptible to manipulation by social movement organizers.[42] But the time for the theoretical eviction of moral feelings and shared normative meanings is over. A vast literature has in fact taken up the "framing processes"[ii] at the heart of social movements, starting from the following principle:

If the combination of political opportunities and mobilizing structures affords groups a certain structural potential for action, they remain, in the absence of one other factor, insufficient to account for collective action. Mediating between opportunity, organization, and action are the shared meanings and definitions that people bring to their situation. At a minimum people need to feel both aggrieved about some aspect of their lives and optimistic that, acting collectively, they can redress the problem.[43]

Ultimately, the initiation of social movements, just as much as their development, presupposes the conjunction of affective and cognitive components within what we can call a "framework of injustice," meaning an ensemble of shared representations within a mobilized group that make it possible, first, to *identify* a social situation as *unjust*; second, to *ascribe* causes to the *injustice* and to assign responsibilities to other social groups; and finally, to envisage a transformation of the situation.[44] The idea of a "moral grammar of social movements" is interesting precisely because it proposes a model with which to analyze the dynamics that go through the elaboration of such frames of injustice, and to articulate their affective (a feeling of injustice) and cognitive (the identification and expression of the injustice of a situation, and demands for its transformation) factors.

What, then, is the experience of a denial of recognition? It is a matter of an experience or an impression that my value is at play, an impression that is given in the form of a moral feeling. In social movements, experiences and moral feelings crop up simultaneously as practical reasons (or as what Honneth terms "the emotional raw materials") and as demands directed towards the suppression of factors that produce the nonsatisfaction of different fundamental expectations defined by the need for recognition.[45] Just as it rejects the utilitarian approach to social movements (by insisting that

ii. In English in the original.

their motivations are never merely of a utilitarian order, even if they can indeed be so in part), the theory of recognition refuses to accept the intellectualist view reducing the growth of social movements to the desire to see that normative rules consciously accepted as valid are respected.

This intellectualist conception suffers the general shortcomings of intellectualist conceptions of action: action is generally guided by dispositions in a preconscious way, and it is only in problematic situations when those dispositions are thwarted that reflection crops up as a factor in the redirecting of action.[46] Furthermore, this intellectualist conception of social movements also suffers a more specific failing: it postulates that abstract moral principles are immediately available without inquiring about the processes that lead individuals to make use of them. Social movements emerge in response to problematic situations that initially appear in feelings of injustice before being understood as situations that contravene principles of justice. Here too, the abstract use of principles of justice is most often secondary and instrumental. Their primary functions are in fact to explicate what is at stake in this feeling and to manifest the legitimacy of the demands that follow from it. We know that they sometimes fail to fulfill these functions. To say that unjust situations are first given in the form of a feeling is thus to say that the normative content of social movements depends upon the nonsatisfaction of expectations which are not necessarily present to consciousness in a perfectly explicit way (one of the issues for reflection upon the problematic situation is to understand what is at issue therein), and even less so in the form of rationally articulated propositions (another issue for this reflection is to give them a coherent form that is justifiable in others' eyes).

At the same time as it follows from the disappointment of certain expectations, the feeling of injustice triggers reflective action by the individual upon her own expectations. In Honneth's terms, "[when one's normative expectations are disappointed,] with the shift of attention to one's own expectations, one also becomes aware of the cognitive components—in this case, moral knowledge—that had informed the planned and (now) hindered action."[47] Here we find an idea already developed in the introduction: the negative feelings involved in the experience of injustice, like shame or indignation, have a specific cognitive content, an "opportunity for moral insight"[48] that, in certain conditions, can lead individuals to a clear awareness of the injustice that they endure. To specify what should be understood by the cognitive potential of a feeling of injustice, we could add that the knowledge here bears both on the situation lived as unjust (consciousness of injustice) and on the normative expectations that make it possible to describe this situation as unjust (realization of the nature of the thwarted expectations). This double object (an unjust situation, and thwarted expectations) gives its specific form to this cognitive potential. It simultaneously falls under a reflexive consciousness (of the subject's return upon expectations' non-satisfaction) and an imperfect hermeneutic (of an understanding of the nonsatisfaction of these expectations as a principle making the situation unjust, without these expectations being posited, for all that, as principles of justice). Two consequences follow from such a connection between the disappointment of expectations and reflection oriented toward a definition of the situation's injustice.

First, this model makes it possible to articulate the affective and cognitive elements of frames of injustice. The analysis of social movements in terms of "frame construction" presupposes, on the one hand, that our social experience is always predetermined by socially accepted cognitive frames (construction of experience by the frames), and on the other hand, that social movements are the occasion for a transformation of these frames (construction of the frames of experience).[49] It thus presupposes that in the specific situations of social movements, those that matter for situations of lived injustice, social experience contains within it an element that could thwart the framing of experience, as well as affective and cognitive resources capable of entailing a transformation of the frame of experience. These two factors are joined—if the origin of the experience of injustice is explained by the disappointment of certain normative expectations, and if this disappointment leads to a reflection on these expectations as elements that make possible a definition of the situation's injustice. According to this hypothesis, the "frame of injustice" is constituted in an inseparable way of an affective element (the feeling of injustice through which we experience the disappointment of these expectations) and a cognitive element (the meanings that we project upon the situation in order to identify it as an injustice). These two factors are inseparable in the "frame of injustice" not only because they contribute to its definition, but also because they reciprocally presuppose each other: on the one hand, the disappointment of normative expectations produces emotional effects which only take the form of a feeling of injustice if the representations of the situation's injustice are associated with manifestations of its effects (emotions like anger, feelings like suffering, are among other possible effects); on the other, the reflexive work of making these expectations explicit and of identifying the situation is initiated by the emotional effect of having these expectations not met. We might ask how a feeling of injustice could simultaneously presuppose representations of a situation's injustice (a first frame of injustice) and contribute to the construction of a frame (a second frame of injustice). This difficulty goes back to a problem we have already discussed: one can have a feeling that what is at issue in a problematic experience should indeed be explained through the vocabulary of justice and injustice by drawing upon the most general and imprecise senses of these notions, while simultaneously finding it difficult to adequately and precisely express those issues by means of the socially available principles of justice.

Secondly, the idea of cognitive potential in the experience of injustice offers a response to those theoreticians who would stress its unproductiveness. The feeling of injustice, even in the case of a wrong (an experience of injustice that does not have the cognitive means available to be expressed as an injustice), cannot be reduced to muted speech—as for example in the expression "silence in the face of injustice," as Lyotard argued.[50] When the injustice is tied to an irreparable catastrophe, as in Lyotard's example of the Holocaust, silence probably functions by itself simultaneously as a statement denouncing the injustice and as the inability of any statement to do so. But in the case of social injustice, it is rare that one would give up one's demands and resign oneself to silence in the face of a discourse insisting that an injustice is not one: the feeling of injustice by the victims of a massive layoff is generally accompanied by protests even when the law and a whole host of reasons are there to say that the idea of justice has nothing to do with it. In the case of social injustice that takes the form of a wrong, the feeling of justice is generally carried out by a normative dynamic that can ultimately lead to demands and that always at least contains a doubt about the principles of justice that discredit its articulation. The fact that the cognitive potential of the experience of injustice takes the dual form of a reflexive knowledge and an imperfect hermeneutic also makes it possible to answer all those who think that theories of justification are capable of accounting for the full range of meanings that we attribute to demands for justice. In fact, the cognitive potential of the feeling of injustice cannot be reduced to reasons that justify this feeling, contrary to what Avishai

Margalit suggests, for example, when he asserts that it is impossible to feel humiliated without having a valid reason to feel humiliated.[51] In the case of a wrong, the feeling of injustice is accompanied by a reflexive effort aimed at the explication of what is at play in this feeling, an effort that stumbles upon the lack of an adequate justification and does not necessarily lead to the formulation of alternative justifications. The theory of recognition extends this reflexive moment by making explicit the different kinds of normative expectations that are at stake in the experience of injustice. And it attempts to complete this imperfect hermeneutic of injustice by integrating these normative expectations within the definition of justice.

As Richard Rorty has noted, there are many reasons to think that the established normative vocabulary is always too narrow to adequately express the full set of moral experiences and that its portrayal of these experiences, always too narrow, always leaves behind an irreducible residue of silent pain.[52] As we will see later, it is difficult to express the injustice tied to contempt for collective identities or to social suffering in the language games of justice. From this general theme, Rorty draws a conclusion that is both skeptical and relativist: only the multiplication of private languages will make it possible to account for the different aspects of our moral experiences. However, if the experiences of injustice are endowed with a specific cognitive potential, it is possible to escape from these skeptical or relativist conclusions. The experience of injustice must be interpreted as an experience of consciousness (in the Hegelian sense of the term, already specified in the introduction), as a dialectical process that allows one to achieve a higher knowledge. As a general rule, and in particular for normative philosophy, there is no direct access to the truth—it is by examining the tensions that traverse our experiences and our knowledge that we arrive at a path towards it.

When it takes the form of a wrong, the experience of injustice presents a particular case of tension between a moral knowledge and a moral experience, which turns them into a dialectical experience that falls under the form of a negative dialectic, in the Adornian sense of an awareness or "sense of nonidentity" of a concept and its object.[53] In this type of negative experience, we understand a situation of nonsatisfaction of normative expectations associated with determinate normative ideas or principles (in this case, as ideas of justice), without it actually being possible to adequately describe this situation by means of these normative ideas or principles (in this case, as an injustice). To take another example, we could say that, in contrast with experiences of freedom or non-freedom where we live in situations that adequately correspond to the idea that we hold of freedom or its denial, we could speak of the dialectical experience of non-freedom when we live in a situation that we consider to be a denial of freedom, without being able to adequately describe it with the help of our ideas of freedom and its denial. This kind of experience can occur whenever our moral vocabulary is too narrow for our moral experiences.

The Hegelian concept of the "experience of consciousness" adds that this moment—of a "sense of non-identity" between a situation and the terms that designate it—carries with it a demand for a joint transformation of the terms that describe the situation and of the way in which it is described. In the particular case of a dialectical experience tied to injustice, the specific cognitive potential of such an experience results simultaneously in a critique of the normative validity of the available ideas of justice and a hermeneutic effort aimed towards a different definition of justice. "Frame analysis" attributes just this sort of experience of consciousness to social movements when it interprets them as the place for "signifying work," understanding that to mean a dynamic of "amplification and extension of existing meanings" and of "generation of new meanings."[54] The socially available normative frame is always partially inadequate not only because it generally entails a structural *devaluation* of social rights demanded by *social struggles* to the advantage of the liberty rights upon which the justification of the social order rests (we will return to this question in chapter 2), and because it entails an *exclusion* of the demands of *identity struggles* and of *struggles of the deprived* beyond the scope of justice (we will return to these points in chapters 4 and 6), but also—and more specifically—because every social movement works toward institutional transformations while the normal institutional functioning is justified by socially accepted principles of justification (we will return to this point in chapter 3). The framing that initiates the social movements and that develops within them thus supposes a cognitive struggle against this devaluing, this exclusion, and this justification of the status quo within the framework of what we could just as well call a "politics of signification."[55] The theory of recognition extends this very politics of signification by attempting to transform the definitions of justice in light of experiences of injustice.

The theory of recognition thus makes possible an account of the motivations and the specific dynamics that are proper to social movements.

It also makes possible an account of the fact that social movements can pursue negotiable objectives when they are characterized by a quantitative dimension, as in the case of a struggle for better wages, but can also pursue objectives that are more difficult to negotiate, or even nonnegotiable.[56] This is the case when the quantitative dimension of their objectives is reduced to nothing or almost nothing, as in the case of a struggle for the preservation of a cultural identity (for example, in the demands connected with the authorization or the defense of regional languages). The theory of recognition allows us to understand that qualitative demands are present even within negotiable conflicts. When they respond to a denial of recognition, the demand for recognition is of a qualitative order: in the face of social contempt or disregard that has become unbearable (whether it takes the form of starvation wages, mass layoffs [*licenciements boursiers*], the elimination of social welfare support, etc.), the demand is never to be less scorned; it is always to no longer be so. Even in the most negotiable social conflicts, the demand is always partially nonnegotiable. This is probably why the end of a social movement judged to be victorious by some is always also experienced by others as a failure, and why it is so difficult to terminate a strike.[57]

But a philosophical description of the motivations, dynamics, and objectives of social movements is not the only task of a theory of recognition. It also aims to articulate a theoretical frame that will allow us to reflect upon what distinguishes legitimate from illegitimate social movements. The specificity of this theoretical frame is connected to the fact that it adopts the point of view of normative dynamics immanent within social movements, while distinguishing the different levels at which their legitimacy can be debated: legitimacy of motivations, legitimacy of demands, legitimacy of the means employed and the objectives pursued.

NORMATIVE EXPECTATIONS, PRACTICAL DYNAMICS, NORMATIVE DYNAMICS

We could describe the dynamics of social movements thus: they start from a disturbance of social life[58] that must be seen as unbearable enough for a group of individuals to decide to undertake a complaint or protest (speaking up, or "voice") rather than bearing this disturbance ("loyalty") or simply fleeing from it ("exit").[59] In order for this voice to be accompanied by a collective action, it requires not only that multiple interests converge and that repertoires of collective action adapted to the situations encountered be socially available,[60] but also that the voice be accompanied by the construction of a normative frame that will permit identification of the situation as unjust, assignment of responsibility, and legitimation of a struggle against the situation. As Arlette Farge and Jacques Revel have stated, revolts should be interpreted not as a simple reaction nor as the result of calculation, but "as a persistent, a piecemeal, search for a meaning which is not given at the beginning, and which only gradually reveals its true significance."[61] This revelation happens through an explication of the motives and objectives that make possible the elaboration of a common language of demands (one possible extension of the reflexive dynamic and the imperfect hermeneutic that follows upon the denial of recognition).[62] When it is imbued with this twofold normative dimension (responsibility/ legitimacy), the voice can take the form of a demand addressed to institutions or social groups, a demand whose natural language is that of injustice. To the extent that the social problem in question profoundly impacts the lives of a particular group of individuals, it can appear as a form of illegitimate inequality. And when this illegitimate inequality appears as the result of determinate institutions and social relations, it must appear as a socially produced inequality or as a social injustice. This is precisely where we should look for the dynamics that animate collective protest actions: within an initial reference to injustice; that is, in the construction of a frame of injustice.

The passage that leads from the experience of injustice to effective struggle against the elements of injustice can thus be considered as the development of what we can call a practical dynamic and a normative dynamic. Social movements are traversed by a *practical dynamic* because following within them are the disturbance that has been suffered, an attempt to react, and then action with transformative purpose. This dynamic brings into play behaviors that are rooted in a feeling of the intolerable. It is accompanied by what we can call a *normative dynamic*—in this case, a cognitive process in the course of which the frustrated expectations suddenly come to consciousness before being integrated into normative discourses concerning the responsibilities at issue in the unjust situation and the demands that should be defended—a discourse that then feeds a collective reflection about the aims to be pursued and the means to be employed to achieve

them. Here it is a matter of a complex cognitive process that is one constituent part of the process of "frame construction" that initiates the social
movement and that subsequently develops within it in the form of explanatory efforts and internal group deliberations and conflicts with the frames
mobilized by the enemy groups.[63]

It cannot be insisted enough that the theoretical language best suited
for describing the politics of social movements is a *dynamic* language. The
normative factors never appear in actions as abstract and frozen formu-
las (objects of practical reason? intuitions of moral consciousness?), but
always as ways of explaining what is at issue in problematic experiences
and as means to resolve practical problems whose nature is never immediately clear. In the case of social movements, an account of the dynamic
dimension of normative factors is even more necessary because, first, it
has to move from situations experienced as problematic at the individual
level to collective demands; second, it must guide the analysis of what is
at stake in the problematic experience through the formulation of collective demands; and third, it must articulate the justification for demands
that are judged illegitimate by those who are *interested in maintaining the
status quo* and who rely upon principles of justice that already organize the
social world that the social movement works to transform.

These practical and normative dynamics can develop in different forms,
according to what we can call a *continuum of protest actions*. Its lower
boundary is defined by the forms of protest action that make use of a feeling of injustice without for all that formulating expressly political demands,
as in the case of "urban riots," which are not strictly speaking social movements in the sense that has been given to this term. Its upper boundary
is the social movement articulated upon a politically coherent discourse
entailing a justification of demands, a justification of the aims to be pursued to best see these demands succeed, and a justification of the means to
employ to achieve these objectives.

Not all instances of collective violence have a direct connection to the
feeling of injustice, as is evidenced by the case, for example, of dramatic
violence by hooligans. But there are also cases of collective violence whose
motivations do resemble those of social movements: riots. They stand out,
however, as much because of their objectives as by their type of internal
organization. The example of urban riots in response to illegitimate police
violence provides an example of collective movements stripped of stable

organization, where it is a matter of responding with violence to an injustice rather than collectively engaging in an enterprise aimed at resolving an unjust situation by transforming the factors of injustice. We could say that in this case, the protest action is only authorized by the legitimacy of its motivations (a refusal of injustice), not by a demand allowing it to assign a positive and specific content to the struggle against injustice. In order for protest action to take the form of a social movement strictly speaking, it must be endowed with specific forms of organization and an internal public space (an auditorium, a general assembly, discussions around a fire pit) in which the work is done of reflection about the normative expectations and values that animate the movement, as well as about the demands that should guide the collective action, the objectives to be achieved, and the means to be used.

Such a project of reflection about what is at stake in the feeling of justice and about the best way to respond to the situation's injustice can be interpreted as the extension of the experience of injustice in the form of the experience of consciousness. It constitutes a process of challenging values by practical means (critique) and creating values (making demands).[64] Social movements are simultaneously characterized by their critical and creative aspects: on the one hand, they yield effects of demystification and truth that explain, for example, the profound traces that they leave in the individuals that participate in them; and on the other, they are the site for a work to correct socially established values in the frame of a process of renewal of the meaning of these values,[65] this creativity of collective action constituting moreover one of the keys behind the unpredictable character of social movements' development.

Thus we can say that social movements are in fact traversed by a three-fold dynamic: the practical dynamic that leads from a situation undergone to the struggle against this situation; the normative dynamic that leads from the frustrated expectation to the reflective explication of this expectation and of its legitimacy, as well as its transformation into a reason for action; and the normative dynamic that extends the explication of these expectations' legitimacy by putting them into the form of demands, and which will eventually lead to the articulation of justifications for the means employed and the objectives sought. If the first two dynamics are already present in riots and in certain kinds of urban violence, in a more or less inchoate way, the third dynamic is unique to social movements.

From a sociological as well as a political point of view, it is important to stress that each of these dynamics can claim to have a first form of legitimacy: it is always legitimate to react practically in situations of contempt and humiliation; it is always legitimate to refuse to accept a feeling of injustice when it is socially produced. This leads to a first level of justification: if it is always legitimate to reject injustice, then it is also possible to justify an action by the humiliation or the feeling of injustice that led to it. But it is important just the same to carefully distinguish these first types of legitimacy and this first level of justification from forms of legitimacy and justification that refer to what falls under what we have designated as the third dynamic. On the one hand, in fact, we must distinguish the legitimacy of motivations (such as that of rejecting injustice) and the legitimacy of demands: it is in fact clear that a legitimate motivation can lead to illegitimate demands (the fact that xenophobic populisms are based upon denunciations of the injustice suffered by the working class provides one illustration). On the other, it is also evident that legitimate demands could be associated with more or less illegitimate objectives, which, in turn, could be pursued by more or less legitimate means (the end does not always justify the means).

To illustrate these different points, we can take the example of what is ordinarily designated by the too-vague category of "urban violence," understanding it to mean collective violence in neglected or "bad" neighborhoods. To be sure, it is difficult for residents of "better" neighborhoods to make sense of attacks whose victims include firefighters, teachers, doctors, and bus drivers, and the temptation is great to see these acts either as completely irrational or pathological behavior or as immoral behavior that ought to be forcefully denounced and severely reprimanded. Therefore, generalizing and stigmatizing judgments most often drive discussions of urban violence. By refusing to recognize even the least bit of legitimacy in these various behaviors and by assigning an absolutely negative value to them, it is easy to stigmatize the residents of "ghettos," reproducing the social contempt they have witnessed within a bad social philosophy. This is social contempt raised to the second power, for it is possible to accord a first level of legitimacy even to forms of urban violence that appear as (and undeniably are) the most illegitimate—even to attacks on doctors, bus drivers and firefighters.

As a result of the increasing precariousness of work and of social exclusion, residents of neglected neighborhoods are subjected to a denial of recognition that saps the very bases of the idea that they could realize their own value. How could individuals who are trapped in neighborhoods abandoned by all those who are able to leave such a social environment, and who are subjected to various forms of stigmatization as soon as they try to cross its borders—how could they be protected from the feeling of "being degraded" or "unwelcome anywhere"?[66] How could such a structural denial of recognition possibly lead to anything but the feeling that society has no place for them, that they have been stripped of everything that gives value to life? These questions lead us to interpret acts of urban violence as a response to the social violence that is carried out through social contempt.[67] Moreover, these questions make it possible to shed light upon the constellation of ethical and political problems that manage to express themselves in this demand for "respect" that, in the parlance of some "suburban youth," seems to have been established as the highest value. More broadly, these questions broach the problematic of the moral motivations behind certain violent behaviors.

To be sure, it is psychologically less disturbing and morally more comfortable to keep this problematic closed—either by accepting a repressive analytical table of violence (moral or legal analysis), or by interpreting it as the effect of a loss of cultural reference points (culturalist analysis) or even of self-destructive tendencies (psychoanalytic analysis). None of these explanations is sufficient. The category of "a loss of cultural reference points" underestimates the weight of socialization upon individuals and the fact that, even in the context of negative (devaluing or stigmatizing) socialization, individuals internalize logics of social action that provide "reference points." Moreover, the category of "a loss of cultural reference points" presupposes a social philosophy that is just as questionable because it seems to presuppose that every society displays a consensus founded on everyone's adherence to shared values such that everyone should have the same reference points. The explanation in terms of self-destructive violence[68] could lead one to compare the Los Angeles riots with those in French suburbs. According to this approach, it would be characteristic of collective acts of violence that they are directed against the residents' own living environment (public services, stores, housing). Founded in self-hatred, violence's only goal would be destroying one's own life by destroying its conditions.

Another interpretation is more plausible even taking into account the apparently most irrational forms of violence, like those that would lash out at parts of one's own living environment or at representatives of the rest of society, independent of any collective mobilization against an injustice in the form of a riot. Just as incitements addressed to other residents of one's neighborhood, or violence directed against the residents of other neighborhoods and symbols of the outside (like buses) should be interpreted as attempts to claim a territory,[69] likewise, violence against elements of one's living environment can be interpreted as being directed against those things that symbolize a denial of recognition, rather than as the destruction of a valued space. Destruction of housing can be understood as violence directed against the environment as it reflects a degraded image of oneself.[70] Attacks victimizing firefighters, doctors, shopkeepers, or even teachers could also be interpreted as violence directed against the representatives of a social order from which one is excluded. We can thus discern that this violence, which at first glance appeared completely irrational, can nonetheless be based upon a refusal to accept the degradation of one's existence. In this sense, it can be supported by a practical dynamic aiming to reestablish one's personal integrity, a dynamic that carries the hope of a better life, a dynamic that can claim a certain legitimacy—even if this hope is expressed in a way that is itself irrational because the targets of urban violence turn out to be very far from the real vehicles of social contempt.

As for urban violence that manifests as riots, these can bring a second form of legitimacy into play, as in France where, typically, they follow from what is deemed to be illegitimate police violence. Collective action is thus accompanied by an elucidation of the reasons to answer violence with violence and an assignment of responsibility, although the threshold into making demands is not really crossed and this elucidation does not serve to organize the mobilization. It is no longer only the right to react against injustice that makes it possible to attribute some kind of legitimacy to violence, but the right to lash out against those one judges (rightly or wrongly) to have caused the injustice (the police), and the right to no longer obey a legal order that one judges (rightly or wrongly) to support injustice. It is still clear, however, that this second form of legitimacy, if it can make use of a better right than the first, remains relative and limited, as much because of the absence of a demand that would give a positive and specific content to the collective mobilization as because of the political stupidity of the (counterproductive and illegitimate) means employed.

A political attitude that is careful to avoid elevating the experience of injustice to the second power (by denying any legitimacy to conscious refusals of injustice)—just like a comprehensive sociology that is careful to capture the immanent logics of behavior—should be able to account for the specific normative potential of such protest actions. They should also bear in mind that only the normative dynamic that leads from a frustrated normative expectation to its reflective articulation, and to its transformation into reasons to act (assigning responsibility and granting legitimacy), is present in these violent and collective reactions against the "blunders" and abuses of law attributed to the forces of order. It is not accompanied by the normative dynamic that leads to defining the demands liable to be publicly defended in order to discuss legitimate ends and means. However, this second dynamic is indeed an extension of the first, which limits the applicability of the opposition between the political logic of a riot and that of a social movement. In the same way, reflection upon the political stupidity of riots can constitute one element in the establishment of social movements, and even in that of structured political organizations.[71] Conversely, the failure of political movements, or of social movements, can always give rise to violent collective actions analogous to riots.

Thus, a continuity exists between these different forms of protest action. On the one hand, there is a form of continuity between the most irrational forms of collective violence (which lash out at their own environment or at sacrificial victims) and riots grounded in a feeling of injustice. This continuity becomes clear when the most irrational forms of violence *reappear* in riots grounded in a feeling of injustice (as was the case in the Los Angeles riots, as well as the suburban riots in France in 2005). On the other hand, there is continuity between riots and social movements that can themselves be transformed into structured political movements. All this illustrates the *continuum* of protest action; and within this continuum, social movements represent the most reflective forms—and those which can claim the highest levels of legitimacy—since political movement as such does not belong to the genre of "protest action."

The theory of recognition makes it possible to describe the relation that exists between the practical dynamic of refusing an unjust situation (triggered by a feeling of injustice produced by a denial of recognition) and the two normative dynamics, in which the elucidation of recognitive expectations make it possible to elaborate demands and justifications. The theory thus makes it possible to explain the continuum of protest action while distinguishing different kinds of justification from a point of view immanent in the normative dynamics of the action, and not from an external and absolute point of view of a legal or moral normativity. It makes it possible to ask the question of the legitimacy of motivations while distinguishing it from the legitimacy of demands, of objectives, and of means of action. But is the theory of recognition really able to measure the value of these demands, objectives, and means of action?

This question is often posed as an objection. In fact, even if we grasp how a theory of recognition can serve to explicate what is at stake in experiences of injustice and describe the practical and cognitive dynamics that find their origins therein, and even if we also grasp how it leads us to see a first level of justification for action in the feeling of injustice, it is still difficult to see how it could determine the legitimacy of action. The apparent consequence is that a theory of recognition would need to be completed by an independent theory of justice. Before presenting in the next chapter a detailed examination of the kind of conception of justice to which the theory of recognition can lead, I can note here that the idea of recognition defines one way of discussing legitimacy. In fact, the idea that the struggle against different forms of denial of recognition is legitimate cannot be separated from the idea that it can only truly be so if such a struggle does not produce even greater denials of recognition. Consequently, every social movement that is directed at the transformation of institutional vehicles of social contempt will appear to be legitimate, on the condition that neither their general demands, nor the particular objectives that they seek, nor the means that they employ result in aggravated forms of social contempt. This in itself is probably not enough for a criterion of legitimacy, but as we shall see in the next chapter, it is unlikely that questions about criteria are fundamental in the political confrontations over justice and injustice.

Chapter Two

THE APORIAS OF SOCIAL JUSTICE

The fact that the "ought" is a concept expressed in relation to action is important for the practical dimension of the concept of justice. In fact, this concept is inseparable from two kinds of relation to action: justification, and the refusal of injustice. Justification is a practical relation because it constitutes one of the communicative and motivational elements of social action. To be able to act in a morally problematic situation, I must be able to justify my action in my own eyes and in those of my interaction partners. Many theories of justice capture this practical dimension. But a theory of justice must also be able to explain the second practical dimension of the concept of justice, that connected to a refusal of situations experienced as unjust. In other words, a theory of justice cannot simply accept a definition of justice based on conditions of justification and the dynamics of a communicative resolution of conflicts, but must also account for the dynamics proper to the refusal of injustice.

Now, normative political philosophy has only rarely met this requirement. Of course, it is not uncommon to encounter attempts to define justice starting from injustice. At the very beginning of his book on justice, *The Just*, Paul Ricoeur declared, "Was not our first entry into the region of lawfulness marked by the cry: 'that's not fair'?"[1] And in the preface to *Spheres of Justice*, Michael Walzer also ties justice to equality while defining equality as the negation of socially imposed inequalities: "The root meaning of equality is negative; egalitarianism in its origins is an abolitionist politics."[2] Ricoeur and Walzer both establish an essential connection between justice and injustice, but this connection remains psychological (the entryway to the domain of law) or logical (the meaning of justice) without analyzing justice's practical connection to the unjust situation itself. To do so, the analysis must shift to the terrain of the experience of injustice—this is where the nonsatisfaction of normative expectations sets in motion the dynamics that define a practical relation to injustice, the traces of which are carried by the type of normativity associated with the notion of justice.

The preceding chapter identified the practical and normative dynamics that are born from the experience of injustice, but not much has yet been said about the normative characteristics that should be associated with the struggle against injustice—the type of normativity that is proper to social justice, the criteria that characterize it, and its domain of application. To clarify these normative characteristics means that we must consider the logical and political problems of a particularly controversial concept: social justice.

INJUSTICE AND THE SOCIAL QUESTION

The meaning of the concept of social justice is not clear. Friedrich Hayek, for one, stresses this point in the brief history that he offers of the notion.[3] But to grant him this point does not necessarily entail that we must accept the conclusions he draws from it:

What we have to deal with in the case of "social justice" is simply a quasi-religious superstition of the kind which we should respectfully leave in peace so long as it merely makes those happy who hold it, but which we must fight when it becomes the pretext of coercing other men. And the prevailing belief in "social justice" is at present probably the gravest threat to most other values of a free civilization.[4]

To deduce from a notion's uncertainty its necessary rejection is to fail to realize that logico-political aporias are essential to political concepts. But Hayek is hardly representative of the general attitude toward a concept that seems so self-evident that it is rarely subjected to critical examination. As the concept of social justice no longer seems to pose real difficulties, and as the authors are few and far between who deem it necessary to specify the precise form of justice that it designates and how it concerns the social, it will be useful to lay out a few aporias.

One can note, to begin, that there are two ways of situating the concept of social justice within the polysemy peculiar to the term justice. The first makes reference to actual meanings of the idea of justice and is based upon the concepts of personal justice, legal justice, political justice, and social justice. The second is related to Aristotelian concepts and the distinction between legal justice, corrective justice, distributive justice, and justice within exchange (or commutative justice). Let us start by following the first approach.

Justice can be understood, firstly, as the moral value of particular actions; this sense of the term can be called personal justice, or justice as a moral obligation. Justice can also designate what is encompassed in conformity with positive law, whether it is a matter of behaviors that are subject to the law (it is said to be just to respect the rights conferred upon individuals by law) or judicial decisions themselves (we sometimes speak of "justice" to refer to judicial institutions). To distinguish these two senses, the latter can be called legal justice, or justice as a legal obligation. Furthermore, the term "justice" can be applied to another kind of object: institutions, speaking in this respect of institutional justice. Two conceptual choices are then possible. The first is to hold that the entirety of institutional justice (that of social *and* political institutions) defines social justice. This is Rawls's position, when he states that social justice concerns the "basic structure" of society. In *A Theory of Justice*, the first principle governs constitutional arrangements (or, if you will, "political justice"), whereas the second principle governs economic and social politics; that is, the problems posed by economic and social institutions (or, if you will, social justice in the strict sense).[5] An alternative conceptual choice holds, on the contrary, that social justice is a particular form of institutional justice, thus distinguishing between political justice and social justice (or social justice in the strict sense).[6] This conceptual split cannot be explained simply by the terminological choice in which society is understood to mean either the entirety of institutions, or simply the institutions of civil society as distinct from the state. In philosophy, in general, conceptual choices are always philosophical choices; in political philosophy, they are always philosophical and political choices. Behind this split lies a fundamental political issue, tied to the implications that the distinction between society and the state has historically had for the very idea of justice.

To grasp this, it suffices to observe that previous distinctions, which seem so natural to us, are in fact just as recent as the concept of social justice. Within the context of modern natural law, for example, the question of institutional justice has principally been concerned with the legitimacy of positive law. If we acknowledge, in fact, that the whole of society is governed by juridical relations, it is logical to conclude that a society administered by just laws is also a just society. However, the actual modalities of our experience of politics rely in particular upon the fact that this sort of vision is not self-evident. Alongside the birth of the concept of social justice, in fact, we find the claim that just laws and a political order that is in conformity with them does not suffice to guarantee the justice of social institutions. This claim emerged in the middle of the nineteenth century, under the phrase "the social question," when it became clear that a political and legal order in conformity with the full set of fundamental political and private rights could be consistent with the existence of an unbridled injustice in different social spaces.

The term "social justice" is often defined in a different way, by reference to the Aristotelian typology of forms of justice. Among the many terminological distinctions of Book 5 of the *Nicomachean Ethics*, we need only recall the distinction between complete (or universal) justice and partial (or particular) justice; and the difference established between the three forms of partial justice. Complete justice pertains to actions' conformity to the laws, when the laws are aimed at the political community's good. Partial justice stems from the matter of receiving or not receiving more than what one is owed, and it takes three forms: (1) distributive justice, related to "the distribution of honors, of material goods, or of anything else that can be divided among those who have a share in the political system,"[i] which can be said to be a matter of geometrical equality (honors and riches being divided according to merit); (2) corrective justice, which rectifies the situation when harm has been done in private transactions—here it is assumed that a judge's intervention is a matter of arithmetical equality; and (3) justice in exchange, termed "justice as reciprocity" (or later "commutative justice"), which is concerned with a new form of equality—a "reciprocity in terms of a proportion and not in terms of exact equality"[ii] (the differential

i. Aristotle, *Nicomachean Ethics*, trans. Martin Ostwald (Englewood Cliffs, NJ: Prentice Hall/ Library of Liberal Arts, 1962),117, 1130b31–33.

ii. Aristotle, *Nicomachean Ethics*, 124, 1132b34–35.

value of various kinds of labor implies that exchanges cannot be governed by a strictly arithmetical equality as a function of time spent, but rather that the quantity of labor must be offset by the value of each kind of labor).

The identification of social justice with distributive justice is quite typical in contemporary debates. We find it in the very first paragraph of *A Theory of Justice*, and in the Preface to *Spheres of Justice*, where Walzer describes society as a vast distribution system. It is, to be sure, indisputable that the distribution of goods poses a fundamental political problem, and that it calls for a definition of just distribution. The controversy hinges on the forms that such a claim can take today, and on the appropriateness of generalizing a model of distributive justice to cover the entire domain of social justice. Iris Marion Young has made what is probably the most thorough critique of this generalization.[7] She showed that the paradigm of distributive justice rests upon three questionable presuppositions: an individualist social philosophy; a reification of the objects of social expectations; and a conflation of the problem of justice with that of the choice of institutional structures.

To Young's first point, the paradigm of distributive justice is tied to an individualist social philosophy, insofar as it conveys the image of a social world composed of a set of independent individuals externally connected to each other by individually possessed goods (the distributed goods)—the paradigm of social justice thus passes over in silence both those problems of justice that are linked to the social relations in which individuals are situated, as well as those tied to institutional effects that cannot be analyzed in terms of distribution. Furthermore, this paradigm claims that all of our expectations with regard to society should be conceived as expectations oriented toward goods—as in Rawls, who understands the term "social goods" to encompass values as diverse as rights, opportunities, wealth, and the social bases of self-respect; but who, by the same token, has difficulty accounting for the specificity of expectations regarding irreducibly social (relational and nonsubstantial) and cultural (symbolic and nonmaterial) objects. Moreover, this distributive paradigm has the disadvantage of obscuring the institutional context of justice. Applied to institutions, the framework of distribution can only account for the problem of distribution of wealth and social positions, whereas the question of injustices within institutions is larger, as we naturally intuit (a point to which I will return in the next chapter): injustice within institutions is connected both to contexts of interaction and to effects ofsubjectivization. Furthermore, given that the concept of distribution presupposes the existence of an institutional mechanism that effects the distribution, the distributive paradigm tends to reduce the question of justice to a choice for the most equitable institutional settings. This way of framing the problem as one of choice does not allow us to account for the fact that social injustices are not only produced by institutional structures, but also by the transformative dynamics of social relations (as illustrated by the contemporary terms *disaffiliation* and *precaritization*—I will return to these). Nor does it allow one to take account of the fact that the struggle against injustice linked to the social question is one of transforming existing institutions rather than of choosing social orders.

Nevertheless, as soon as this social question became a part of public discourse, people have tried to translate the new problems into the old Aristotelian vocabulary of justice. One of the first philosophical instances of the term "social justice" is to be found in *Utilitarianism*, where John Stuart Mill makes the concept of social justice a synonym for distributive justice. Social justice thus designates a social duty, analogous to the duty of justice that defines justice as a moral obligation—in this case, for a distribution of utility and goods in proportion to merit:

If it is a duty to do to each according to his deserts, returning good for good, as well as repressing evil by evil, it necessarily follows that we should treat all equally well (when no higher duty forbids) who have deserved equally well of *us*, and that society should treat all equally well who have deserved equally well of *it*, that is, who have deserved equally well absolutely. This is the highest abstract standard of social and distributive justice, toward which all institutions and the efforts of all virtuous citizens should be made in the utmost possible degree to converge.[8]

How can a society have duties? What, precisely, does "distribution" mean here? How does the call for a just distribution apply to the various institutions? All these questions serve to indicate the insufficiency of the distributive definition of justice and, more generally, that attempting to translate new problems into the language of old solutions is a dead end.

The problems indicated by the emergence of the expression "social question" clearly cannot be reduced to problems of distribution. Rather than the distribution of wealth, they are primarily concerned with injustices linked to the functioning of the labor market, to the increasing precariousness of work, and to salary and wage levels. Even more than endemic unemployment and the competition among workers that it entails, the social question historically designates a situation in which workers' wages do not allow them to live a decent life. From an Aristotelian point of view, it is thus a question of commutative justice (a question of just wages) rather than of distributive justice. Moreover, it is not certain that in modern societies the question of distribution of wealth can be compatible with the meaning of the Aristotelian concept of distributive justice. For Aristotle, the concept of distributive justice refers only to goods held in common by the political community and by private associations. The goods held in common, of which it is entirely legitimate to ask how they should be distributed, are wealth and honors. If wealth could be considered as one of the goods held in common, that is because "[i]n Greece . . . , the citizen regarded himself . . . as a shareholder in the state rather than as a taxpayer; and public property, e.g. the land of a new colony, was not infrequently divided among them . . ."9 This definition of wealth is hardly compatible with a capitalist economy in which wealth is seen as an accumulation of material goods. Here, wealth takes the form of individually owned particular goods, whose distribution is principally a matter of exchanges, such that distributive justice does not seem to apply. To try to show that it does nonetheless is the subject of a controversy concerning the relation between distributive and redistributive justice. On the one hand, it will always be possible, in fact, to maintain that market-based distribution of wealth rests upon the rewarding of individual virtue, such that the market achieves, at least imperfectly, the ideal of distributive justice.10 Yet on the other hand, it is just as possible to maintain that distributive justice cannot have any contemporary meaning except in the form of redistributive justice. It is then a matter of the redistribution of income whose distribution is initially determined by the market. This redistribution itself supposes taxation as a form of collective appropriation that makes it possible to establish an income held in common that will then be the object for distribution in a just way. There is at least a twofold normative problem that must thus be resolved. First, there is a conflict of legitimacy between individuals' rights to the wealth that they have legally acquired, and the rights of the less privileged to benefit from a redistribution of that wealth. Second, there is a question as to whether a social injustice (tied to wages, working conditions, or loss of employment and the various reductions in quality of life that result) can be adequately addressed in a compensatory justice, given that social aid, for example, can be experienced as a particularly painful form of social stigmatization. Still other problems arise, concerning the retroactive effects of taxation upon the production and distribution of wealth, or even concerning an adequate definition of contributors—economic actors (businesses, families); social classes (based upon levels or types of income)? Understanding social justice in terms of distributive justice most often means proposing redistribution as an answer to the social question. But the concepts thereby introduced have very little to do with those that the Aristotelian concept of distributive justice attempted to address, and it is not at all clear that they can fulfill the functions to which they are assigned.

This point—that Aristotelian concepts are hardly applicable to the questions raised since the middle of the nineteenth century by the term social justice—was underscored by Catholic groups opposed to the integration of the concept of social justice within the social doctrine of the Church. This opposition could point to the Thomistic reinterpretation of the Aristotelian theory of justice, as in the pamphlet "On 'Social Modernism': 'Social Justice' and 'Catholic Doctrine.' "[11] The author attempts to show that the social question must not be understood within the framework of problems of social justice for the following reasons: (1) the fate of the poor must be addressed not only through justice, but also through charity; (2) as social conflicts concerning wages are conflicts between different parts of society, they should be addressed through commutative justice and charity, not though distributive justice (contrary to what the advocates of social justice maintain); and (3) the idea of social justice is dangerous because it claims to displace older models of legal justice by approaching the general organization of society for the common good, while reducing the question of the common good to the economic question of distribution of wealth. The idea of social justice would thus consist of a web of confusions between legal justice, commutative justice, and distributive justice—confusions linked to the exorbitant extension of a concept claiming to speak about society in general—whereas we should distinguish different kinds of relations within society, each of which calls for a specific kind of justice. Without subscribing to this reactionary point of view, we can acknowledge that it quite rightly sees that the framework of distributive justice does not make it possible to account for the diversity of institutions and relations that are answerable to justice.

The meaning of the concept of social justice must not be sought in Aristotelian concepts but rather in the social injustices whose abolition it envisions within the specific framework of the social question. The term "social question" really entered into the public sphere in the 1830s,[12] in connection with the discovery of a new form of poverty then called "pauperism." We have to grasp how much intellectual upheaval was caused by the discovery of pauperism, and the resultant shift in the meaning of the ideas of justice and the social. Robert Castel describes the problem in this way:

This was an essential moment, when the divorce first appeared between a juridico-political order founded on the recognition of the rights of citizens and an economic order that carried with it widespread misery and demoralization . . . This split between the political organization and the economic system allows us to note, for the first time with clarity, the place of the "social": to be deployed in this gap, to restore or establish new bonds that obey neither a strictly economic logic nor a strictly political authority.[13]

The problem is that the simple respect for individual rights put forward by classical political liberalism does not seem able to guarantee conditions of existence that are acceptable for all members of society: a society's value seems, at least in part, to be independent of the liberal conception of political justice.

This problem raises an objection to liberalism by claiming that justice should be defined by rights over social institutions and not only by protections of liberty; and by claiming that we must take claim rights and not merely liberty rights into account. The conflict between these two conceptions of rights must be grasped in all its radicalness. The idea of social rights does not merely express a different interpretation of rights; it is the assertion of a properly political demand. It answers the demand directed against injustices grounded in social institutions. A demand means a legitimate claim, and a response to social injustice means a right over society; that is a claim right. Ultimately, the specifically political practical dimension of the idea of social justice is indeed located within the idea of social rights. But it is nonetheless marked by a profound ambiguity, because it could lead to demands either for a set of measures to compensate for social injustice or for the transformation of social institutions that produce injustice—an ambiguity that sustains political confrontations.

Social rights found their legitimation and legal recognition in France, which made possible the establishment of the welfare state,[14] through the intermediary of Léon Bourgeois's Solidarism.[15] Solidarism tried to resolve the conflict between these two conceptions of rights, not through a normative theory of rights but through a social theory. Solidarity was then understood according to a Durkheimian model that presupposed, on the one hand, that individuals only exist through their inscription in collectivities that are defined through forms of solidarity; and, on the other, that modern societies have passed from a mechanical solidarity to an organic solidarity founded upon the division of labor. Bourgeois concluded therefrom that every individual owes a debt to society—the fact that he benefits from an organic solidarity makes it possible to depict his rights as dependent on an original debt. Because this solidarity is fragile (as it is a kind of indirect solidarity, that of the division of labor), it is always at risk of being broken, such that the state must always ensure its maintenance—in particular, by providing aid to the various "losers" of social cooperation. To this end, the state can place levies on wealth, by virtue of the debt that everyone owes to society as a whole. The idea of a social right is thus emptied of any subversive significance and social justice is reduced to a compensatory justice. Social rights are no longer presented as subjective rights (of legitimate demands), but only as objective rights (as legally guaranteed possibilities). That which governs an individual's relation to society is no longer the rights that one could assert, but rather one's debt with respect to society.

This solidarist conception of social justice rests upon a conception of social aid and a conception of the social, both of which are quite debatable. In a certain respect, Marx had already rejected them. In his 1844 article, "Critical Marginal Notes on the Article 'The King of Prussia and Social Reform. By a Prussian,'"[16] he stressed that the social question cannot be ruled by a compensatory justice. The article begins by explaining that pauperism is not uniquely German, but is a characteristic of all contemporary societies. By "pauperism," Marx writes, we must understand "universal distress, a distress whose general significance is shown partly through its periodic recurrence, partly through its geographic extension, and partly through the frustration of all attempts at its alleviation."[17] We see here the two characteristics of the new poverty that is linked to the social question: periodic crises; and the growth of poverty tied to work (no longer simply to the absence of work). Marx endeavors to show, through a brief history of the measures that have been employed, that every attempt aimed at remedying this new poverty has failed: encouragement of charity, legal beneficence underwritten by a poor tax (or an obligation on the part of parishes to give aid to destitute workers), confinement in English work-houses[iii] or French maisons de dépôt. Public authorities were constantly imagining poverty as a fundamental problem to resolve, even developing cumbersome administrative infrastructures, veritable "ministries of poverty." However, governments never managed to eliminate it, and had to be satisfied with addressing its effects with a view to social regulation:

In the course of its development and in spite of administrative measures, pauperism has raised itself to the status of a *national institution*, thereby inevitably becoming the object of a wide-spread administration, with many branches to it, an administration which, however, is no longer charged with suppressing pauperism, but rather with *disciplining* it, perpetuating it. This administration has given up trying to stifle the source of pauperism by means of *positive* measures; it is satisfied with digging a grave for it, with police-like charity, whenever it bubbles to the surface of public life.[18]

The institutions of the welfare state fall under this now-classic critique. At least in part, they indeed constitute a set of techniques aimed at disciplining poverty and mastering the political danger that it entails. This critique of the institutions of public assistance serves, in Marx, to justify a revolutionary position. More precisely, it announces the demand for a social revolution. If the regulatory policies have failed, it is because they do not address the structural causes of poverty and inequality—the dynamics of modern industry.

Thus we find in Marx a critique of the definition of the social that inspired solidarism's compensatory understanding of social justice. This critique rests on the claim that social life cannot be considered as a harmonious whole in essence, only unjust by accident. Society is always traversed by class conflicts and by a struggle to maintain inequalities that were obtained through violence. As Max Weber would later note (following Georg Simmel), conflict is a mode of structuring the social,[19] which implies in particular that the latter cannot be understood in a substantive way: there is

iii. In English in the original.

no such thing as "the social," but rather different kinds of social relations, different kinds of social institutions that do not have any essential link with the idea of solidarity.[20]

The conception of social justice as solidarity has played a fundamental role in the establishment of the twentieth-century social welfare state [*État social*], and it is not surprising that we should find traces of this conception in thinkers (like Rawls) who seek to legitimate the welfare state [*État providence*]. In § 2 of *A Theory of Justice*, Rawls claims that in order "[f]ully to understand a conception of justice, we must make explicit the conception of social cooperation from which it derives."[21] Examining "The Circumstances of Justice" in § 22, he explains that questions of justice can only arise if two conditions are met: first, a conflict of interests as to the distribution of the benefits of social cooperation; and second, a convergence of interests tied to the fact that in a context of resource scarcity, social cooperation is necessary. In Rawls, cooperation is thus the site of an objective solidarity, not a conflict, as conflicts are only concerned with the distribution of what results from it. The goal of cooperation is immediately presented as advancing "the good of its members"[22]—that is, their capacity to enjoy the "primary social goods" together. As for justice, it is introduced as an instrument that makes it possible to maintain the benefits of social cooperation. Thus we learn, as early as § 3 of *A Theory of Justice*, that "the division of advantages should be such as to draw forth the willing cooperation of everyone taking part in it, including those less well situated."[23] We find here the old conflation of social bonds and solidarity, masking all those aspects of the division of labor that can be described as domination (the sexual division of labor; the division between manual and intellectual labor; the division between city and country; the delegation of "dirty work"; etc.) and exploitation.

If we consider the facts that, first, basing social rights upon a social debt is unable to resolve the problems posed by the structures of the division of labor (whether this is deceptively conceived in terms of cooperation or solidarity); second, that it is unable to account for the specifically political dimension of social rights (namely, the expression of demands upon society); and finally, that this move is grounded in a particularly problematic social theory, our conclusion is self-evident: the concept of social justice must rather be articulated in light of a demand for the transformation of social institutions that produce injustice; and the only thing it can favorably recommend is a society caught up in such a process of transformation. What the social question requires is a social justice understood as the demand for the equal (the meaning of which has to be explained) satisfaction of a set of legitimate (the meaning of which has to be explained) claims, understood as a set of rights bearing directly on those social institutions upon which the satisfaction of these claims depends, and which justify their transformation. Only a definition of social justice that begins from the demands born out of the experience of injustice will succeed in achieving a sufficiently dynamic and institutional definition, one whose practical import includes not only proposing a public justification for a choice among different institutional settings (an objective that doesn't seem at all to correspond to those situations where important political questions arise), but also giving explicit legitimacy to projects that aim to transform the existing institutional frameworks (an objective whose significance for effective politics is clear).

RIGHTS AND JUSTICE

Every demand posits a claim and asserts that this claim is legitimate, or that it is a right. This is why the most important problem for a theory that would account for the political dimension of the concept of social justice is the relationship between justice and rights. The problem can be posed in two different ways, depending on whether one aims to articulate a theory of justice based upon a theory of universal expectations, or upon a theory of law. In the first case, the legitimacy of demands (the rights that we can enforce with regard to them) is based upon universality, not upon the law. In the second case, the legitimacy of demands is based upon a higher law.

Rawls provides an illustration of the first approach. In a certain respect, rights are precisely what the theory of justice determines, as is explicitly shown in the very phrasing of the first principle: "each person is to have an equal right to the most extensive basic liberty compatible with a similar liberty for others."[iv] The first principle establishes rights, while the second considers the conditions that impact "the value to individuals of the rights that the first principle defines."[24] Nevertheless, this first stage of the deduction of rights presupposes a preliminary form of reflection

iv. John Rawls, *A Theory of Justice* (Cambridge, MA: Harvard University Press, 1970), 60.

about the legitimacy of expectations, in the form of a theory of primary goods. It is upon the basis of this theory that justice is defined as the equitable distribution of primary goods such as individuals could imagine it in the original position. The question of their legitimacy is posed in terms of universality and not of a law. The primary goods are posited as "things that every rational man is presumed to want."[25] If we identify the question of legitimacy as that of rights, we will probably say that this appears as a theory of two kinds of rights: the rights that we can claim regarding the objects of our legitimate expectations, and the rights that are granted to us regarding the distribution of these objects. However, for Rawls, only the second kind of rights figure as such when their legitimacy is derived. This is why he stresses that his work *A Theory of Justice* does not constitute a theory founded on rights.[26]

In fact, the concept of rights entails several difficulties in Rawls's argument. Legitimate expectations are defined within the frame of a theory of rational life and of individual plans of life, whereas justice is not supposed to arrive until later, at the same time as rights, in order to determine how different legitimate expectations can coexist. Following the logic of contractarianism, rights can certainly be introduced as the result of a compromise between individuals' demands. But to account for their specific normative claims, the normative expectations that are the objects of compromise must themselves be based upon legitimate claims or rights—and it is not so easy to accept that a theory of primary goods could very readily take the place of natural law for this purpose.[27] Furthermore, in order to explain expectations specifically tied to life in society, Rawls is led to reintroduce rights themselves in the list of primary goods: "the chief primary goods at the disposition of society are rights and liberties, powers and opportunities, income and wealth . . . [and] self-respect."[v] The concept of rights thus figures in the list of primary goods to which the theory of justice appeals in order to determine to what extent we have rights! These theoretical problems have their political counterpart: the problems of social justice present themselves not only as problems that apply to the mediation between expectations recognized as legitimate, but also as conflicts in which the very legitimacy of those expectations is challenged. With Rawls, it is always possible to maintain that we can only find a satisfying solution to political

v. Rawls, *A Theory of Justice*, 60.

conflicts by adopting a point of view in which the irreconcilable character of demands disappears. But we must then be sure that such a consensus-based approach does not lose the properly political meaning of a conflict among demands, and that it preserves what is at stake in such conflicts.

As I have already noted, the concept of social justice was forged within the constraints of a political conflict pertaining to the clash between two opposing kinds of rights. Even today, the majority of debates concerning social justice are determined by this conflict between formal rights (as liberty rights) and social rights (as claim rights), or more precisely, between property rights and social rights.[28] The idea that social rights are fully fledged rights is generally acknowledged, and the question most often is one of the respective scopes of social rights and formal rights. The question of whether either of these kinds of rights is legitimate is generally avoided. On this point, too, Rawls provides a good illustration. The first principle is concerned with the legal guarantee of formal rights and proposes a definition of justice understood as equal respect for rights to liberty—or liberty rights—among which must be included the right "to hold (personal) property."[29] It is clear, moreover, that the second principle, addressing the conditions that make liberty valuable, concerns all those demands that, in the name of social rights, would stand in contrast to the restrictive definition of rights as freedom rights. For the majority of them, the sorts of demands that are traditionally encompassed by the idea of social rights are excluded from the list of fundamental rights, but are nevertheless preserved within the second principle by virtue of a consequentialist analysis. The distribution of primary goods apart from liberty is not presented as a rights claim, but as a reasonable claim that individuals should be accorded so that they may maximize the chances of realizing their life plans. Here again, Rawls's consensus-based strategy is carried out through the application of a procedure designed to avert the problem. His concern is not so much to try to address the problem raised by the conflict between liberty rights and social rights, as it is to provide a coherent articulation of the various elements in our representation of justice—to achieve a "reflective equilibrium" between our intuitions and our rational reflection. But avoiding a decision still constitutes a kind of decision. In this case, it is making a decision in favor of liberty rights. Once the principles of justice have been established, it seems in fact that only liberty rights are rights in the strong sense. To reconcile liberty rights and social rights without raising the problem of which kinds of rights each person is entitled to, is in effect to unreflectively go back to the least debatable and most restrictive possible understanding that could be given to the concept of fundamental rights; it is to conclude, quite simply, that social rights are not rights in the strict sense of the term.

Instead of connecting formal rights and social rights within the framework of a philosophy of law that would encompass all forms of rights and analyze their legitimacy, Rawls attempts to reconcile these two rights within the framework of a theory of the distribution of primary social goods (among which are included, we can recall, rights, liberties, opportunities, income, and wealth). This attempt is *conceptually* problematic for at least two reasons. First, rights, liberties, and opportunities on the one hand; and income and wealth on the other, are not goods in the same sense of the term, and it can be doubted whether the idea of distribution could be unequivocal if it refers to goods that are so different. Second, the paradigm of distribution is connected to a schema of possession (possessing goods and wealth), whereas rights are exercised or are claimed—in the same way as liberties can be exercised or can define opportunities for action. Furthermore, the Rawlsian attempt to reconcile formal rights and social rights is also *theoretically* questionable because it is not at all clear that one could account for the conflict over legitimacy that is inscribed within the problematic of social justice without inserting oneself into the battlefield over legitimacy; that is to say, without engaging arguments concerning rights.

All this leads us to think that if we are to take seriously the problems at the origins of the very idea of social justice, we really have to undertake a critical reflection upon rights. The problem of reciprocal limitation between property rights and social rights cannot be rigorously addressed without an explanation of the reciprocal legitimacy of each, nor without examining the conditions of their commensurability and their reciprocal subordination. To do so thus entails not only confronting a theoretical problem, but also preserving the political significance of the concept of social justice. As the demands made in the name of social justice are introduced as demands for rights, these demands always have to confront modes of justification of the existing social order that employ arguments of legal legitimacy against them; and what is at stake in these political confrontations is the institutionalization of the demands of social justice in a legal form. A critical theory will only be able to fully grasp those disputes in which the idea of social justice weighs heavily if it takes the form of a reflection upon rights. An understanding of social justice in terms of rights also makes possible an explanation of the all-inclusive character of demands concerning social justice. The latter are addressed to society as a whole, and to the state insofar as it has the power to act upon society; but they are concerned with neither the social as a specific reality (as in the solidarist version), nor this or that particular institution (as in the Aristotelian model that distinguishes between legal institutions, institutions of exchange, and institutions of distribution). It is true that different institutions establish specific principles of justice, but it is experiences (experiences of a wrong) that test the untruth of established principles of justice; and they do so then in the name of general claims—in the name of rights—that ought to be valued by all institutions and not only by one particular institution (and in this way we can understand the ease with which sectorial social movements come to speak of society in general and to affiliate with other sectorial social movements). To be sure, the claims of justice cannot be applied in the same way to different spaces of social life, but the demands concerning social justice do not begin from an objective analysis of the social world. They start from experiences of injustice—that is, from the particular effects of institutions on our lives—and they confront them with general claims in the name of which they demand a right to transform the vectors of injustice. The concept of rights makes it possible to adequately express the generality of the normative expectations that are thwarted in experiences of injustice.

If the concept of social justice must stay connected to political conflicts anchored in different forms of the social question, and to the language in which political demands are articulated, it thus cannot be understood in the sense of a (liberal) claim for equality of liberty rights that would furnish the legitimation principle for different social institutions; nor in the Aristotelian sense of equal exchange or proportional distribution; nor yet in the sense of principles of justice that specifically govern particular institutions. It can only be understood in the sense of respect for an ensemble of social rights—in a word, in the sense of a right to transform those institutions that thwart legitimate expectations. I have already suggested in the introduction that the theory of recognition makes it possible to produce such a concept of social justice. I must now demonstrate how it can succeed in doing so. The logical constraints that weigh upon such an undertaking are tied to the ways in which rights and freedom are interconnected.

RIGHTS AND FREEDOM

Since the concept of human nature no longer seems able to ground legal normativity, legitimate law is generally conceived as starting from freedom and its conditions. For this reason, the conflict between liberty rights and social rights has also been conceived as a conflict between two conceptions of freedom. It is most often by starting from a theory of the value of freedom that one tries to determine if rights over society (claim rights) can be recognized as rights, and what relations they may have with rights to exercise certain freedoms (formal rights). The respective positions of Kant and Hegel provide a typical illustration of this debate. As Kant explains in *The Metaphysics of Morals'* "Introduction to the Doctrine of Right," right must be understood as the condition for the coexistence of everyone's freedom; and, more precisely, of freedom as *Willkür*.[vi] By *Willkür*, Kant means a power of choice (a power of self-determination independent of one's inclinations) and an external freedom (the absence of external constraints). Freedom is thus conceived according to the model of what will be called negative liberty, and only those protections for the exercise of this freedom are recognized as rights. Right is thus conceived by Kant according to the model of liberty rights, and it is again for this reason that he vigorously rejects the idea of a right to well-being that, as a right to the material conditions of well-being, constitutes a claim right. His hostility with respect to such a right rests, moreover, on the idea that it is incompatible with the right to freedom. The second part of the essay "On the Proverb: That May Be True in Theory, But Is of No Practical Use" develops this idea in the form of a denunciation of paternalism: it is each individual's responsibility to freely seek his own happiness and to freely determine what is needed for it. The public authorities can in no way claim to do so without restricting their subjects' freedoms, without asserting to know better than the subjects themselves what constitutes their happiness, without treating them as minors—"such a government is the worst *despotism* we can think of."[vii] Everyone must be free to choose whether he wants to be happy or

---

vi. Immanuel Kant, *The Metaphysics of Morals*, ed. Mary Gregor (Cambridge: Cambridge University Press, 1996), 23–28.

vii. Immanuel Kant, "On the Proverb: That May Be True in Theory, But Is of No Practical Use," in *Perpetual Peace and Other Essays: On Politics, History, and Morals*, trans. Ted Humphrey (Indianapolis, IN: Hackett, 1983), 73.

not, and to choose the means he will employ to that end—by placing a poor individual in a hospice, it is likely that he will be forced into a life that he does not wish to lead, because perhaps he prefers his poverty to this kind of well-being. A second argument[30] is then added to this one, which insists upon the fact that a right to assistance would come about through the levying of taxes, property taxes being incompatible with the right to ownership.

In Hegel, on the contrary, the freedom that guarantees rights is conceived as a positive freedom understood as "being at home with oneself," or as the possibility of finding within the system of social institutions the conditions for the realization of one's freedom. It follows that rights are defined as rights to the conditions for the realization of freedom (as conditions of "the existence [Dasein] of freedom") following the model of claim rights: "An existent of any sort embodying the free will, this is what right is."[31] It follows not only that there is a right to well-being and that "that *particular welfare*" must be "*treated as a right* and duly *actualized*,"[32] but also that the entirety of social institutions come under the jurisdiction of the philosophy of right. The actualization of freedom demands that society establish a legal order guaranteeing the coexistence of negative liberties, along with a set of social settings like the family, a market regulated by the state, trade groups and corporations, etc.

The conflict between these two philosophies of right makes it possible to state the problem in its sharpest form, because it opposes the one thesis—that only freedom rights are rights in the proper sense—to the other that conceives of freedom rights as the most abstract claim rights. Ordinarily, intermediate positions confront each other in debates about social justice. The most common view acknowledges that we are dealing with two kinds of rights in the proper sense, while asserting that negative liberty must be recognized as a higher right for two reasons: first, because freedom cannot be legally defined except as the opening of a possibility for choice (freedom to vote, freedom of enterprise) and behavior protected from illegal constraints (freedom of conscience, freedom to use or misuse one's possessions); second, because only such negative freedoms can have a universal form ascribed to them, whereas the modes of actualizing freedom in the social world cannot be the object of any form of agreement. What is generally deduced therefrom is not that claim rights are stripped of any value, but simply that they are on a subordinate level and can only be recognized as rights insofar as they make it possible for a larger number of individuals to make use of their negative freedoms. This is the significance of the structure of the two principles in Rawls, and of Habermas's assertion that social rights "can only be justified in relative terms."[33]

The theory of recognition makes it possible to bring out the inadequacies of these arguments by underscoring that all negative liberties presuppose forms of positive freedom. It is only if my existence manages to integrate itself in a favorable social context (a form of "being with itself") that I can gain access to a positive relation to myself that presupposes the very idea of choice and of external liberty. As Charles Taylor has noted, the idea of negative liberty as the absence of external constraints presupposes the idea of liberty as the absence of internal constraints—the latter falling under the logic of an affirmation of a noncontradictory self through action; and thus, of positive freedom.[34] It must be added that what is true about negative liberty as external freedom is equally true for negative liberty as a power of choice. It presupposes a positive relation to oneself without which the idea of a choice regarding what is preferable among various possible options loses its meaning for the potential author of such a choice—as does the idea of choice itself. When the intersubjective, or institutional, environment constantly reflects back an image of oneself that is liable to undermine one's positive relation to oneself—or even transform it into a negative self-relation (or into a negative identity), shattering the positive self-image—the conditions of possibility for negative liberty collapse: Why make a choice if nothing truly matters for me anymore? The problem here is no longer just that a formal liberty (the freedom to work) is truly possible only if the social conditions for a choice are truly filled (one could choose to leave the paid workforce only if one had other financial means). The problem is that the very idea of a choice (between working and not working, even if the latter would be detrimental to me) presupposes a positive relation to myself that makes it possible to ask myself which of these choices is preferable. The value accorded to negative liberty, and its very possibility, thus depends upon relationships of recognition that maintain the positive relation to oneself, and that depend as much upon a certain kind of relation to others as upon a certain kind of relation to institutions. Recognizing negative liberties as rights can, in one sense, lead to the idea that recognitive expectations that support the fundamental forms of a positive self-relation also define rights over institutions. If we have a right to freedom, we must also have a right over the conditions that make these rights formal (possibilities for choice)—and those rights over conditions constitute social rights.

Let us review and summarize: On the one hand, the expectations for recognition that ground the fundamental forms of one's relation to oneself appear as legitimate expectations, or as rights, insofar as they belong to the conditions that open the horizon of valued choice—and in the same way, the domain of law, morality, and politics. On the other hand, the theory of recognition leads to a Hegelian sort of position, by subsuming liberty rights within claim rights. Recognition of the value of my freedom of choice itself is one of the conditions for a positive relation to oneself; it defines a recognition for which positive rights (private rights and constitutional rights) constitute the institutional medium. In other words, the legal guarantee of forms of negative liberty (freedom to choose one's profession; freedom of movement; freedom of association, of thought, etc.) is a part of the conditions for a positive relation to oneself, just as much as economic and social institutions are. But only those expectations for recognition directed at specifically social (not legal) institutions constitute those claim rights whose specific character is to be social rights, and which come under the scope of social justice (in the strict sense).

The demand for legal institutionalization of freedom rights can obviously come into conflict with the demand for legal institutionalization of social rights, just as a liberal definition of social justice can come into conflict with a socialist definition of justice. The theory of recognition serves not to demonstrate that such conflicts should not take place, but, on the contrary, to underscore that they must be taken seriously because the various rights in conflict express legitimate claims. By itself, a defense of the concept of social rights does not make it possible to resolve the conflict between liberty rights and social rights, no more than it makes it possible to propose a complete definition of social justice. Moreover, in the face of fundamental political problems (such as those at the heart of the opposition between liberalism and socialism, which come into sharp focus in the idea of social justice), the philosopher's task is probably not to decide between these rights; but to propose a definition of justice that will manage to account for what is at stake in the conflict, and to conceptually motivate siding with one of the two positions in dispute. In order to move toward this definition, we must now take up the question of what kind of normativity can lead back to social rights. In the philosophical debates about justice, this question has generally been posed by means of the conceptual distinction between the just and the good.

THE JUST AND THE GOOD

Can it be granted that the perspective of social justice suffices to encompass the set of questions upon which social values depend; or must another kind of normativity, different from that of the just, be acknowledged? And in the latter case, what sort of relation is there between these different kinds of normativity? It is impossible to explain the nature of this problem without once again making reference to Rawls. Section One of *A Theory of Justice* begins by asserting that "[j]ustice is the first virtue of social institutions, as truth is of systems of thought," before adding that "[b]eing first virtues of human activities, truth and justice are uncompromising."[35] He then adds that the question of social justice only refers to one of the virtues that define the value of social institutions: "A complete conception defining principles for all the virtues of the basic structure, together with their respective weights when they conflict, is more than a conception of justice; it is a social ideal. The principles of justice are but a part, although perhaps the most important part, of such a conception."[36] What are the other virtues only alluded to here? Section One explains that the function of principles of justice is to resolve distributive questions, but that "[t]here are other fundamental social problems, in particular those of coordination, efficiency, and stability"; it also maintains that "it is evident that these three problems are connected with that of justice";[37] moreover, the question of the social ideal refers back to the connection between the just and the good. Ultimately, a social ideal should be a model of society that achieves a perfect balance between justice and the good life within an institutional framework that ensures efficient coordination and stability.

Rawls thus indirectly indicates that a society can be critiqued from perspectives other than that of justice—such as, in particular, those of the good and of economic efficiency. The fact remains that some have attempted to replace the perspective of justice either with that of the good life,[38] or with that of economic efficiency.[39] Adopting the perspective of the experience of injustice requires that both of these positions be rejected. Economic efficiency is compatible with a proliferation of injustice, and it does not in fact provide any defined practical orientation, for there are various ways of institutionalizing and directing economic dynamics. Of course, not every-thing is compatible with the constraints imposed by the material basis of society; but economic theories only articulate laws of possibility, and leave it to politics to later steer the results toward possibilities that are compatible with a just and good life. Moreover, dogmatically presupposing a vision of the good life, in the name of a model of human nature or human excel-lence, does not make it possible to recover what is at stake in the experi-ence of injustice. It is difficult to see how a conception of human excellence or human essence could explain what is contained within the feeling of injustice and the demands that emerge therefrom, except by stating truisms like "it is an essential human quality to prefer the better over the worse," or "avoiding suffering is an essential human trait."

But the sharp distinction drawn between what is a matter of justice and what is a matter of the good, whose terms were set by Rawls, is no more satisfactory. We have already seen that social movements draw their origins from a disturbance to ways of life, and that they envision the transforma-tion of social forms that stand in the way of a satisfying life. What holds for social movements also holds for social demands in general: they are con-cerned as much with what is recognized as unconditional rights as with the conditions of life. Social rights, such as a right to employment or a right to housing, address the conditions for a satisfying life. They lead to a concept of the good life that is most likely not defined by starting from a conception of human nature (a perfectionist conception of the good life), or from judg-ments closely connected to collective goods (a communitarian conception of the good life); but they do take account of the conditions that distinguish between a satisfying and an unsatisfying life. The viewpoint of the experi-ence of injustice leads, of course, to the idea that justice constitutes the principal virtue of society, but it also implies that justice and the good do not refer back to two independent models of social critique.

How is the relationship between the just and the good presupposed by this approach to social justice to be understood? Thus framed, the question warrants a conceptual clarification. Justice and the just are understood here in different senses. *Justice* generally designates what is valued by societies, or the principal virtue of a society, whereas *the just* designates a specific kind of normativity, of which the question arises whether it is sufficient for a definition of justice (in the wide sense of the first virtue of societies), or whether it must be conjoined with consideration of a second kind of normativity, that of the good. The problem is thus to know which types of normativity belong to the good and the just, and what relationship obtains between these two types of normative scales. Among those who admit this conceptual distinction's relevance, the just and the good are contrasted by appealing respectively to the normativity of *legal and moral* imperatives, and to that of *ethical* values. We have, on the one side, the principles guaranteeing the exercise of our individual freedom as a *right* (the just is defined by these principles of freedom); on the other, the principles describing the *ends* that we must pursue (the good, or the good life, being defined by these ends). To assert a right is to demand of others or of society that it be respected; it is to state a rule of action that does not obligate only me. The principles that articulate rights thus present themselves as *duties*. On the contrary, the ends pursued by an individual or a group of individuals aimed at a good life can only be expressed as simple *values*. As they have to do with the conditions for others' respect of one's individual liberty, moral and legal imperatives have *a universal claim*; whereas ethical values would be *devoid* of any such claim. In fact, to claim that others must respect my right to individual liberty is also to claim that they must recognize it as a general right, and thus must also respect everyone's rights; whereas to regard some end as a good for my own life does not imply thinking that everyone must also seek it.

The liberal position, for which Rawls has become the standard representative, begins from the "fact of pluralism"—from the observation of a "diversity of comprehensive religious, philosophical, and moral doctrines"[40]—from which it follows that *values* do not authorize a definition of the principal virtue of societies. Justice must be defined from a universal perspective, that of the *rights* of individual liberty. To say that justice is thus defined starting from the right to liberty amounts to maintaining that various depictions of the good are only acceptable to the extent that they are in conformity with equal respect for these individual liberties. In other words: the just takes precedence over the good. Against this view, Charles Taylor makes a twofold argument, both ethical and metaethical, that aims to illuminate the inseparable aspects of the just and the good. A first argument—ethical—develops the idea that the questions linked to justice do not always have the same value, and that it is only as a function of a theory of the good that one can determine which questions of justice truly have value. Taylor insists on the fact that "under the heading of justice we find, at one extreme, problems as serious as the protection of fundamental human rights or protection from brutal exploitation, and at the other extreme, the question whether you did your share of the housework last week."[41] He concludes therefrom that the demand for equality contained within the idea of equal respect for liberties does not always hold the same significance for us. If we take this argument to its limit, we arrive at the idea that if the question of justice is so important, this is because it is linked to some of our fundamental interests and is rooted in a conception of the good, in the sense that it is inseparable from our representation of a complete life. The perspective of the experience of injustice leads to the same conclusion, because injustice is experienced in many cases as that which drains any value out of life itself. The theory of recognition makes it possible to express this intuition: the very possibility of a positive relation to oneself is at stake in the recognition of our liberty rights.

Taylor supports this conclusion with an argument that could be described as metaethical (to clarify that it is focused on reasoning regarding the just and the good, rather than on the just and the good themselves). According to Taylor, every definition of justice presupposes an anthropology from which the criteria of the just are defined: "[t]he affirmation of certain rights involves us in affirming the worth of certain [human] capacities . . ."[42] The definition of the just by a universalizing procedure (Habermas), or by a procedure that should lead to a consensus (Rawls), presupposes an anthropology that makes it possible to valorize language and reason as mechanisms of such procedures.[43] What consequences are to be drawn from these arguments? To maintain that a definition of justice presupposes an anthropology does not mean that every anthropology offers a definition of justice, nor that said definition is wrong. In some of his texts, Taylor derives a critique of the universalism of liberal definitions of justice from the inseparable nature of the just and the good. The argument is as follows: because the just is dependent upon the good, and because the good is historically determined, the just must be defined as a function of historical givens.[44] An analogous argument is articulated with respect to the concept of distributive justice. The definitions of distributive justice twice presuppose a historically determined conception of the good: first, in their definition of what is to be given to each person (as a function of criteria that go back to particular anthropological assumptions); second, in their interpretation of the nature of the objective pursued through social cooperation and the goods of which it is a matter of distributing.[45] In other texts, Taylor seems rather to maintain that is necessary to broaden the definition of justice by taking into consideration those representations of the good that are not incompatible with respect for individual liberties.[46] Adopting the perspective of the experience of injustice leads to a defense of this second option, because the demands tied to social justice function precisely to enlarge the domain of rights through a consideration not only of liberty rights but also of the social conditions for an undamaged life. As we have seen, the theory of recognition makes it possible to express this position theoretically, by distributing the right to negative liberty and social rights across two spheres of recognition (different but cognate in their legitimacy)—those of self-respect and self-esteem.

A DEFINITION, OR CRITERIA?

In proposing to connect the just and the good as required by the concept of social justice, the theory of recognition nevertheless finds itself open to two objections, both of which have been articulated by Nancy Fraser: it is simultaneously overdetermined (from the perspective of its content) and underdetermined (from the perspective of its form).[47] On the one hand, the theory of three fundamental forms of recognition supporting self-confidence, self-respect, and self-esteem, deduced from expectations concerning the institutions that fall within each of the three spheres of recognition, would be too specific to be able to provide an account of the particular kind of universality that characterizes the normativity of justice. Too tied to particular institutions, it would not articulate principles of sufficient generality to be able to distinguish between just and unjust societies in general. Finally, such a project would thus disconnect the concept of justice from one part of its significance. Honneth's response is framed at the level of historical development, stressing that the concept of social justice has not functioned so much to pass judgment on societies in general as to determine which social transformations are legitimate in a particular social context. In this sense, to begin from particular recognitive expectations with respect to a certain number of particular institutions does not constitute a disadvantage, but rather a strength. Honneth adds that the theory of recognition does not reject the demand for universality, but instead reformulates this demand in dynamic terms: to be able to claim legitimacy, every transformation must make possible a more complete recognition for a larger number [of people].[48] Fraser ultimately accepts a rationalist model that conceives the political dimension of philosophy according to a foundationalist model; and the practical dimension of the demand for social justice through reference to both a decision (in a situation of choosing between institutional frameworks) and a justification (of social critique—or, conversely, of a criticized institutional framework's validity). Adopting the perspective of the experience of injustice leads, on the contrary, to conceiving social critique as an extension of the dynamics of effective struggle against injustice, and to understand the normativity of social justice starting from the practical and cognitive dynamics linked to the refusal of injustice.

The second possible criticism is tied to the fact that when universal claims are articulated by the theory of recognition, their form is too imprecise to be able to decide between conflicting demands to which the idea of social justice could give rise. For Honneth, the *recognition claims* that can be accorded a universal validity (because everyone expects intersubjective and institutional confirmation of what makes self-confidence, self-respect, and self-esteem possible) are expressed in purely qualitative terms. It is impossible to deduce from them criteria that would make it possible to measure the extent of legitimacy with respect to a demand for social justice. Inasmuch as it fails to articulate the contents of its definition of justice in the form of operational criteria, the theory of recognition fails to distinguish between just and unjust projects of social transformation. In the end, it turns out to be unable to satisfy the very conditions of its own definition of political philosophy as taking sides.

This objection rests upon the presupposition that philosophy's task is to merge a definition of social justice with a set of operational criteria. The presupposition is widely accepted; it is, nonetheless, debatable. In fact, as regards social justice, the disputes about legitimacy that accompany conflicts among demands are not so much about criteria that make possible the application of shared normative principles as about the very legitimacy of normative principles. The emergence of the problem of social justice provides an illustration. Social movements born from the social question had required that social rights—those that the liberal camp refused to acknowledge as such—would be recognized as fully fledged rights. The dispute was not about the criteria that would make it possible to decide between demands recognized by both sides as falling within the scope of justice. The confrontation instead had to do with two definitions of justice, the more restrictive of which would lead to the exclusion of one side's demands in the struggle over justice's scope. The most significant political disputes of political modernity fall under this model. In the dispute between liberalism and socialism, the contested question is whether demands in terms of "social rights" are included within the scope of justice. In the dispute between liberalism and communitarianism, demands in terms of "collective rights" are contested in the same way. In feminism's dispute with certain forms of liberalism, socialism, and communitarianism, the extension of justice into the private sphere and private life is particularly at issue. The normative problem that philosophy must address if it wishes to participate and take sides in these disputes is one of determining *the extension of justice's scope*, not of deciding between two demands that mutually acknowledge they both are legitimately included within that scope. To undertake such a project amounts to situating the debate at the level of the very *definition* of social justice, not at the level of *criteria*—a more fundamental level because any posited criterion presupposes a definition; in this case, an explication of the concept of social justice's content and extension.

To claim to make judgments regarding social justice presupposes an understanding of what social justice is, as well as a determination of the area within which social justice and injustice can be distinguished. As the Port-Royal logic states, concepts' extension and content are inversely proportional. Starting from the experience of injustice amounts to trying to determine the content of the concept of social justice from its extension— one first presupposes that the domain of justice overlaps with that of the feeling of injustice before then investigating whether there are good reasons to narrow this extension. This approach takes seriously the hypothesis that the concept of justice has a larger extension than is generally admitted, and that the content of the concept of social justice must be reformulated as a result. At the same time, starting from the experience of injustice amounts to giving the content of social justice a formulation that is sufficiently deflationary to account for the fact that many conflicting demands based upon different principles of justice are possible within the area defined by the extension of social justice—the same experience of injustice can give rise to different cognitive dynamics that would lead to its being explained in terms of different principles of justice. The real difference between these principles of justice—a difference that could lead to conflicting demands—nevertheless presupposes a shared concept. As for which side to take within such disputes, as we have already said, this cannot be deduced in a purely speculative way if we admit that concepts are essentially contested—this, too, falls within the scope of a political engagement.

The theory of recognition makes it possible to enlarge the domain of social justice while at the same time providing a deflationary definition of the content of the concept of social justice, by identifying qualitative claims that are sufficiently flexible to be open to interpretation in different ways. Moreover, it offers a sufficiently pluralist definition of the content of this concept to explain the fact that different elements of the concept of social justice can come into conflict with each other (as in the case of the conflict between "liberty rights" and "social rights")—disputes that can turn into confrontations over the scope of justice. But it does not offer criteria to determine how the expanded definition of social justice should be applied to historical reality, nor to explain how conflicts between different rights to which the concept of social justice makes reference can be connected to each other. By what right can philosophy claim here to have a better understanding of these things than the individuals and groups confronted by specific injustices and conflicting demands? One might ask in response: Then why shouldn't we immediately hand over not only the criteria, but also the very definition, to collective deliberation? Precisely because a restrictive definition of justice is one of the elements opposed to the possibility that some of the demands born from the experience of injustice could enter the institutionalized political public sphere—it is thus one of the elements prohibiting collective deliberation from completely fulfilling its role.

The theory of recognition thus gives the concept of social justice a content deflationary enough, and an extension broad enough, to explain how it is essentially contested. But the theory of recognition also embarks upon the path of connecting a logical solution and a political solution, as all essentially contested concepts demand. By describing the content of the concept of social justice in a negative way—by starting from the experience of a denial of recognition—it accepts a commitment in favor of those who are subjected to social contempt, those whose demands rarely gain entry into the institutionalized political public sphere.

Chapter Three

THE INSTITUTIONS OF INJUSTICE

The preceding chapter claimed that a theory of recognition could fulfill the conditions for an approach to justice capable of explaining the particularity of demands associated with the idea of social justice. It remains to be demonstrated that it also makes possible an account of the different forms of the experience of injustice. How can the experience of being denied recognition entail a social dimension and thus fall within the purview of social injustice? The question arises because the idea of recognition seems to refer primarily to a relation between an I and a Thou (that is, an interaction), whereas the issue of social injustice points toward institutions. This question is at the intersection of two debates in social theory. The first has to do with the relations between interactions and institutions: is interaction primary or secondary with respect to institutions? The second concerns the principles of institutional critique: are they immanent within institutions or do they transcend specific institutional contexts?

THE RULES OF INTERACTION

To put the problem of the relation between interaction and institutions on relevant bases, we must begin by dismissing the false dualism of the individual and society, and the false opposition between individualism and holism. The individualist position is based upon two theses, one of which maintains that the ultimate components of social life are individual behaviors (an atomist hypothesis), while the other claims that all social phenomena can be understood as the aggregation of individual actions (a hypothesis of composition). These two theses thus imply that the primitive elements are individual elements and that every collective phenomenon is derivative. The holist position consists, conversely, of positing the existence of an irreducibly collective dimension of social life, a collective dimension established independently of individual behaviors and sometimes designated by the term "institution," this term being thus understood in a wide sense (a hypothesis of the collective, or of the institution). The holist position adds that individual behaviors are conditioned by elements that specifically refer back to this collective reality (a hypothesis of holist causality).

The corresponding flaws of these two positions are evident: on the one hand, the socialized individual is the product of social processes which cannot be explained as merely aggregations; on the other, it is difficult to see from where collective phenomena could draw their reality other than the validity they are accorded in the eyes of individuals and the individual actions that contribute to their reproduction. We should thus overcome the opposition between individualism and holism, but there are different ways of doing so. One of those ways can take its inspiration from the definition that Max Weber gave to the specifically social dimension of social phenomena. In *Economy and Society*, social activity is defined as action or behavior whose "subjective meaning takes account of the behavior of others and is thereby oriented in its course."[1] Weber thus maintains that the social world is constituted by actions endowed with a meaning for social agents and, more precisely, of actions whose meaning depends upon an individual taking account of an other's action. This definition makes individual action the first element, without actually being strictly speaking "individualist," because it shows that action only becomes social insofar as it is inscribed within interactions, and that the meaning that an individual gives to his action depends upon the meaning of the interactions within which it is inscribed (the primary unit is not the individual, but the interaction). To be able to meaningfully direct one's actions as a function of others', in fact, one must be able to presuppose rules of action that are shared by the different interaction partners. However, if these rules make it possible to anticipate others' behavior, that is because they are imposed upon agents as socially legitimated rules, already established before they are recognized as valuable, even if they only maintain their social legitimacy through the use that individuals make of them. The hypothesis of holistic causality is the only one that can explain this condition of interaction.

It is tempting to develop this holist argument by drawing inspiration from Ludwig Wittgenstein, who asserted specifically that "the *speaking* of language is part of an activity, or of a form of life" and that meanings are defined by "*customs* (uses, institutions)."[2] In this quotation, the term "institution" only designates an example of a custom, but it is possible to regard every custom as an institutional product and, consequently, to hold that the institution is the very principle of meaning: every meaning is institutionalized in the sense that it is part of an institutional context. It is in this sense that Vincent Descombes asserts[3] that the question of meaning refers back to that of institutions, which he understands in a Durkheimian sense as "the set of instituted acts or ideas that individuals find before them and which are imposed more or less upon them."[4] For Descombes, shared meanings are imposed upon individuals because they are immanent within modes of social activity through which individuals are socialized and interact. The term "institution" designates these modes of social activity. Hence, linguistic acts presuppose institutions and, in return, institutions must be understood on the model of grammatical rules and shared meanings at the heart of a particular form of life. This Wittgensteinian model has the virtue of highlighting that collective meanings embodied in institutions cannot be conceived as the objectification of meanings constituted independently of individuals' use of the rules—for example in a transcendental consciousness, in a spirit of the people, or in collective representations that exist by themselves. This leads to a reformulation of the hypothesis of holist causality in a form that makes it possible to overcome the opposition between the individual and the collective, and the spirit of the opposition between atomism and holisim.

However, this Wittgensteinian model presupposes a concept of the institution that remains too indeterminate to explain the full range of institutional settings that the term encompasses, as well as the diversity of problems that individuals are likely to encounter in institutions and, as a consequence, the variety of forms of social critique that said individuals are likely to employ to resolve them. In fact, this Wittgensteinian model can only explain institutions in the most general sense of the term: institutions in the sense of customary usage, not in the sense of organizational frameworks specific to social life (school, the market, the family, corporations, hospitals, etc.). The latter social frameworks are distinguished from simple customary usages ("usages" in the Weberian sense of the term[5]), in that they are not only defined by ways of being and behaving with respect to an other, but also by frameworks of action coordination. Understood in this narrower sense, the term "institution" encompasses two types of social frameworks that it is again useful to distinguish: simple frameworks of indirect and decentered coordination, like the market (which correspond in particular with "legitimate orders" in the Weberian sense[6]), and local and centralized frameworks, where action coordination takes place in specific social spaces, like the family, the school, the corporation, the prison, army barracks, etc. (in the Weberian terminology, "organizations" based upon "agreement," and rule-governed organizations like "voluntary associations" and "compulsory organizations"[7]). The latter type of institution, the local and centralized framework, simultaneously supposes a hierarchy in power relations (they constitute "ruling organizations"[8] in Weber's terminology) and specific principles of justification (the principles defining "legitimacy" and "domination"[9]). On this point, Weber has to be more fully fleshed out by Foucault: power in institutions cannot be analyzed solely in terms of its ability to provoke obedience (according to the Weberian definition of domination[10]) and to legitimize it; it must also be analyzed in terms of technologies of power—technologies of normalization, of surveillance, and of punishment. Institutions, in this narrow sense, are composed of highly elaborated social frameworks that can only be very partially explained by the Wittgensteinian model.

This model is only applicable to the extent that institutions are understood in the widest sense of customary usages. We can indeed hold that individuals obey customs in the same way that they obey the grammar of a language or a language game: by interpreting the rules in light of the usages that are associated with them. And it can certainly be acknowledged, moreover, that every institution supposes the existence of specific rules of action coordination, and that the principles of justification particular to an institution constitute specific rules for the resolution of problems that emerge in interaction. It is in this spirit that Luc Boltanski and Laurent Thévenot have suggested that institutions mobilize various principles of justification whose function is to resolve the disputes that arise within them.[11] But as soon as institutions anchor the rules of interaction within power frameworks, the objectivity of those rules of interaction can no longer be understood only according to the model of rule-usage; neither are the processes of forming expectations and conditioning effective bodies (for example, the bodily rhythm and the kind of attention that a machine imposes upon workers, or again, the conditioned bodily posture of a student at his desk and the techniques used to focus and control his attention) simple cases of the application of a customary rule. To understand institutions by starting from rules and justification is to fail to grasp both the power relations that traverse institutions and the specific effects of normalization and subjectivization that they produce, as well as the particular kinds of conditioning of action and investment in action that they arouse.

The Wittgensteinian model thus suffers from a descriptive inadequacy. This is accompanied by a threefold political inadequacy. First, by understanding the usage of an institution as a case of rule-usage, the Wittgensteinian model bases institutions' value upon the shared meanings and authoritative ideas, rather than upon the satisfaction of normative expectations. It thus tends to reduce the acceptable function of an institution to its normal function (the correct usage of the rule), thus leading to a conservative picture of the social. Second, by conflating institutions and rules, the Wittgensteinian model proscribes an analysis of the logics and specific effects of the technologies of power that organize interactions in the institutions. It cannot account for the manner in which power relations can suffocate actors' sense of injustice (fear of sanctions or reprisals) or atrophy their critical capacities (through a process of subjectivization pushing one toward conformism), nor the ways that the onerousness of positions that are the objects of power (of its arbitrariness or its violence) can contribute to break the habits produced by the institution and push individuals to revolt. Third, to understand institutions in terms of the model of shared meanings and authoritative ideas is, in effect, to remain silent about the fact that within institutions there are conflicts between quite different problems, only some of which can be resolved with the available principles of justification. To understand institutions in terms of the model of inscribing rules within positive usages is to disregard the fact that when the normal functioning of an institution disappoints normative expectations, at the same time as it is legitimated by the available principles of justification, the very value of those principles of justification can be called into question. In other words, this model does not allow the following question to be asked (a question whose importance for the experience of injustice has been demonstrated in the preceding chapters): Under what circumstances could rules of interaction, and the resolution of problems of interaction, be experienced as satisfactory or unsatisfactory?

Recall that in institutions, as more generally in interaction, the experience of injustice can take different forms. A first kind of injustice is concerned with an incompatibility between actions or the rules of interaction, and explicitly articulated normative principles with legal or regulatory force—either in the form of a generally valid principle or in the form of principles that are only valid within an institution (think, for example, of the regulations internal to a school or factory). An individual action, or a social practice (governed by tacit rules), can be determined to be unjust because it violates a legal principle (consider, for example, hazing at a school), or because it violates internal regulations (consider an arbitrary abuse of power in a factory), just as an internal regulation can be declared unjust in light of a legal principle. This is the kind of justice that the Rawlsian and Habermasian models take as their guiding thread, but there are other kinds of justice that are defined in relation to normative principles other than those taking the form of universal demands that can be legally or administratively formalized.

There are implicit principles of justification, too, that can also claim general validity (as in the case of shared moral intuitions) or a merely local validity—principles of justification proper to an institution. These kinds of principles, too, can make it possible to identify unjust behavior. In the interactions of ordinary life, individuals often draw upon principles of courtesy and morality to articulate and resolve the problems that they confront. In institutions, too, it is possible to have recourse to these principles to manage their disagreements as well as to criticize the tacit rules of particular social practices or even explicit rules like internal regulations. Within institutions, moreover, it is also possible to appeal to internal principles of justification in order to resolve disputes. These principles of justification, not articulated in the form of laws or regulations, are taken up within locally determined modalities of interaction, and they seem to condition the ways in which actors make use of other principles in analyzing the problems that they confront within the institutions. This is why Boltanski and Thévenot maintain that social critique must take the form of a theory of justification.[12] Taking up an argument from critical hermeneutics, they maintain

that critique is to be understood as a social activity and not as the preroga-
tive of scholars or lawyers, an activity upon which, moreover, the social
validity of moral and legal principles depends when they are employed in
a critical way. Rather than criticizing an institution from the outside, starting from transcendent principles, or from the inside, choosing one side or
another of a conflict, social critique should espouse the "increasing generalization" by which agents relinquish their particular interests in order
to rise up to a form of situated universality. They should use principles
of justification as a support that will make it possible to arbitrate their
disagreements. Conceived as a social competence, critique would thus be
identifiable as the capacity to adequately employ the implicit grammar of
justification that is associated with each institutional order.

In order for such a model of social critique to be generalizable, it must
be conceded that the experience of injustice is only concerned with simple
litigation [*litiges* in Lyotard's sense]; that is, conflicts inscribed within the
ordinary operation of an institutional order and capable of being regulated
by the simple and ordinary application of normative principles inscribed
within it. But there are also injustices that take the form of a *differend* rooted
in a wrong; that is, situations that cannot be articulated within the available normative grammar because the principles of justification and the rules
of interaction that they oversee are compatible with intolerable experiences.
These are precisely the experiences of injustice with the greatest critical
potential, those that lead—if the crisis that they open up is followed by a
successful revolt—to the transformation of an institutional order. In the case
of such differends, "increasing generalization" toward the unjust order's normative principles is a political mistake, as it avoids what really constitutes the
problem and searches for a solution in a false consensus. The only politically
relevant solution is to take the side of one of these two irreconcilable parties—those victims of injustice who cannot express themselves as such in
the socially accepted normative language—by showing that the disappointed
expectations in their experience of injustice are legitimate, and that their
experience calls for a recasting of the socially accepted principles of justice.

It remains to be seen how the theory of recognition could appropriate
this conception of the institution as founded not only upon rules but also
upon frameworks of power, as the site for experiences of injustice that can
sometimes be expressed in explicit principles but are sometimes just as
likely to cast a critical light upon those principles.

RECOGNITION AND INSTITUTIONS

How are we to take account of what is at stake within our experiences of injustice, while accepting the fact that we exist in and through institutions? Initially, Honneth portrayed this question as the heart of his critique of Habermas and it appeared as the principal motif of his theory of recognition.[13] On his account, the process of rationalization, which constituted for Habermas as well as for Weber the principal characteristic of modernity, must not be understood as the autonomous development of two forms of rationality, as a twofold and impersonal learning process taking place in the independent social spheres of system and lifeworld (the first becoming ever more practical, the second more reflective). The rationalization of the social world must rather be understood as a process within which social groups engage in a struggle to construct institutions that make possible the forms of life to which they aspire. Institutions should not only be understood as forms of action-coordination, but also as the object of some of the most fundamental normative expectations. The theory of recognition thus has the objective of describing these expectations, while pointing out the relations they maintain with institutions. The recognition of our psycho-physical value (at the basis of self-confidence) is preferentially directed toward familial institutions or other institutions of intimacy, whereas the recognition of the value of our freedom (at the basis of self-respect) is preferentially directed toward legal and political institutions, and the recognition of the social value of our existence (at the basis of self-esteem) is preferentially directed toward the market and places of work.

The theory of recognition thus accounts for the fact that different dimensions of our social existence are tied to institutions, and it explains the normative expectations that apply to different institutional spheres, while distinguishing those that intervene in a decisive way within a specific institution (for example, those concerning self-confidence within the family, or self-esteem within a company) and those that intervene only secondarily (recognition of spouses' and dependents' freedom, as well as recognition of the value of domestic labor within the family;[14] recognition of the value of family life and citizenship within a company). The rationalization of the social world is thus interpreted as underpinned by a set of struggles for recognition in order to transform these different institutions so that they might better satisfy individuals' expectations for recognition.

This leads to an analysis of the relations between recognition and institutions that rests upon what I will term an *expressive* conception of recognition (a conception of recognition as *being expressed* in institutions). In fact, Honneth analyzes the relationship of recognition at two levels: that of the expectations of an I with regard to a Thou, and that of the ways in which institutional frameworks facilitate or stand in the way of said expectations. Institutions and the social relations that they condition *express* (more or less) the satisfaction of recognitive expectations. Pushing this to its extreme, it can thus be said that "to express" here means that institutions should not be considered as settings that by themselves produce a positive recognition or a denial of recognition, but rather as the institutionalization of relations of recognition that are as such part of a preinstitutional level. Institutions constitute only the conditions, either for the stabilization of positive recognition-relations between individuals or for the perpetuation of obstacles to their development.

This expressive conception can boast of its descriptive capacity and its critical potential. At the descriptive level, it has the virtue of underlining that the institutional context cannot guarantee by itself the satisfaction of recognitive expectations, and that with regard to recognition, individual behavior is never entirely reducible to institutional constraints. Furthermore, if we wish to give critical force to the idea of recognition, it seems necessary to presuppose, on the one hand, that an ensemble of fundamental expectations is identifiable independently of institutions; and, on the other, that these institutions are liable to fail to satisfy these expectations, thus giving rise to experiences of the denial of recognition or to insufficient forms of recognition that can transform into experiences of the denial of recognition. The thesis that an ensemble of recognitive expectations constitutes the engine for the rationalization of the social world also adds that these expectations are too basic to remain unsatisfied in the long term.

This expressive conception can nonetheless be seen as facing the classic objections that were raised against efforts to construct a social theory from a theory of preinstitutional intersubjectivity.[15] A comparison from the Habermasian and Honnethian points of view makes it possible to illustrate the problem. Just as Habermas maintains that social interaction is underpinned by the normative principles of linguistic understanding, Honneth maintains that social interaction is underpinned by the normative principles of nonlinguistic communication that develop in recognitive relations. But the normative demands of understanding, for Habermas, are directly constituted from the background assumptions that are embodied in ordinary language and constitute the institutional moment (in the broad sense of social usages), whereas Honneth tends to interpret the conditions of recognition as normative expectations that structure institutions according to a psychosocial logic, that of the confirmation of a positive relation to oneself—a logic that already exists in the most inchoate social relations, those of the most elementary forms of primary socialization. This amounts to assuming that intersubjectivity can be analyzed independently of its institutional structuration, and that the particular processes that characterize it as such also provide a critical perspective upon institutions. This presupposition is challengeable because, abstracting from the first forms of an infant's interactions with its parents, recognitive expectations themselves always exist in the *habits* of expecting recognition in a particular way within a particular institutional context.

The challenge that a *constitutive* conception of recognition must address is how to understand the critical potential of recognitive expectations at the same time as their conditioning by institutional contexts. To do so, it can be useful to refer to the Deweyan distinction between *impulse* and *habit*, and to the idea that if impulses are fundamentally indeterminate and liable to be directed in a great number of ways in the form of habits, they can nonetheless come into conflict with habits in particular problematic situations and thus constitute a transformative element for habits.[16] Recognitive expectations should be understood simultaneously as impulses and habits, and in accordance with a conception that simultaneously stresses both impulses' flexibility and their capacity to transform habits. As John Dewey has emphasized, there is a fundamental need for recognition, but in its current form this need is largely undefined, in the sense that it can be satisfied in various ways. When Dewey maintains that it "is the deepest urge of every human being, to feel that he does count for something with other human beings and receives a recognition from them as counting for something,"[17] "urge" is a synonym for "impulse." Pierre Bourdieu had something similar in mind. When he presents the "*search for recognition*" as the reward for an abandonment of narcissism at the root of all processes of socialization,[18] he simultaneously emphasizes both its fundamental character as an impulse and its plasticity. There is an impulse to search for recognition whose origins can be understood in

Meadian and Deweyan terms, or in Bourdieuian terms—two theoretical perspectives that are not in conflict on this point.

Moreover, as long as they are not confronted by problematic situations involving a denial of recognition, these recognitive expectations always exist in the form of habits—a habitual expectation of recognition from this or that individual, a habitual expectation of recognition in this or that way. According to Dewey, habits should be interpreted as modes of internalizing a social environment composed of individual actions, institutions, and social customs.[19] In conformity with this understanding of habits, recognitive expectations are structured by socialization processes, in the course of which we grasp from whom we can hope to be given recognition and in what ways. The institutions that govern the socialization process thus channel impulses for recognition by orienting them toward various objects and giving them various forms. But the plasticity of recognitive impulses is not infinite, and the recognition made possible by habits of recognition is not always fully satisfactory.

The distinction between impulses and habits of recognition makes it possible to explain the fact that institutions make a twofold intervention in the constitution of positive recognition and in the denial of recognition. We have already noted that the concept of recognition is a relational concept. To speak of positive recognition is to speak of a situation in which an expectation of recognition directed toward another individual or an institution is satisfied. This implies that the recognitive effects produced by the other's behavior or the institutional workings correspond with the recognitive expectations. A denial of recognition implies, on the contrary, that these expectations are unsatisfied by the individual or specifically institutional recognitive effects. The relation of recognition is always a relation between the *expectations* and the *effects* of recognition. And yet, the recognitive expectations, just like the recognitive effects, have institutional conditions—including when they are carried by individual behaviors.

It is clear that recognitive effects depend upon institutional settings, on the one hand because individual behaviors likely to obtain recognition are always conditioned by current or past institutional elements, and on the other because institutions produce specific recognitive effects (think, for example, of the classification of individuals by regulations or laws: authorization or prohibition to engage in a particular action, attribution of a particular status, etc.). They thus produce indirect and direct recognitive effects. Their *indirect* effects should be understood in terms of habits: habits of recognizing a particular individual in a particular way. In the course of the socialization process, which mainly occurs in institutions, individuals learn who they should recognize and how they should do so: they gain habits of recognition which are conditioned by the social relation of domination (according to derogatory classist, sexist, racist, or ethnic prejudices), as well as by the rules pertaining to social situations where they experience these social relations of domination. As for the *direct* effects that institutions produce, they should be understood in terms of status and power: recall the hierarchies of status and power (for example, in the family or at school)—the exercise of power as the right to give some reward or sanction, even to promotion to a superior status (as in a business). One can speak of a direct effect here in the sense that, even if institutions act through the intermediary of individual behaviors (and in this sense indirectly), it is none other than the institution that authorizes individuals to impose hierarchies, rewards, and punishments; and in the sense that when these effects give rise to a denial of recognition, the latter can be experienced as produced by the institution itself—and not solely by the habits that it has produced, or by some particular rules of its working and its overdetermination by the social relations of domination—one can thus come to hate the family, the school, or the capitalist business as such, instead of condemning a particular rule in effect therein, or a particular behavior that they authorized or encouraged.

Institutions also act upon recognitive expectations. Within recognitive expectations, to be sure, there is something that does not directly depend upon institutions but rather on our nature as social beings, and that falls under humans' impulsive character (to use Dewey's term); but the way in which research on recognition is carried out depends upon the ways that we have been habituated to expect recognition (from whom and how) in the different institutional spaces where socialization occurs. If the recognitive expectations are unarticulated until they are confronted by problematic situations, this is because they are still incorporated in the preconscious factual and normative expectations that are constitutive of our habits. And they remain preconscious as long as these habits are adapted to the institutional contexts in which they are formed; that is, as long as an individual does not confront a problematic social situation.

The distinction between impulses and habits of recognition also makes it possible to understand that there are two different forms of denial of recognition. A first form of denial of recognition occurs in situations in which habitual recognitive expectations are contradicted. The expectation of recognition that we are accustomed to be able to hope for, and which corresponds to promises of recognition inscribed in the normal working of institutions or in socially accepted normative principles, is contradicted. In these cases, we can rely upon that institutional working or those normative principles to explain why and how a given situation is problematic and to try to transform it, possibly by articulating a demand for recognition. But there is also another kind of situation denying recognition in which the promises of recognition immanent in social life, and the ways that they have been internalized in the form of habits of expecting recognition and habits of according recognition, themselves become problematic. These situations correspond to different kinds of negative experiences. One can have the feeling that there is something false or profoundly unsatisfactory in the way that recognition is promised and expressed in an institution (as in the experience of the fact that one's recognition at work is based upon ignorance about the nature and value of the work performed). One can experience profound disappointment in the kind of positive recognition that one receives, even going so far as to find intolerable the way in which an institution defines the criteria for recognition (for example, in institutions marked by strong sexist, classist, or racist oppression). These two kinds of experience are sometimes explained by the fact that habits of recognition expectation, constituted in other institutions, are disappointed. But the impulses for recognition are not infinitely malleable—there are also cases in which the habits of expecting and receiving recognition are themselves experienced as unsatisfactory, false, or intolerable. It is a fact that one is not easily habituated to contempt, even when one is always subjected to it. It is also a fact that this experience of contempt has fueled struggles against social relations of domination. It is true that domination produces unequal and asymmetrical habits of recognition, as Bourdieu has stressed.[20] But various elements could end up making these habits intolerable (the burden of giving up, the fact that intimidation by authorities has become too strong), thus causing recognition impulses to overflow their banks. In this sort of situation, the denial of recognition divides recognition impulses from habits of recognition, and gives rise to the appearance of demands for recognition that could find it difficult to assert their legitimacy in terms of socially accepted normative principles.

A TYPOLOGY OF INSTITUTIONAL RECOGNITIVE EFFECTS

I have thus far distinguished two large forms of denial of recognition, in function of the kinds of recognitive expectations that are contradicted (impulses or habits). I have also indicated that the modalities of denial of recognition vary according to whether the recognitive effects that institutions produce are direct or indirect. I would now like to distinguish different kinds of institutional recognitive effects by adopting the perspective of the experiences of being denied recognition to which they can give rise. I have already indicated that institutions are simultaneously the site for the constitution of specific *rules*, *values*, *statuses*, and *habits*; these all occur in a different way in the experience of being denied recognition. Institutions have an effect, first of all, on behaviors as instances of rule-directed action coordination. But they also produce effects that are tied not only to *interaction* but also to *subjectivization*. As they internally promote different values, they also expect individuals to steer their actions as a function of particular definitions of how to respect rules of interaction, and to identify themselves as much as possible within these definitions. Moreover, as soon as institutions are composed of hierarchies of status and of power, they produce *habits* of assuming the roles associated with these *statuses* and these *powers*—habits that impact the construction of identity in socialization. There are thus three institutional recognitive effects: first, those tied to the identification of partners in action; second, those tied to the mobilization of subjectivities; and third, those tied to identity construction within institutions. And hence there are three correlated kinds of denial of recognition, which I will call depreciative recognition, maladjusted recognition, and unsatisfactory recognition.

TABLE 3.1

Institutional mechanisms	Identification of action partners	Mobilization of subjectivities	Identity construction in socialization
Genres (genus) of denial of recognition	Depreciative recognition	Maladjusted recognition	Unsatisfactory recognition
Subgenres (species) of denial of recognition	• Devaluing • Disqualifying • Stigmatizing	• Misrecognition • Invisibilization	• Unstable • Splitting or tearing apart

Action coordination is clearly a matter of recognition. In fact, insofar as rules of interaction condition the ways in which another behaves with respect to me, these rules influence the ways in which that other recognizes (or not) the value of my existence. In contrast to technical rules of action, rules of interaction presuppose a classification of agents, a classification of actions, and a classification of the action contexts in which the other intervenes. They are subject to what could be termed a "triadic"[21] logic that implies the possibility of a differentiated classification and evaluation of interaction partners (what one thinks, for example, about the master-student-lesson relation in educational and academic institutions). The classification of an agent and her action-partners through rules of interaction produces specific recognitive effects and denial of recognition. The type of denial of recognition tied to this first kind of institutional effect can be called depreciative recognition. This depreciation can take the form of (1) *devaluing* recognition (the identification of an individual as a subordinate partner in the context of a hierarchized action—for example, a worker in relation to a manager or supervisor); (2) *disqualification* (the identification of an individual as not meeting the criteria for being an action partner in a specific action context—for example, an immigrant "youngster" at the entry to a nightclub); or (3) *stigmatization* (the identification of an individual as the agent of harmful or reprehensible actions—the Roma people, throughout Europe and even today, are paradigmatic victims of this kind of judgment.

A second kind of institutional effect addresses the fact that the interpretation of roles one plays is always determined by values, while every institution aims to promote particular values. This aim sometimes gives rise to specific frameworks of power that strengthen the institutional coordination of action by processes serving to orient expectations toward the institution's own ends and the values linked to them. The business world provides many examples of techniques of power meant to direct desires in accordance with the business's success (through profit sharing, merit pay, or frameworks for promotion), to control the ways in which employees play their professional roles (instructions regarding self-presentation and interpersonal interaction, and the "corporate" attitude), and to foster identification with a company's specific values (the "culture" of the firm). The subjectivization effects that result therefrom are connected to a new form of denial of recognition that can be termed *maladjusted*. This denial of recognition appears in two forms. In institutions that only give recognition to individuals who endeavor to adhere as closely as possible to a particular interpretation of socially determined roles, denial of recognition takes the forms of misrecognition and invisibility. The experience of *misrecognition* corresponds to situations in which individuals see themselves as compelled to play roles in such a way that they cannot make sense of the positive recognition associated with these roles. This happens whenever employees are required to obey prescriptions concerning interpersonal interaction and self-presentation that are foreign to them (and which can go so far as to demand that they lose their identity, as for employees of foreign descent who are asked, in call centers, to use a "French" name during their telephone conversations). The experience of *invisibility* arises when individuals subject to such prescriptions have to accept that despite everything they do, the value of their activity is truly invisible to those who would give recognition. The invisibility of domestic work provides an example: one of the particular characteristics of domestic work is that when it is done well, it is invisible to those who reap its benefits without having to perform it—this is the case for all the work associated with housecleaning and housekeeping, but also for the various types of care work. It is obvious, moreover, that there are other ways that invisibility is experienced, and that the most radical forms of invisibility are experienced by people who do not exist for an institution. They can have such an experience either because they do not act within it [the institution], or because they do not serve any socially identifiable function (which is too often the case for many who are homeless, who can remain invisible even unto death[22]).

Finally, the way that one brings into play the roles and values that one sees as goods depends upon how the process of socialization presents the problem of our identity to ourselves. Over the course of socialization, different institutional spaces impart to each individual a representation of the specifics of her existence and its value. In this sense, they are the formative sites for different elements of personal identity. What can be called an individual's character (that is, a particular sort of combination of habits) is constituted in them [these spaces]. They are also the sites where identification with ways of playing certain roles is connected with assumption of a particular status. In what follows, I will speak of "elements of personal identity" (or "identity components") to designate these various dimensions of one's existence, dimensions that are taken into consideration in specific problematic situations where an individual asks herself: "What am I, really?"; "What is my life really worth?"; and "What must I do with my life?"

Institutions thus produce new recognitive effects, effects that in fact constitute a *process* of recognition, because the socialization and the constitution of identity components must not be understood as the imposition of social norms upon a formless subjectivity, but rather as a process in which a subjective transaction (the individual's own unification of different elements of her identity) accompanies an objective transaction between the individual's own expectations and those of the institution. An individual's action in a particular action context is never determined solely by this action context, but always also by the weight of her past and the various forms of her social existence.[23] Just as a child tries to be recognized at school as the self that has been created within the family, she tries in return to be recognized at home as the self that has been created in educational spaces. This process characteristic of the first phase of socialization also continues in later phases where it is a matter of a relationship maintained between different non-familial institutions (a point to be taken up in Chapter 5). The different phases of socialization can thus be interpreted as the unfolding of a process in the course of which the individual takes on new identity components, at the same time as she finds herself in particular kinds of problematic situations that call for a form of reflexivity in terms of personal identity. And it is through this process that she comes to demand of institutions, in a more or less explicit way, that they recognize the specificity of her personal identity. In such a dynamic of subjectivization, recognition both determines and is determined by the institution: on the one hand, institutions are the site where identity components that alter recognitive expectations are taken on; on the other, identity components are the starting point for demands for recognition that are specifically addressed to institutions and that aim to transform the way they function.

Whence comes a new form of denial of recognition, that we can term *unsatisfying* recognition. In a given society, different institutions can produce subjectivization effects that are mutually incompatible. Then, not only is an individual unable to have the way that he interprets the roles he takes on be recognized (misrecognition), but these different roles are superimposed upon each other within him, while he is unable to effect a personal unification of them which would give him the feeling of being recognized through them. Such a denial of recognition can take two forms. The first is *unstable* recognition, corresponding to a situation where the individual floats between different social roles without managing to unify them in a coherent narrative: he does not manage to give a biographical coherence to his life. Richard Sennett has argued that this situation corresponds to "flexible" kinds of employment in the new capitalism: "The conditions of the new economy feed instead on experience which drifts in time, from place to place, from job to job . . . [S]hort-term capitalism threatens to corrode . . . those qualities of character which bind human beings to one another and furnishes each with a sense of sustainable self."[24] Sennett adds: "The conditions of time in the new capitalism have created a conflict between character and experience, the experience of disjointed time threatening the ability of people to form their characters into sustained narratives."[25] Unsatisfying recognition can also take the form of a *splitting* or *tearing-apart* recognition, when an institutional context enables powerful but incompatible identifications. Pierre Bourdieu stresses that such a tearing apart of individuals between incompatible habitus is a not insignificant source of social suffering: "Habitus is not necessarily adapted to its situation nor necessarily coherent. It has degrees of integration—which correspond in particular to degrees of 'crystallization' of the status occupied. Thus it can be observed that to contradictory positions, which tend to exert structural 'double binds' on their occupants, there often correspond destabilized habitus, torn by contradiction and internal division, generating suffering."[26] Recognition is splitting, or tearing apart, in cases of relegation upward or downward—or when, from initial socialization, individuals are taken up in incompatible institutional frameworks (as in immigrants' experience of a "two-fold absence"[27]; or in the experiences of second- or third-generation immigrant youths who struggle to unify their familial cultural codes with those in their schools and other spaces of social life).

INSTITUTIONAL CRITIQUE

Taking seriously the institutional dimension of social life makes it possible to shift from a theory of institutions as an expression of recognition to a theory of institutions as the constitution of relations of recognition—and to a description of different types of denial of recognition produced by institutions. The adoption of such a constitutive conception of recognition is crucial for a critical theory of society, for two reasons. Firstly, confrontations between demands for recognition and institutions most often take place within the regular functioning of institutions themselves—they draw the institutions either into a process of internal evolution or into crises or public conflicts that seem, to those who are denied recognition, as the only possible way out. Thus the constitutive conception of recognition makes it possible to adopt a critical perspective immanent in institutions' dynamics. Secondly, a description of the different ways that institutions can produce a denial of recognition is an indispensable condition, if we are to explain the full gamut of injustices linked to denial of recognition.

To show how the theory of recognition can explain injustice in institutions, I now need to more precisely describe several typical experiences of injustice. In the first chapter, I stressed that the institutions that structure the political public sphere can actively contribute to the production of injustice, an injustice that can be called social insofar as it is produced by institutions but only falls under the scope of social injustice in the broadest sense of the term. The specific forms of injustice produced by political institutions are linked either to the nonrecognition of rights (whether it is a matter of devaluing recognition through identification of individuals with citizens of inferior rank, as in the case of legal permanent residents; or of stigmatization, as in the case of illegal immigrants), or to the masking or "making invisible" [*invisibilisation*] of social problems suffered by particular populations (residents of blighted neighborhoods, workers, prisoners, and many others) that are thus viewed as second-class citizens. Political institutions are thus liable to produce an injustice tied to a direct denial of recognition—through exclusion from the political public sphere—but also to an indirect denial of recognition, and to raising an initial denial of recognition to a second power, by proscribing the political recognition of a social injustice. This denial of recognition to the second power can itself take two forms: (1) exclusion from the political public sphere through the affirmation of principles that amount to restraints (for example, making political and social problems that are not encompassed within the technical principles of "good governance" invisible); and (2) a contradiction between the self-proclaimed principles of the political public sphere and the principles that effectively structure the social practices (abstract affirmation of the republic's uniqueness *versus* privatization of public services; abstract affirmation of the value of work *versus* dismantling of all sorts of worker protections, etc.). Rather than elaborating on these questions, in what follows I will examine social injustice in the narrower sense of injustice produced by social institutions as distinguished from political institutions.

In this area, the theory of recognition is most obviously fruitful in explaining experiences of injustice arising in familial institutions (in the general sense of intimate institutions). Indeed, it is not difficult to acknowledge that the forms of injustice specifically produced by familial institutions result from denials of recognition linked to gender differentiation (whether as a denial of recognition resulting from the invisibility of domestic labor, from the devaluing of the ethical principles of care, or from different forms of devaluing recognition of women); or forms of stigmatization of individuals whose sexual mores do not conform to the hetero-procreative norm that continues to prevail in familial institutions (i.e., homosexuality, bisexuality, transsexuality). As a patriarchal institution, the family provides the typical example of a social setting that, by carrying out the institutionalization of a cultural model based upon the devaluing of a social group, structurally produces a denial of recognition.[28] No excess of critical awareness is needed to see that if a shared will were enough to do away with domination, the marriage contract would have long ago transformed the family into an institution of freedom. If we merely open our eyes, we can see that in the sphere of emotional intimacy too, and perhaps even more so than elsewhere, communication is fundamentally distorted by asymmetrical relations of recognition that remain below the surface of what is discussed. One of the advantages of an approach based on recognition is the ability to analyze the ways that domination is carried out by this kind of implicit communicative relations. It occurs, for instance, through self-presentation and the affirmation of one's identity—quite simply wanting to be oneself is already an affirmation of the symbolic domination that permeates gendered identification. It also occurs through a structural flaw in communication that accepts as given that the qualities generally coded as feminine (tact, gentleness, discretion) are invisible and are thus unrecognizable, in contrast to "masculine qualities."[29] To say "I acted tactfully, as you observed," or "I've cleaned the house, as you can see," is always tactless, whereas a demonstration of strength saves one the trouble of later having to note where one is strong. It occurs, too, though the general devaluing of ethical principles that are associated with jobs typically performed by women (the ethic of care associated with social work, and the protection of children and other vulnerable groups), a devaluing that implies a fundamental asymmetry in the expression of the normative stakes in men's and women's experiences.[30]

Finally, the theory of recognition makes it possible to explain the multiplicity of issues demanding recognition within the sphere of emotional intimacy. In the familial order, concern for recognition of one's bodily and emotional integrity undeniably takes precedence over recognition of one's spouse's or children's freedom, or over recognition of the value of domestic labor and professional activity. We know what kind of feeling of injustice can come of this: in intimate relations, one does not generally want to be recognized only as a child or a partner, but also as a free individual capable of giving social value to one's life. But still today, this latter recognition is often accorded to adult men rather than to other members of a family. Forms of recognition outside the familial unit can also weigh upon the distorted forms of communication that were mentioned above, as is shown by the strengthening of stereotypes of virility (evidenced by the recent emergence of a "masculine press" and a "masculine pride" that promote them), led to by the worsening of certain working conditions (because virility implies the acceptance of risk and suffering, rather than a rejection of working conditions that aggravate them), with the consequence in return of restricting one's spouse to feminine stereotypes (since the more a man resolutely puts up with such work, the more he demands a stereotypically feminine support in the private sphere).[31]

In order not to lead to what I have termed maladjusted recognition or unsatisfactory recognition, each member of a couple must attempt to accommodate the other's expectations for recognition, which presumes not only a negotiation of roles but also work on the effects of subjection entailed by the institutions of the couple and the family, as well as on the recognitive relations that surround the couple and the family. This is why a critique of the family that would take as its guiding thread demands for recognition immanent within institutions of intimacy should do much more than acknowledge each one's right to know one's place and to collect a material or symbolic remuneration (a bouquet of flowers as compensation for housecleaning, or maternity pay to get women into the house!)— to demand equal, rewarding, nondisplaced and satisfying recognition is also to demand a transformation of the entirety of institutional conditions (material and symbolic) that structure this denial of recognition.

Critique of intimate institutions in terms of recognition can thus claim a certain political relevance, but it is far from obvious that one can make such a claim to the same extent with respect to socioeconomic institutions. Indeed, it seems reasonable to question whether the recognition model could adequately explain forms of injustice that are linked to the production and distribution of wealth. Many leftist critics have rebuked Habermas for entirely losing sight of a critique of political economy.[32] And this reproach has been directed at Honneth himself as well, for example by Nancy Fraser.[33] For her, the concept of recognition makes it possible to address injustices that are linked to different forms of symbolic domination, but not those that concern the distribution of wealth, because the latter are not at all the result of denials of recognition of social groups' identities, but rather of class differences that structure the capitalist order. The concept of recognition could only have critical value with respect to injustices carried through institutionalized normative models (dominant cultural codes; religion; particular sexual ethics or morality; racist, sexist, or classist customs). Unjust distribution would only depend upon production structures and the capitalist market, which themselves neither create nor deny recognition. And thus, only an analysis of capitalism as a mode of the production and distribution of wealth could constitute a relevant perspective upon such injustices. Axel Honneth is correct when he replies that the question of recognition is much larger than one of injustices carried through institutionalized normative models and that it also leads to a critique of economic institutions that deny the social value of lives. However, in the face of an objection that bears more specifically on the theory of recognition's ability to generate a critique of economic institutions that would be politically and sociologically relevant, this kind of response cannot suffice. It must be supplemented, and in order to do so, the principles must be specified by means of which a theory of recognition can be applied to a critique of political economy.

There is no debate that economic phenomena are characterized by a specific logic that is not of the same order as that of recognition. Whether this specific logic is interpreted from a Marxian approach (as in terms of the production of surplus value), or a neoclassical approach (in terms of maximization of utility and profit), or from a Keynesian approach (functional relations between macroeconomic factors such as global investment, global consumption, etc.), it is clear that it cannot be explained as such in the

framework of a theory of recognition. But these arguments are not sufficient to dismiss the possibility that institutions of capitalist production and
distribution create specific recognitive effects. It is quite clear that, by itself,
a theory of recognition is incapable of producing a theory of capitalism;
and for that matter, has never tried to do so. But by relying upon theories
elaborated by the sociology of work and economic theory, it can nevertheless engage in an analysis of the recognitive effects produced by the institutions of paid labor and the capitalist market. It is not out of the question
that it could thus manage to articulate a critical model that is as politically
relevant as models that rest upon descriptions of class inequalities and divisions in the world economy. Nor is it out of the question that these models
could be in a complementary relationship, insofar as the theory of recognition focuses on the experience of injustice and needs to be filled out with
a theory of the causes of experiences of injustice. Finally, it is not out of
the question that a description of the forms of denial of recognition could
lead to a more defined critique of political economy than would a description of the functional logic and the contradictions of capitalism in general,
and in the mode of post-Fordist regulation in particular—more defined in
that it brings an analysis back down from structures to the social experience proper to contemporary capitalism. To be sure, a critique of political
economy developed within the framework of a theory of recognition will
be content to analyze effects, but it does not for all that pass in silence
over the structures that produce them, precisely because it aims to evaluate
these structures in light of their effects. Why should we, with respect to the
economic basis of the social, begin our analysis from normative principles
or structural causes, rather than starting from its effects? Isn't an analysis
in terms of effects the only way to escape the dichotomy in which social
theory always risks becoming entrapped—a dichotomy both sides of which
are unsatisfactory: on the one hand, a reflection starting from principles
that does not manage to grasp the productive mechanisms of injustice; and
on the other, an analysis of causal structures that does not manage to get
back to the experience of injustice?

Any critique of the capitalist economy must focus on the connections
between institutions of paid labor and those for the exchange of goods; in
other words, the connections between the firm and the competitive market.
These two institutions create specific injustices, and neither one of them
can be the object of an adequate critical discourse except on the condition

that it is brought into relation with the other: for example, a critique of markets takes the form of a critique of labor markets whose recognitive effects relate to labor which is supposed to happen outside of the market, within a firm. As for a critique of labor within a firm, it is concerned with denials of recognition that vary according to forms of employment (a continuing, short-term, or temporary contract) that were specified through the labor market.

If the theory of recognition is led to engage in these two critical projects (critique of labor and critique of markets), that is because it confers a certain importance upon recognition through work. On the one hand, a positive relation to oneself is inseparable from recognition of the social value of one's life—self-esteem is one of the fundamental forms of a positive relation to oneself. On the other hand, labor, as an effective activity coordinated in order to produce useful goods (and not merely an income!), is the principal form of recognition for the social value of one's life. A critique of markets and firms stems therefrom, insofar as these two institutions are the site for specific forms of (denial of) recognition related to normative expectations attached to the activity of labor.

This thesis takes a point of view in opposition to an entire school of thought that argues for the end of work through three different arguments: first of all, work occupies an increasingly smaller and smaller role in social life and in individuals' lifespans; next, it is less and less understood by individuals as a means for self-realization and as an essential part of one's life; finally, the only modes of emancipation that can fit with the real world have to do with life outside of work. None of these arguments is fully convincing. While it is true that a rise in unemployment and a reduction in working hours universally characterizes the current era (at least in the old centers of the world economy), these phenomena go hand in hand with an intensification of work and a lengthening of work well beyond the official hours of paid work (in the form of overtime, work done at home, the need to maintain one's technical knowledge base and social networks, etc.). If it is true, moreover, that a reduction of job security and new forms of management are accompanied by an increase in work's unpleasantness or suffering, it appears to lead rather to an ambivalent relation to work rather than a flight outside of work. Further, labor remains a central factor in the construction of identity.[34] Strategies to escape paid work are certainly tempting for young employees, but this kind of escape is generally too costly in terms of identity for a large number to be able to effect it long-term. Moreover, it seems politically difficult to maintain that struggles promoting escape from work should take the place of struggles for better wages and against unemployment, for it is difficult to see how one could then critique the trends aiming to reduce labor to a cost which reduces shareholders' profits, the dynamics of labor-market deregulation creating an increasingly precarious workforce, and the intensification of work within firms. Taking a step back from this debate concerning the end of work, one can have the sense that most of the time it is based upon a conflation of work and paid labor. It is true that recognition of the social value of one's life can be based upon other factors besides one's financially compensated activities but it seems difficult to imagine that recognition of the social value of one's life could be obtained apart from activity or use of different skills aimed at producing goods and services that are useful for others. But this is precisely the definition of work.

THE MARKET

It is well known that labor markets exist and that other markets have their roots in one way or another in the products of labor. But—and Marx was the first to have made this point—the market must not be understood solely as an institution of exchange of goods and allocation of resources, but also as the site for social validation. The market is not only, in fact, the site where products are exchanged, or where wealth is invested in one or another productive sector; it is also the site where capital and the labor contributing to the production of particular merchandise agree to a wage (or retail price) for the labor that can be deemed competitive in comparison with other offers— it is the site where the value established within the productive sphere obtains an objective form by virtue of a social "validation."[35] Talking about social validation amounts to talking about recognition. It is only in the market that commodities are recognized as values. It is in the very nature of markets' functioning to present them as values that are interchangeable with other values. The market thus produces a double recognition of the value of labor.[36] In the labor market, a first form of recognition of the value of employees' labor (that of the value of their capacity for work), a first measure of their skills and the usefulness of their activities, is manifested in their wages. In other markets, a second form of recognition of the value of employees' labor, a recognition of the value of the goods and services that they produce, is manifest in the price of the goods and services. Insisting on the fact that the wages are more than the price that is paid for the commodities, because it is also recognition of the value of the individuals who labor, allows us to understand that struggles for better wages are never just purely utilitarian struggles, but also always struggles for recognition of the social value of their lives. And, in truth, this is the only way to fully grasp what is at stake in the experiences of injustices borne by those paid disgraceful wages—the fact that those wages do not make it possible to live decently, or that they do not reflect the social utility or the onerousness of the job.[37]

To understand work as the site of an ensemble of fundamental normative expectations and wages as the institution of one form of recognition that could satisfy them (or not) leads to a first form of critique of markets. Indeed, markets do not necessarily suffice to satisfy some of an individual's most fundamental normative expectations. Their functioning must thus be domesticated by the addition of external interventions to mechanisms of self-regulation. To deprive individuals of work is to condemn them to a profoundly unsatisfying life, because it constitutes depriving them of the possibility of gaining recognition of their social value through their own activity. For, as Hegel had already observed, only recognition obtained through one's own activity is a satisfactory recognition.[38] When the market does not provide enough employment, volunteer agencies or government programs, along with the domestic sphere (though the latter always runs the risk of reproducing domination and alienation rather than egalitarian recognition), can take its place. Demands associated with recognition through work thus lead to the idea of regulation of labor markets accompanied by public support for a strong nonprofit sector and a dynamic public sector—in a word, these demands advocate that recognition of the value of work through wages take not only a marketized form but also an unmercantile form, that they are answerable not only to capital but also to the state and voluntary associations.

Understanding work as an essential vehicle for recognition leads to a second kind of market critique, which is addressed not to labor markets but to markets for goods and services. In fact, measurement of the value of goods and services is a second form of measuring the value of work. If work is the very form of recognition of a life's social value, that is because it produces goods and services that are capable of meeting social needs, which are the objects of a market validation. It is thus also by means of the market

value of these goods that the value of work is measured (and this affirmation is by no means a purely theoretical affirmation, as is shown by workers'
traditional attachment to well-done work and the products of their labor).
And yet, it is hardly disputable that not only does the market barely make
it possible to measure the social value of goods and services, but also that
it can also direct labor into industries that either do not make it possible
to meet the most fundamental social needs (think of the pharmaceutical
industry's policies) or that destroy the conditions needed to satisfy social
needs (pollution, ravaging of natural resources, etc.). Left to itself, the market cannot be understood as a space for recognition of the social value of
work. To demand recognition of this value is thus to demand, again, that
market mechanisms be domesticated (that the self-regulatory mechanisms
should not be the only means of allocating resources) and that they should
not be the only means of recognizing the value of goods and services. To
demand recognition of the social value of work is to demand that market
activity be confined to areas in which it is socially useful and that socially
useful activities that are incompatible with the requirements of market
competition are directed by a voluntary or public sector.

The theory of recognition thus makes it possible to explain experiences
of injustice produced by market deregulation (wage reductions, unemployment, unequal access to care, etc.) and, at the same time, to articulate a
twofold critique of the market that is sought by various social movements.
Given that it is no longer possible to critique markets in light of an alternative which will take their place (central administration of production
creates new forms of inequality and bureaucratic domination, as well as
new illusions which are comparable to those produced by commodity
fetishism—this approach is thus just as undemocratic as the market, while
being less economically efficient), given further that it is difficult to see how
a global master plan could take the place of globalized markets, critique of
markets can only take the form of a theory of their domestication, through
regulation and by the strengthening of a nonmarket sector, composed of
nonprofit and public firms or state institutions.

THE FIRM

The growing interconnection between markets and the advancement of
deregulation at the global scale have served in recent years to focus critical

attention on the most obvious effects of globalization: the appropriation of nonmarket wealth, and the exclusion of vast populations from markets for consumable goods and the labor market. But the current stage of globalization also has consequences for the integration of labor markets (such as the increasing precariousness of employment as a result of deregulation and new organizational models) that bring with them new forms of injustice. Before examining how a theory of recognition is liable to explain these new forms, we must recall how critics have attempted to analyze such disruptions.

When it takes the question of labor as its guiding thread, a critique of political economy can be based either upon the progressive (or even revolutionary) possibilities implicit within new forms of the organization of work, or upon an interpretation of the neoliberal firm as a more sophisticated technology of domination. The first approach finds its most developed articulation in the work of Antonio Negri and Michael Hardt, in particular in *Empire*. Their principal argument is that the ever-more immaterial, cooperative, digitalized and autonomous character of work implies that employees exercise an ever-larger collective control over their working conditions. Likewise, the wealth that they produce is more and more difficult to appropriate within the system of private property. The result of all this is that the reality of work and its products challenges the very forms of capitalist production just at the moment when the latter exercises an ascendancy over the lives of almost every individual (disappearance of the division between paid labor and private activity; instrumentalization of subjectivity and feelings within work).[39] We would thus be dealing with a new contradiction between the form and the content of work, and we would have to place our bets on this contradiction in order that a new revolutionary subject (the "multitude" as a new collective subject of this new organization of work) may come into being that would be likely to liberate the contents of production from its capitalist form. The principal objections to be raised against Negri and Hardt address precisely these contents' ability to subvert the form in which they have developed. It can, in fact, be asked whether they underestimate the strength of the forms in which working activities are institutionalized by the new capitalism—and, conversely, whether they overestimate the contents' capacity to resist those forms. It can thus be held that the transformations of work (a shift from Fordism to post-Fordism) have been carried out in a context so unfavorable to employees that the positive potential of the new forms of work has only rarely been realized; and that, more often, the neoliberal business model has installed heavier and less tolerable constraints than those of the Taylorist business model.[40]

To count on the contradiction between form and content is to wager on an anticipated future: the organization of work is interpreted on the model of information-based work, which is presupposed to be generalizable in restructuring the entirety of production processes. Once the existence of such a historical trend is admitted, it is of course possible to put forward the hypothesis that principles of social critique are to be found in the norms of intangible work. But this hypothesis is not entirely convincing. In fact, the development of the digital economy seems to lead less to a restructuring of the entirety of production following the logic of immaterial work than to a polarization of production between an innovative digital sector and a sector comprised of all activities excluded from the first (handling, maintenance services, etc.); and production of goods and services where competitiveness is only sought in quantifiable ways—[such as] through reduction of production costs, simplification and intensification of work, and outsourcing. This new economy does not seem so much to necessarily lead to individuals' increasing control of their work so much as a twofold movement in which this emancipatory trend is accompanied by a tendency to reduce employees' activities to the use of a totally instrumentalized capacity for hard work. If it seems difficult to claim that nothing has changed and that it therefore is enough, now as always, to denounce the exploitation of labor, it seems just as difficult to claim that the contemporary organization of work is only to be described by structural progress. Consequently, social critique must gauge the advances made possible by an emancipatory trend, in light of the pathologies and injustices that go along with it, and bring it down to size—without which it runs the risk of losing the perspective of those who are actually interested in a transformation of the real social order, because they suffer from it.

In a certain way, the methodological choice made by Luc Boltanski and Ève Chiapello in *The New Spirit of Capitalism* seems to answer this demand. In fact, they aim to provide a description of the values that structure the new organization of work in order to explicate the rules of justice that could be applied to new forms of injustice. They begin by remarking that the new forms of organizing work are centered around employment "by projects," which implies both a valorization of employees' mobility and adaptability, and measurement of the value of their work through evaluation of the direction of their projects. They assert that the generalization of assessment that follows is based upon rules that are just as vague as the distribution of honors and wealth that results. They thus attempt to make explicit the rules to which individuals appeal in their justifications, in order to define principles of justice that make it possible to restrain the new forms of exploitation created by these new circumstances for work. But this theoretical construct ultimately serves only to displace the problem.[41] In fact, the emergence of employment by project relates to highly skilled workers and does not truly apply to a less-skilled workforce, which generally continues within Taylorist prescriptions. To be sure, the new organization of work attempts to bring this workforce, too, under the demands of a flexible company, but in that case the values of autonomy and self-realization that are advanced by management to justify this transformation lose all their meaning. In effect, when individualized evaluation of performances is applied to a low-skilled workforce, it is in a purely quantitative form that serves no other purpose than to increase productivity. The effects of "total quality management" (TQM), which requires individuals to follow a set of written rules (to comply with a dream of the complete rationalization of production[42] that fails to understand that the experience of work is precisely one of the disparity between prescribed and real work[43])—in the same way that the effects of service work subject to very powerful constraints (like working from a "script" in call centers) come with constant inspection and qualitative evaluation (by means of the computer that serves as one's work station)—fundamentally produce the same consequences as individualized performance evaluations: new forms of denial of recognition of the reality and value of work emerge. Not only do these forms of evaluation prevent individuals from having the value that they give to their efforts recognized (whether that be the merits of the efforts made, or the value of the contribution to the production process), but they also contribute to a denial of recognition of the reality of the work activity, for it is very often the case that those who control and formalize it completely misunderstand it.[44] This denial of recognition is simultaneously a devaluing, a misrecognition, and a making invisible of the work that has been done. This leads to a feeling of being dispossessed on the part of those whose activities are subject to a set of even tighter constraints than the Taylorist prescriptions, which at least could be circumvented.[45] This also leads to a typical example of the experience of injustice in [what Lyotard called] a "wrong," for even if employees grasp that the rules according to which they are evaluated are duplicitous, there still aren't any other alternative evaluative rules at their disposal.

In addition to these various mechanisms of formal evaluation there is also an informal evaluation tied to the culture of the new management and the generalization of organizational frameworks such as working in "open space." By means of subjective incentives and employees' self-regulation, corporate culture is an effective vehicle for dissolving the too-inflexible hierarchies of the Taylorist model of work, because it is based upon norms to which each individual is ostensibly required to comply around others, when presenting oneself as a typical employee. The modernization of the workplace thus takes place by means of a "battle of identities" whose aim is to replace a rebellious and paradoxical employee self-understanding with one that unequivocally identifies with the company.[46] By means of open office spaces and others' constant surveillance of whether one's image is in alignment with the company's, individuals themselves are compelled to submit, as much as possible, even in their bodily comportment, to roles and norms that they quite often disapprove of or only pretend to value while they are at work. The fundamental result of all this is misrecognition (recognition through norms with which employees cannot identify) and a splitting or tearing recognition (when employees do identify with certain norms without actually integrating them with other aspects of their identities).

Low-skilled workers' experience of injustice in the neoliberal corporation does not only depend upon forms of evaluation, but also on a gap between principles of justification and the reality of working conditions. The new organization of work is based upon principles of justification that draw upon a notion of responsibility—responsibility understood as concomitant with autonomy and self-realization—made possible by the fact that the worker is no longer bound to a tedious routine and skillset that effectively imprison his entire professional life. At the same time, however, flexibility is accompanied by the loss of specific expertise that comes from long tenure at a particular workstation. As a result, it limits opportunities for self-realization made possible by pride in proficiency, and renders demands for productivity and hard work even more unbearable. Injunctions to take responsibility for one's own work are often empty, because they are put forward in situations without real liberty. Their only effect is thus, for those who would have the value of their work recognized, an internalization of this conflict over standards: "One's whole self must be committed in order to take it upon oneself to reconcile the irreconcilable: consistency, speed, quality, safety. The psychological internalization of conflicts over standards linked to too-often unrealizable goals leads to new dissociations."[47] And this leads to effects of splitting recognition, to which are added new effects of devaluing recognition. The reduction of the organization's managerial hierarchy is in fact accompanied, in labor-intensive industries, by the disappearance of the professional worker and a more rigorous division between unskilled positions and skilled positions. In such a context, flexibility is only the mask for a definitive imprisonment within a devalued position: "In fact, possibilities for advancement are limited to a few skilled or maintenance positions. This sharp break, simultaneously professional and social, between machine operators and other employees (technicians, engineers, managers) increases for the former a low self-perception, the feeling of belonging to a profoundly devalued group."[48] In the case of low-skilled workers, the principles of justification are definitively invalidated by the institutional frameworks with which they are associated, as evidenced by the feeling that sometimes can be seen to develop in a professional universe that the workers themselves call "a trap" or "perverted."[49]

Nor is the model of social critique that Chiapello and Boltanski take to be well adapted to the new organization of work able to explain the new forms of injustice borne by high-skilled workers. To be sure, investment in a project makes it possible to give meaning to principles of autonomy and self-realization, but here again, powerful invisible hierarchies take the place of subordinate relations in the old corporation,[50] and effective constraints take hold that are at odds with autonomy and self-realization.[51] Power relations take form beneath these principles of justification, and deprive these principles of their value. Moreover, the subjective cost of identification with these principles in the context of flexible work is heightened. The multiplication of projects establishes flexibility and mobility as criteria that define the value of one's activities and the just distribution of wealth and reputation. It follows that the ideal worker is caught between contradictory demands: portrayed like a nomad who has given up everything that could inhibit his availability, including putting down roots or even his personal identity,[52] he is simultaneously subject to demands for a complete identification with his employer and for self-realization through his work. Recognition here is simultaneously splitting and unstable. In fact, the fragmentation of work (moving from project to project, from job to job) does not allow one to integrate the episodes of one's professional life into a coherent narrative[53]— [a narrative] that would serve to alleviate the onerousness of work, or in other words, to validate the psychological investment that follows from the imperative for autonomy and the demand for complete investment in the project. The increasing fragility of identity fundamentally takes the form of an expenditure of mental energy that is pathogenic because it is stripped of meaning.[54]

A theory of recognition founded upon a constitutive concept of recognition will be able to more appropriately describe the forms of injustice created by the new organization of work, for it makes it possible to bring together individuals' normative expectations with respect to work and to the different kinds of recognitive effects created in a business. The first recognitive effect produced by the organization of work has to do with *workers' rights*. It is well known, at least since Marx, that a labor contract gives rise not only to a market transaction, but also to the use of the exchanged labor power in a space other than the market. A labor contract implies a temporary assignment of the labor power to the employer, but the worker retains rights over his working activity—rights that are the object of a twofold institutional recognition. Labor laws define a first set of rights to which are added agreements governing the exercise of work, whether they are collective bargaining agreements or merely implicit agreements.[55] That the denial of recognition linked to violations of workers' rights, to a failure to honor the agreements or to degrading agreements (think, for example, of provisions regulating break time and bathroom breaks), could give rise to a feeling of injustice is a point that has often been repeated.[56] These aspects of denial of recognition are very real parts of the neoliberal corporation's struggle against workers' rights, and its potentially limitless quest for an intensification of work.

A second recognitive effect is linked to the specific modes of interaction in the corporation and has to do with the *utility* of the *work activities*. Individuals encounter it through the roles they take on and the status associated with those roles. They thus find themselves recognized according to the particular duties of their work and according to the ways an organization portrays the value of the work associated with those duties. A feeling of injustice can result from this—one that is tied to a feeling of dissonance between the usefulness of their work for the organization and the feeble recognition that it is given. This experience of injustice, connected with the effects of devaluing recognition, is typical of nurses' work in hospitals, and motivated the nurses' strikes in France in the 1990s. We have just seen that it takes different forms in the neoliberal corporation.

A third recognitive effect is connected to recognition of the *reality* of *work activities* themselves: recognition of the value of work comes about through a judgment not only of its utility, but also of its technical quality (one is not only proud of having done useful work, but also of having done "good work").[57] We are indebted to Christoph Dejours for having taken seriously the numerous grievances put forward by workers with respect to the nonrecognition of the reality of their work:[58] individuals do not merely want the usefulness of their work to be recognized; they want this recognition to stem from the reality of their activity itself and not merely from a professional status, a particular role, or conformity with instructions that are out of sync with the experience of work. Any such recognition is problematic insofar as real work is always different than prescribed work. But it is nonetheless possible, from one's "work collective"[i] (one's co-workers and colleagues) as well as from management. This recognition of the reality of work, along with the pride that can be attached to (recognition of) the social function of a trade and its usefulness within the work organization, is to be counted among the principal factors that make it possible to tolerate the onerousness entailed by any work activity. Conversely, nonrecognition of the reality of work is at the heart of various types of the experience of injustice. It has been shown that the growth of various forms of formal and informal evaluation contribute to their development today.

The experience of injustice at work is thus linked to various recognitive effects that themselves correspond to different normative expectations: recognition of my rights, of my physio-psychological integrity, of my contributions to society, of my usefulness in action coordination, of the reality of my activities. Various recognitive effects can be superposed upon and compensate for the nonsatisfaction of one expectation or another. Quite often, in order for one to have an experience of injustice, various denials of recognition must be conjoined. This explains the explosive appearance of an experience of injustice at work. Anyone who has observed or participated

---

i. See the translator's note for a discussion of this term, "work collective."

in the growth of social struggles linked to wages and work knows this: as soon as the lid is off, a whole host of demands spew out.

By taking these different demands for recognition into account, the theory of recognition makes it possible to articulate a critique of injustice in work that connects with different dimensions of the experience of work. Thus, transformations of the Taylorist system cannot so easily be portrayed as progress. Within a framework of Fordist organization of production, everything associated with individual subjectivity represented a potential obstacle to the scientific organization of work. Reduced to a role and a professional position, an employee saw the reality of his activities misunderstood by management and had difficulty finding recognition for aspects that expressed personal identity and creativity in his work. He had to find some compensation in recognition by his work collective, as well as in social recognition of the work's value as represented by salary increases; and he had to maintain insofar as possible an instrumental relation to his work by making employment the means for personal realization outside of work. This was possible, first of all, because stable work made it possible to think of work as a relatively unproblematic condition of life; secondly, because legally established rights allowed employees to make work a relatively positive element in their construction of identity; and thirdly, because membership in a work collective offered a relatively stable and rewarding network for recognition. The modernization of business practices has completely altered this situation by fostering an institutionalization of recognition of subjectivity destined to motivate individuals and to draw upon their creativity. But this process has taken on contradictory forms in areas of highly skilled employment just as much as in unskilled work.

Unskilled workers are subject to demands for autonomy and flexibility in a context where room for maneuver is limited, where work collectives (or labor unions) are weakened, and where they are aware of evaluations' arbitrariness. They are severed not only from some of their activity, as in a Fordist model, but also "from part of its motivations,"[59] for they must give the impression of being committed to work whose meaning is harder to discern.

Recognition of one's own subjectivity is greater for highly skilled workers. It is not so much a matter of motivating them to work harder as it is to galvanize their innovativeness by rewarding personal initiative and driving workers themselves to take responsibility for the appropriate organizational forms. The recognition of subjectivity that results does not come without a price, however. Workers shift from being recognized ex ante, because of an a priori aptitude linked to having a profession, to an ex post recognition that is largely independent of the reality of their work because it depends principally upon the success of a project; that is, upon how one's projects are evaluated by management and the market.[60] Their work no longer being subject to rigid prescriptions, its value becomes defined by workers' personal investment in the project's success. But because this commitment is difficult to measure, it is necessary that the employees themselves work to have it recognized. They must perform their own identity at work by giving evidence of their complete personal commitment to the project, their ability to enlist and work with a network of competent collaborators, and their ability to go along with any organizational changes that may become necessary. In a way, the new management model is management of recognition: the employee only has value if he is able to obtain recognition through his own means. But this recognition is false.[61] Recognition is a technique of power whose principal function is to foster a more subtle and efficient control of production, but the conditions in which this power is exercised undermine the conditions that allow individuals to satisfy their fundamental expectations with regard to recognition. The management of recognition instrumentalizes recognitive expectations by means of unrealizable promises of recognition—ultimately it only constitutes an ideology of recognition.[62]

To conclude, it is indeed possible that new models of organizing work are characterized by a more communicative/interactive aspect of work, for unskilled as well as for highly skilled work—but here again, the reality of linguistic and explicit communication is distorted by institutional settings that lead to modes of informal communication; and modes of subjection that turn a heralded recognition into a distorted recognition. To be sure, the new forms of work organization tend to draw upon the deliberative dimension intrinsic to all workplace cooperation, but they undermine the two prelinguistic communicative conditions that make possible the emergence of an undistorted deliberation: recognition of the reality of work, and forms of solidarity that build work collectives and workplace community.[63]

When a theory of recognition portrays work as the object of a fundamental normative expectation, it does not thereby merely entail demands for access to employment. It also articulates a demand with another aim, one that has been repressed in the name of struggles for employment, especially within a policy intended to reduce unemployment: the aim to improve working conditions. Whether we consider neoliberals, who adopt the classic conception of work as a disutility, a simple displeasure that is sufficiently compensated by a salary; or the official discourse of the left, which in recent decades has principally fought against unemployment; or even those advocating the end of work, who hold that the only legitimate political objective is the growth of life outside of work, the activity of work is hidden in the same way. And yet, the activity of work remains the primary activity of the vast majority of the population, and it often poisons their lives. This activity ought to be one of the privileged objects of social critique, but normative social theories prefer to steer clear of it. Are they willing and able to address the activity of work? Surely not! Their definition of justice can hardly apply to it, as long as this definition is unsupported by a critical conception of work that is as differentiated as the one proposed by the theory of recognition.

How are we to imagine a radical transformation—indeed, an overcoming—of capitalism, while granting that central planning cannot take the place of the market? The answer is surely to be found in a domestication of the market from above (through regulation, through certain price controls, and through the subsidization of certain sectors), and in restrictions on markets by strong nonmarket sectors, both public and nonprofit; but also through an alteration in the organization of businesses (private or public). This last political aim would likely come about through the growth of workplace democracy and various forms of self-management. But any workplace democracy will remain empty, and any self-management will remain merely formal, if they are not conjoined with a transformation of the organization of work in light of normative expectations linked to the activity of work—in other words, if they do not enlist a critical conception of work that is sufficiently differentiated to be applied to actual working conditions.

THE QUESTION OF DISAFFILIATION

One part of the experience of injustice related to work results from the massive increase in wage earners' insecurity (short-term work, part-time work, informal work, and the increasing precariousness of formerly stable employment). But, as Robert Castel has shown, this process is inseparable from the exclusion of vast populations from the labor market. It is a matter of two inseparable aspects of a single structural dynamic of "disaffiliation," or of the loss of social supports for individuals' lives. Now, by proposing a normative concept of social integration, a theory of recognition also makes it possible to articulate the kind of social critique corresponding to this kind of structural dynamic that cuts across institutions and recasts social relations of domination into a form that gives social questions their current specificity.[64]

As has been articulated by Castel, the concept of "disaffiliation" has the principal virtue of measuring the devastating effects of neoliberal globalization, while also struggling against the dualist presuppositions of the concept of exclusion. This alludes to an opposition between inclusion and exclusion; and this opposition seems to necessarily lead to an opposition between the disaster of desocialization and the value of integration within the current social order. Interpreted in light of the concept of disaffiliation, exclusion only appears as the extreme form of a process of desocialization that cuts across the social order (including paid work) in such a way that the current state of affairs must be subject to a global critique. An elaboration of the concept of disaffiliation nonetheless falls short in two ways, linked to the fact that (just like the concept of exclusion) it remains trapped within the general logic of a discourse of integration. On the one hand, it leads to treating some social institutions (in this case, those linked with the welfare state) as a social model, while minimizing the injustices and domination that they carry. On the other hand, it tends to see only anomie[65] in everything that strays from this model. In order to maintain the concept of disaffiliation's critical force and descriptive power, two modifications are necessary.

First, to achieve true sociological consistency, the concept of disaffiliation should not be articulated only from the macrosociological perspective of a comparative description of the institutions of the welfare state and their decline, but also from the microsociological perspective of a description of interactions that characterize the loss of social support for people's lives.[66] This description should not merely examine the loss of social programs, for the destruction of the welfare state has also led to the creation of new forms of sociality and, in the same way, to new social support systems. To maintain the idea that disaffiliation actually describes an aspect of forms of sociability typical of the present, it would probably have to be characteristic of each of the various ways that social supports break down (a task, moreover, taken up by the sociology of social precarity[67]). But it must also realize that the loss of the welfare state's protections is accompanied by the integration of particular individuals in specific social relations, which are inherently depreciative and unsatisfying (as is stressed, for example, by approaches in terms of "social disqualification"[68]).

Second, to avoid legitimating non-disaffiliating situations, the concept of disaffiliation should provide a normative criterion that would make it possible to distinguish between good and bad integration. Castel is satisfied with measuring the processes of disaffiliation in light of a model provided by the welfare state (social security + stable employment + sharing of productivity increases), thus giving the impression that the latter constitutes a model of integration because individuals reap the benefits of social supports. However, it seems difficult to concede that the social networks characteristic of the welfare state provide truly satisfying networks of socialization, which must lead us to at least distinguish the question of the stability of social relations that support and protect individuals from that of truly satisfying socialization. Consequently, attention to *stable and rewarding* social supports should take the place of attention to "social welfare," in order to define a normative model of social integration; and attention to insertion within *unstable* (increasingly insecure, or precarious) and *devaluing* (through social contempt and social disqualification) social relations ought to take the place of a loss of social supports, in order to develop a critique of disaffiliation.

The concept of disaffiliation should thus be reformulated in light of a normative conception of stable and rewarding social relations and a microsociological characterization of the effects of structural processes of disaffiliation. The theory of recognition can make a contribution to this reformulation. Starting from the principle that a positive relation to oneself is intersubjectively constituted and intersubjectively vulnerable, it makes it possible to define the general conditions institutions must fulfill to produce a valid integration (by specifying, for example, which kinds of insertion into the family, the labor market, and institutions of work can be lauded). It makes it possible to explain both the importance of rewarding intersubjective relations that allow individuals to find confirmation of positive self-images, and the importance of social support provided by intersubjective relations (or a "supporting effect"[69])—a social support without which individuals are more vulnerable to various forms of denial of recognition and social violence (we shall see in chapter 7 that the loss of this kind of support can explain the growth of what is termed social suffering or psychosocial suffering). By thus elaborating a normative conception of integration along the lines of an analysis of I-Thou interactions in particular institutional contexts, the theory of recognition further makes it possible to offer a model that can be mobilized in the microsociological description of disaffiliation.

In taking up the question of disaffiliation, I hope to have convincingly argued that a theory of recognition grounded in a constitutive concept of recognition makes it possible to explain various dimensions of the experience of social injustice. Elements that can emerge as determining factors of this experience are: (1) the rules, values, and subjectivization effects proper to various institutions; (2) the structural asymmetries of power and status that cut across institutions and constitute structural relations of domination (sexist, classist, racist); as well as (3) structural social dynamics that undermine stable and rewarding social relations and replace them with unsatisfying social relations leading to new forms of denial of recognition, on the one hand, and on the other, leaving individuals more vulnerable to denials of recognition.

The question of disaffiliation makes it possible to expose an important dimension of the contemporary form of the social question, tied to transformations of institutions that are embedded within economic dynamics. However, the scope of the question of stable and rewarding relations is not limited to economic matters. It also is concerned with the stability of identity elements and what can be thought of as the subjective side of social insecurity. To explain this subjective side, we must now turn our consideration to questions of identity and social suffering. This will allow us to investigate new dimensions and new forms of the experience of injustice.

PART II

The Politics of Identity and Politics
in Identity

Chapter Four

IDENTITY AS THE EXPERIENCE OF INJUSTICE

It seems reasonable to agree that issues of identity are at stake in certain experiences of injustice, and that these experiences can give rise to various specific resistance movements having to do with a "politics of identity." But the nature of identity, the interconnections between identity-related demands and the domain of justice, and the value of a politics of identity all remain very controversial. One aspect of the problem stems from a polysemy in the concept of identity. For most contributors to debates about the value of identity and of various identity politics, the term "identity" designates the identity that one *is* or that one *has*, whether in a psychological or cultural sense: identity would be an objective property of individuals or social groups; it would designate permanent character or cultural traits. For others, identity is only a way of denoting individuals or groups; a term amounting to a social construction that doesn't correspond to what they really *are* or the experiences they really *have*. In what follows, I will use the term "identity" in a different sense. In order to take seriously the fact that some individuals have the feeling that their experiences of injustice put their identity at risk, I shall begin from the fact that identity is a category of social experience—a category enlisted in specific social experiences and which thus has the function of resolving particular problems.

Individuals and groups rarely confront the problem of their identity, but it does arise on occasion. The concept of identity thus has the function of designating a certain kind of problem in order to resolve it. However, when it makes reference to social experiences where this problem arises and to the function that it fills therein, the concept of identity can no longer be understood in the sense of an ensemble of permanent traits (whether they are conceived in terms of identification, attachments, or powerful assessments) able to be specified independently of the explicit awareness that individuals can have of them. Neither can it be conceived of as an arbitrary social construction. On the contrary, it designates the reflexive relation that individuals come to maintain, in certain situations, with the problems raised by questions like "Who am I?" and "What am I worth?"; as well as "Who are 'we'?" and "What makes us different from other groups?" These problems arise in certain situations, and people must then try to resolve them through the articulation of reasons and demands in terms of their individual or collective identities.

What sorts of situations are we concerned with here? It could be said that we are concerned with any situation in which one discovers that one's actions disappoint or exceed one's expectations with respect to the course of one's life, and any situation that seems to demand a redefinition of these expectations. This means that challenging situations in which the question of identity arises are not always negative. One's actions can exceed one's expectations: one can discover new capacities by succeeding in taking on new roles or new positions, and this can be the basis for developing the hope that one might change and become better than one has been.[1] Problems related to identity can also arise in situations that are neither positive nor negative but neutral, from the perspective of the satisfaction of expectations—as in the situation where, when facing biographical choices with long-term consequences, one ends up asking oneself which life one would choose to live.

Insofar as it is a question here of reflecting on identity-related dimensions of the experience of injustice, I will focus exclusively in what follows on problematic situations corresponding to negative social experiences. On the one hand, this includes situations in which one can experience the feeling of a loss of self, or the feeling that one's life no longer has meaning. On the other hand, this includes situations where one's biographical coherence seems to be challenged, either because one is no longer able to grasp what relationship obtains between different aspects of one's life, or because one comes to think that particular current social experiences betray one's commitments or past hopes. And this also includes all situations in which one is (or, for a group, we are) faced with negative identifications (tied to one's class, gender or sexual orientation, "race" or ethnicity, etc.) from others or from institutions. In all these situations, one can come to ask oneself the two following questions, which portray identity as a problem: What am I, and what worth do I have? When the concept of identity designates particular social experiences that situations give rise to, identity is no longer what one *is* or what one *has*, nor what one is *supposed to be* according to social classifications, but what one *becomes*—we become someone (or a group) who has this sort of problem to resolve. As Jean-Paul Sartre rather provocatively put it, it is not the Jew who creates the anti-Semite, but "it is the anti-Semite who creates the Jew."[2]

Understood in this way, the concept of identity serves to specify the nature of a problem: an incapacity to live in conformity with strong evaluations; an incapacity to maintain attachments to which one clings; an incapacity to maintain biographical coherence. These problems are concerned with what I will call in what follows the elements or facets of personal identity, understood not as objective characteristics but various possible elements or facets of these problems. These encompass characteristics of individual biography, but also what is sometimes encompassed within the concepts of social identity, professional identity, and culture. In other words, the problem of identity is a problem with multiple dimensions.

The concept of identity does not only function to point out these problems, but also to resolve them. It serves to make explicit a set of normative expectations that are at stake in these problematical social experiences, and these normative expectations provide a possible reference point to help find solutions. Reflection—on the nature of the problem, on what is at stake within it, and on the most satisfactory solutions that could be given—can advance in two different directions. The first consists in trying to change objective elements of the problem—by transforming a social world that is incompatible with our strong evaluations or that renders impossible our attachments, or that produces forms of division or rifts in identity; or by struggling against derogatory judgments about who we are. This is the first of two possible paths for an identity politics. The second path consists in trying to change subjective elements of the problem—when, for example, one comes to give up on certain strong evaluations or particular attachments; when one feels the need for greater distance with respect to certain roles or even a redefinition of oneself; or when one understands that one must learn how to seek social recognition in a different way. We shall see in the next chapter that transforming the world and transforming one's identity are often interlinked in the politics of identity. Just as identity is a problem with multiple dimensions, it is a dynamic one.

For now, however, we must try to understand how identity can intervene in experiences of injustice, and what implications it has for a conception of social justice. What arguments could lead to an exclusion (or, on the contrary, the inclusion) of identity within the domain of justice and injustice? The classic answers to this question are to be found in the debate between liberalism and communitarianism. Just as with the debate between liberalism and socialism, this debate has been sustained by particular forms of the experience of injustice. In return, it has brought out new dimensions of the experience of injustice that are linked to the question of identity. We must now ascertain how a theory of recognition would lead us to reformulate this debate, and how this debate and this theory can be made compatible with the pragmatist conception of identity that has just been sketched.

PRINCIPLES OF JUSTICE OR IDENTITY?

Defenders of liberalism and communitarianism hold diverse and partially irreducible views: Michael Sandel, Charles Taylor, Alasdair MacIntyre, and Michael Walzer among the communitarians; John Rawls, Ronald Dworkin, Thomas Nagel, and Bruce Ackerman on the side of liberalism. The fuzziness of these characterizations allows some of these figures to reject their classification in one of the camps, such as Taylor, when he presents his own view as a form of liberalism;[3] or Walzer, when he attempts to show that the debate between liberalism and communitarianism rests upon a false dichotomy.[4] We can admit, however, as a hypothesis, that these two approaches represent a fundamental choice. The communitarian position asserts that it is impossible to determine what makes a just society without reference to the values shared by particular social groups, whereas the liberal position maintains, on the contrary, that the question of justice can only be answered by abstracting from such values to the benefit of universal rights related to individual liberty. Liberalism asserts that the just is independent with respect to the good (understanding by "the good" shared representations of the good life, or the different values shared by various social groups), and that the former has priority with respect to the latter; while communitarianism maintains that the just is inseparable from the good and therefore that the former cannot have priority with respect to the latter.[5]

The debate opened by these alternatives includes a number of aspects. First of all, it has to do with strictly normative questions, such as that of the normative nature of the just and the good (how they are differentiated) and their respective contents (what rights can be deemed just, and what values can be deemed good?); this aspect of the debate has already been considered in the preceding chapter. Next, it has to do with questions of social theory, such as those concerning the motivational origins of principles of justice (what are the ethical dispositions that allow individuals to subscribe to such principles?) and the stability of just institutions (what are the institutional frameworks that make it possible for principles of justice to take form in a just society?). Finally, it has to do with questions related to the nature of personal identity and its connection to group affiliations.

It can be noted that in this debate, the concept of identity is understood in the sense of a collective identity and not in the sense of personal identity (of which group identity is only one instance), and that group identity is most often identified with cultural identity (without taking into account social and professional identities). It can be further noted that identity, understood in its cultural component, is identified with a set of strong evaluations that are inseparable from individuals' attachments to communities grounded in traditions (the fact that we could care about other commitments is no more taken into account than the normative problems of biographical coherence that could result from them).

For their part, debates concerning the relation between justice and identity develop from two different approaches. The first has to do with the normative criteria of social critique: Is it legitimate to base social critique on the strong evaluations of identity? The second has to do with social stability: Can principles of justice preserve their social validity if they are no longer compatible with strong evaluations of identity? The perspective of the experience of injustice leads to a privileging of the first approach to the discussion, even if it implies that social critique must not be separated from social theory (related to objective contexts that lead to experiences of injustice with implications for identity) and questions related to normative dynamics that can be carried through identity. But it is precisely this connection that Rawls attempts to undo, and the communitarian critique attempts to reestablish. We have already seen that for Rawls, the principles of justice are defined starting from a fictional "original position" in which individuals are supposed to be able to reach universal agreement on the common rules that will govern social life because they are unaware of the position that they will occupy in this society, by virtue of the "veil of ignorance." The condition that makes it possible to formulate a universal definition of social justice is the bracketing of questions concerning the specific effects of social contexts that create injustice. At the same time, the strong evaluations of identity are relegated to questions of the good, which—due to their irreducible pluralism—must be excluded from the domain of justice. One of the most obvious difficulties of the Rawlsian approach is tied to the articulation of this constructivist approach (the abstract construction of principles of justice from an ideal situation) and the critical function of principles of justice (the application of universal principles to particular societies that actually exist). This difficulty constitutes one of the principal focal points of the communitarian critique of liberalism. Indeed, *pace* the constructivist approaches, Walzer maintains that the validity of a normative principle can only be recognized by individuals on the condition that it is already active in their fundamental moral intuitions.[6] It follows that the fact cannot be excluded that strong evaluations of identity play a role in social critique.

From the liberal point of view, this objection boils down to asking about the social validity of principles of justice. Liberals and communitarians agree, moreover, on the fact that adherence to universal principles of justice must be supported by values carried by common ways of life, or by values at least partially compatible with each other. The liberal argument is that in societies marked by the "fact of pluralism," the political community must be understood as a "posttraditional" community, marked by a plurality of ways of life and conceptions of the good, in which it is not possible to obtain more than an "overlapping consensus" reinforced by the universal values of liberalism. Ultimately, this boils down to a wager on the partial compatibility of strong evaluations of identity, and on the capacity of universal principles to transform group identities in order to reduce their partial incompatibility. The communitarian argument consists, for its part, in stressing that the strong evaluations of identity have their own coherence and proper function, and that they are not so malleable. Added to that is the assertion that the breakdown of identities through social and political developments can yield a series of political, social, and psychological problems, at least a few of which fall within the domain of justice and injustice.

The communitarian critique of liberalism thus initiates a twofold challenge for theories of justice. The first is to take account of the dimensions of the experience of injustice that are linked to identity and the normative dynamics that lead to a critique of social injustice from the perspective of identity. The second is to take account of experiences of injustice that are linked to the breakdown of identity and to formulate appropriate models of social critique. Both of these challenges can be taken up by a theory of recognition.

THE LIMITS OF A CONCEPTION OF IDENTITY AS A POSITIVE RELATION TO ONESELF

One of the aims of *The Struggle for Recognition*, clearly, was to put forward a model capable of integrating the communitarian critique of liberalism within the framework of a critical theory of society in the Frankfurt School tradition.[7] For Honneth, who follows Habermas on this point, what must take the place of a *constructivist* social critique is not a hermeneutic social critique (the interpretation of that which is given as just in a particular culture), as in Walzer, but the normative *reconstruction* of principles at work in the social experience of individuals and groups.[8] In fact, the normative principles that structure social life are not merely particular, or linked to mutually incompatible cultural and social contexts. They also contain a universal core. Social action is impossible if individuals do not at least implicitly agree upon the forms of their interaction, which presupposes symmetrical recognition of their rights and their respective worth. It is precisely these demands for recognition, constitutive of individuals' and groups' social experience, which ought to be made explicit in order to elaborate a definition of justice connected to the experience of various individuals who, in an unjust context, are affected by social critique.

The originality of the kind of reconstructive social critique that Honneth proposes is linked to the fact that it is inspired by a pragmatist conception of identity as a problematic relation to oneself. What is always at stake in experiences of injustice is the reaffirmation of a weakened positive relation to oneself. In other words, it is identity in the sense of a problematized question of who I am and what I am worth. The question of identity is thus integrated into the domain of justice according to a strategy that entails three key differences with respect to communitarianism. Firstly, the question of identity is approached by starting from personal identity rather than from group identity (which is but one dimension of the former). It is only when identity is understood by starting from the experience of a problematic relation to oneself that it will become possible to explain the plurality and the dynamic character of facets of identity in the experience of injustice, and to avert the risk, faced by communitarian arguments, of reifying cultural identities. Secondly, group identities, once they are understood as moments of personal identity, can be related not only to cultural identities but also social identities (affiliation with a class or a social position and the set of strong evaluations that correspond to it) and professional identities (affiliation with a profession, a business, or a work collective, and the set of strong evaluations that correspond to it) falling under the third sphere of recognition. We know that one of the primary vehicles for social recognition is work. But, to review, what one wants to have recognized through one's work is not only personal skills but also conformity with a set of values shared by a work collective or even by a business or a profession. This is the source for ambivalence in demands for recognition in the workplace, when work collectives and labor unions are weakened and the values tied to a profession are rendered impractical by the ways in which work is organized. Thirdly, the normative content of personal identity is linked to universal expectations and not merely to strong evaluations unique to particular communities. As an intersubjectively vulnerable positive relation to oneself and as an expectation of confirmation, identity in fact appears as the source for universal expectations, the very ones upon which Honneth grounds his conception of justice.

Honneth's approach to identity thus defines an original way forward for recasting the debate between liberalism and communitarianism. It manages to raise the challenges of communitarian critique while also avoiding several of its most typical pitfalls. It carries with it, however, a number of limits that all hinge upon the identification of identity with a relation to oneself. From the perspective of the pragmatist conception of identity I sketched a bit earlier, identity is simultaneously less and more than a positive or negative relation to oneself. A first limit is tied to the fact that conflating identity with a relation to oneself makes identity into a permanent problem. But if we can acknowledge that confirmation of a positive relation to oneself is the object of a general normative expectation, we must also acknowledge the fact that we only rarely raise the problem of our identity. Most of the time, recognitive expectations based upon an expectation of confirmation of one's positive relation to oneself remain implicit, and even when they become explicit within problematic social experiences, it is rare for reflection on what is at stake in these experiences to be articulated in terms of identity. In the same way, Honneth's model fails to explain the specific features of experiences appearing to those who live through them as having identity-related dimensions—which also prevents it from being able to explain, in starting from the experience of injustice, the specific features of demands that carry aspects of identity. He does not articulate the concept of identity by starting with the functions fulfilled by references to identity within negative social experiences, which means that it is impossible for him to analyze the specific forms and dynamics of experiences of injustice that carry identity dimensions.

A second limit is tied to the static character that is assigned to identity when it is identified with a relation to oneself. To be sure, this identification makes it possible to emphasize that identity can take two opposed forms—a positive relation to oneself (positive identity) or a negative one (negative identity). Moreover, it makes it possible to highlight that a positive relation to oneself can be weakened and can thus give rise to particular practical and cognitive dynamics. But identity is not, for all that, conceived of in its internal dynamics. Only its external dynamics come to the fore. It is conceived as a self-image (an image of what I am and what I am worth) resulting from the integration of others' images of me, and not also as a work upon the self. In other words, Honneth's intersubjectivist approach leads him to understand identity solely from the perspective of "external transactions" between recognitive expectations and recognitive effects, whereas it should also be understood from the perspective of "internal transactions"[9] between different elements of identity. In fact, personal identity is the result not simply of an internalization of recognitive effects produced by "significant others" and institutions, but also of an interaction between the various subjective effects of socialization. It is precisely because this internal transaction has become problematic that one has to ask oneself how to preserve one's biographical coherence, or how to struggle against the effects of a splitting or tearing recognition. Thus identity never appears to oneself as a self-image to be reestablished or confirmed, but rather as a problem that cannot be resolved without some form of self-work. Even when it is our image of ourselves that becomes problematized, what we have to deal with is, in fact, the failure of identity-work. A global image of who we are and what we value cannot be produced without some sort of synthesis of different recognitive effects and different elements of personal identity. One part of this work is probably carried out in a preconscious, or even unconscious, manner; but another part is also carried out consciously, in those stages of our lives when the question of our identity arises. Therefore it can be said, employing the language of theories of narrative identity, that personal identity rests upon a twofold work of making a narrative of oneself. It supposes, first of all, work to bring together and unify what an individual identifies as his own special characteristics. Added to that is work to improve upon the various elements of one's positive self-image. This work can thus be defeated in two ways: by failing either to narratively unify different biographical traits and different distinctive identifications; or by failing to bring a rewarding dimension to this narrative unification. Speaking of work with respect to identity makes it possible to stress that a rewarding unification of identity elements can come about through transformations of personal identity. If there is a point that must be emphasized, it is that identity is susceptible to immanent transformations as soon as it becomes problematized; and therefore there is no reason to maintain that demands having to do with identity are based upon inert identities that can only be transformed from an external point of view (such as that of adapting to a situation, or the view that universal principles alone could legitimize these demands).

The third limit of an identification between one's relation to oneself and one's identity has to do with the fact that it does not make it possible either to distinguish between a preconscious relation to oneself and a conscious relation to oneself, or to analyze the relation between identity and its preconscious foundations. Since the theory of recognition is based upon a correlation between recognitive expectations and forms of positive relation to oneself, as well as upon the distinction between implicit (or preconscious) expectations and explicit expectations (or demands) for recognition, it ought to lead to a distinction between two types of relation to oneself. The pragmatist conception of one's relation to oneself proposed by G. H. Mead moves precisely down this path. If we believe the author of *Mind, Self and Society*, interaction is inseparable from a relation to oneself (or a "Self"[10]) through which an individual monitors his interactions with another by adopting the other's perspective. But this relation to oneself remains preconscious in the normal course of interaction; it does not take the form of a reflexive relation to oneself in which the question of identity (that of the "I" in Mead's vocabulary) arises. To specify the meaning of this distinction, one can add that on the preconscious level, the idea of a relation to oneself designates two different things: a form and a content. On the one hand, it designates a functional relation to oneself: an awareness of oneself as meeting or not meeting a certain number of social expectations. On the other hand, it designates the contents of this formal relation to oneself—namely, an awareness of particular expectations tied to this or that context of interaction, an awareness that is delivered through a social knowledge (which defines the "Me" for Mead). Implicit expectations for recognition are connected to this determinate content: individuals expect that their interaction partners will recognize their ability to play their role appropriately, which also means that they expect to be recognized for their particular way of playing the role. In this sense, the modes of a preconscious relation to oneself depend upon an implicit awareness of one's abilities and skills that is incorporated into one's habits. At the level of an implicit relation to oneself, the "Me" is thus constituted by an awareness of oneself as endowed with a set of abilities, skills, and habits that make it possible to satisfy a set of social expectations. When an individual experiences new abilities or inabilities, or when his actions fall below or go beyond social expectations, or even when his actions are out of step with the affiliations or strong evaluations that have structured his habits—this is when the relation to oneself becomes explicit and when the questions "Who am I?" and "What am I worth?" arise (or when the "I" in Mead's sense, as a new phase of experience, emerges). This is also, therefore, when demands for recognition concerning identity can arise.

A failure to distinguish between these two forms of a relation to oneself makes it impossible to explain the real relation between identity, as an explicit question or problem to solve, and its preconscious materials, which will ultimately end up as the object of a thematization within the framework of a reflection guided by the questions "What am I?" and "What am I worth?" But failing to explain the nature of this relation leaves one open to two classic critiques of the concept of identity: the first condemns the partiality and the illusion of an identity that only grasps the unrepressed part of the psyche; the second stresses that the true "Me" is not so much one of identity but of habits. The first of these critiques asserts that identity is untrue because it is based upon the denial of an essential part of our being. This is Max Horkheimer and Theodor Adorno's claim when they see in identity only a mutilated self-image that can only be preserved through a "self-sacrifice" similar to Odysseus's when he has himself bound to the mast of his ship.[11] The second critique can be associated with Pierre Bourdieu and the idea that our lives are governed by a plurality of habitus, in such a way that the feeling of unity associated with the idea of identity must be understood at best as a "[well-founded] illusion of personal coherence."[12]

To answer these objections, we can begin by noting that they rest upon a sort of epistemological overdetermination of the concept of identity. Reflection upon the self that develops in terms of identity does not have a speculative purpose (defined by self-awareness as its only goal), but rather a practical one: its aim is to resolve ethical and psychological problems concerning the ways and means of conducting one's life. Even if, quite often, individuals pose the problem of the unity and value of their lives in confused terms, the problem is no less essential for the conduct of their lives. It is quite possible that life's most fundamental problems cannot be settled within the framework of self-reflection in terms of identity because the unconscious and a part of our preconscious escape the control of reflection, but some problems can be resolved in this way. Moreover, it is quite likely that the feeling of unity conceals the plurality of habits; but one can also hold, with John Dewey, that habits (which in his view define who we are) always interact, at least in a partial way, with each other[13] (in a sort of preconscious "internal transaction"), and that the feeling of personal coherence supposes a minimum of integration—this demonstrates that habitus are not disturbed or torn apart to the point of throwing an individual into malaise and suffering. These two objections, one concerning the unconscious and the other concerning the plurality of habitus, rest in fact upon the opposition between what falls under the unconscious (repression) or the preconscious (habitus) on the one hand, and the conscious (identity) on the other; whereas the pragmatist conception of identity is entirely consistent with the idea of an unconscious and preconscious conditioning of identity when it makes identity the reflective thematization of a set of preconscious materials produced by processes (in particular, habits) that always at least partially elude reflection. Moreover, reflection is itself a habit, a habit that cannot claim any sovereignty over habits but that can nevertheless contribute to their transformation.[14]

The fourth limit of Honneth's approach is linked to the strategy employed to integrate references to identity within the domain of justice and injustice. Honneth's argument can be rephrased in the following way: normative expectations linked to the confirmation of a positive relation to oneself are sufficiently fundamental and sufficiently general to be able to be integrated into the domain of justice, as long as one takes into account the normative expectations linked to the three general forms of a positive relation to oneself (self-confidence, self-respect, and self-esteem). But this implies a quite restricted account of identity. The impediments to this restriction are as connected to the implicit distinction that it presupposes between the form and content of identity as to the presupposition that universality constitutes the criterion for inclusion within the domain of justice. Firstly, this restriction consists in separating the form of a satisfactory personal identity (a positive relation to oneself) from its contents; namely, the different elements of identity by which an individual imagines who he is and what he is worth. However, as I have already noted, recognitive expectations, whether implicit or explicit, are not associated with the form of one's relation to oneself, but with its contents. There are always particular dimensions of my life that are the object of recognitive expectations, and I must be able to deem them sufficiently important for me, in the framework of a reflection in terms of identity, so that their disappointment would give rise to an experience of denial of recognition (someone who does not identify as essentially French will hardly suffer from Francophobia). Not all recognitive expectations carry the same weight; their respective importance depends upon a hierarchy of strong evaluations and attachments that structure personal identity. The connection between recognition and a positive relation to oneself is thus mediated by the contents of identity. Inversely, it is clear that the institutionalization of depreciation or of invisibility of this or that element of personal identity will be accompanied by a general questioning of one's positive relation to oneself. In sum, it is difficult to see how what is at stake in recognitive expectations, and what comes to be made explicit in particular in the language of justice and injustice, could be related only to the forms of one's relation to oneself, and not simultaneously to its contents; that is, to the different elements of identity.

It is not difficult to understand why Honneth want to relate the stakes of justice only to these three forms. The various biographical, social and cultural components of identity, which give a relation to oneself its concrete form, seem too specific and too contingent to come under the domain of justice. And yet, if recognitive expectations are always at least indirectly linked to the elements of personal identity, and if recognition of the things that give individuals' lives their value are most fundamental for them, there is no longer reason to ascribe such particularity and such contingency to the contents of personal identity. To approach the question of justice starting from the experience of injustice leads one to see the concept of justice as an instrument for explaining a set of fundamental expectations, an instrument for the analysis and resolution of what is at stake in a number of negative social experiences. It is difficult to see why, from a speculative perspective, recognitive expectations connected to the elements of personal identity should be excluded from these fundamental expectations. It is difficult to see, moreover, how to justify such an exclusion from a political perspective. That would amount to holding that experiences of injustice linked to identity, in the eyes of those who undergo them, do not deserve to be taken seriously. Who could disagree that when individuals assert that the values and commitments that have structured their lives are subjected to forms of social contempt, they can feel a form of injustice? Isn't that, for example, one of the reasons for a feeling of injustice linked to the experience of being laid off (where personal attachments to one's coworkers, and even to one's workplace, are also nullified)? Isn't that, to take an even clearer example, one of the reasons for a feeling of injustice created by derogatory views associated with various religions—a feeling of injustice whose mobilizing power is well known?

Furthermore, even when injustices are not experienced as directly linked to identity, the latter can play a fundamental role in the normative dynamics that originate in an experience of injustice. In fact, the values that are carried by group identities can play a decisive role in the sharing of a negative experience and in the construction of frames of injustice.[15] As another example, we can again make reference to injustices linked to transformations of work. It is clear that these are not reducible to a denial of recognition of professional identities, but it is just as clear that they can be *collectively designated and expressed* as injustices that can be transformed, by those who undergo them, only by means of professional identities.

The social demands linked to working conditions are never born solely from a feeling that the value of any particular individual's work, or of work in general, has not been recognized. Rather, indeed, they stem from the feeling that the value of a specific kind of work, whether represented as a positive professional identity or as what is structuring a work collective, is not recognized. In France, the nurses' strikes of the early 1990s, the social movement of November-December 1995, and even the teachers' revolt in 2003, were always linked to a feeling that duties connected to "public service," constitutive of public-sector employees' identities, were not recognized for their full and just value.[16] In sum, professional identity itself provides part of the normative context that makes it possible to understand worsening working conditions as an experience of injustice, and can set dynamics of formulating demands into motion.

Many experiences of social injustice are articulated in the language of group identities, even if they are more closely categorized as social struggles rather than as the politics of identity; and, here again, political philosophy must integrate references to identity into its reflections on justice if its critical models are to remain congruous with the discourse of those practically engaged in the transformation of injustice, and if its critical models are to achieve the particular kind of social validity they seek.

IDENTITY AND JUSTICE

But how is a reference to identity to be integrated into a definition of social justice? To clarify what is at stake in this question, it can be useful to analyze the normative demands that can be associated with concepts of self-respect, dignity, and identity.

With the term "the decent society,"[17] Avishai Margalit has attempted to articulate the normative model of a social order whose institutions do not damage or prejudice the self-respect to which individuals can legitimately aspire. By "self-respect" or "intrinsic honor" (p. 43), Margalit means the feeling of belonging to the human community. He simultaneously contrasts this to dignity, as "the external aspect of self-respect" (p. 51), and to "social honor," or the feeling of social value. The nonrecognition of either one being insufficient by itself to create humiliation, it need not be taken into account in a model of the decent society. However, individuals do not merely look to social institutions to recognize their humanity, but also to allow them to have their humanity recognized through actions that express it. It is difficult to see how a society that deprives men of their dignity could truly be called decent, and we can thus ask if a decent society ought not therefore also be defined by the conditions for dignity. Moreover, it can be asked whether recognition of one's dignity depends only upon the recognition of rights that define respect for each individual's humanity, or also upon recognition of the social value of our lives, or on "social honor." How could a society be decent, if it imposes upon people a feeling of being good for nothing or of being superfluous? This is precisely the thrust of Honneth's critique of Margalit.[18] Nevertheless, Honneth's conception, in turn, seems to remain too narrow if it is a matter of covering the entire spectrum of social injustice. The model of recognition of humanity must not only be expanded to include recognition of dignity and social honor, but also recognition of identity. The argument in favor of such an expansion is twofold.

The first part of this argument rests upon the claim that meaningful recognition from the viewpoint of social justice is an institutionalized recognition. Yet, as institutions embody normative models, they always have the effect of accentuating certain elements of identity and of deprecating or devaluing—even disqualifying—others, or rendering them invisible. The result is that recognition of individuals by institutions is always mediated by their identities. This is the case in institutions in the narrow sense, where subjectivation processes come about through the recognitive effects of group identities. Just as recognition of my psychophysical integrity comes about, in the family, through recognition of my role as a man or a woman, a husband or a wife, a mother or father, recognition of the social value of my work comes about, in businesses, through recognition (from management) of my support for the business's culture or through recognition (by my coworkers or work collective) of my professional competence and conformity with professional values. It is the same in institutions in the broader sense; that is, in the sense of socially accepted ways of acting. I have already noted that the rules of interaction have a tripartite structure that simultaneously assigns both a role and a value to interaction partners. Ordinary interactions are thus the occasion for different kinds of confrontation between different kinds of evaluations about various social positions and various ways of fulfilling certain roles, confrontations in which the commitments and strong evaluations that are constitutive of identity are involved and can arouse an experience of injustice as contempt.

The second part of the argument in favor of an expansion toward identity rests on the claim that institutionalized denial of recognition, when it bears specifically upon identity, involves an injury to a positive relation to oneself that is as profound as the denial of recognition of one's dignity. The denial of recognition bearing specifically on group identities, or on the biographical elements of personal identity, can also entail a weakening, or even a collapse, of a positive relation to oneself. Many examples can be given showing that the kinds of stigmatization aimed at certain social groups that see themselves as unable to live in conformity with the commitments and strong evaluations that they hold can be a factor that contributes to turning a positive identity into a negative one. If the recognitive expectations connected to affirmation of a positive relation to oneself constitutes one of the general issues behind various forms of the experience of injustice, then there is indeed a good case for taking seriously these particular experiences of injustice in which affirmation of a positive relation to oneself by means of recognition plays an important role.

This expansion of the scope of the concept of social justice, however, runs counter to our intuitions of justice, because, according to the latter, the idea of impartiality should play a fundamental role. To say that justice is characterized by some sort of impartiality amounts to asserting that it comes under some sort of universality. But if the three forms of recognition of dignity can appear as universal conditions of the good life, group identities embody by definition nonuniversalizable claims: recognition of identity is necessarily recognition of particulars. This is indisputable, but it is not sufficient to exclude identity from the domain of justice. In fact, the opposition between the universal and the particular presupposed here is based upon a kind of fetishization of logical categories that can be disputed. The fact that the definitions of universal and particular presuppose a distinction between universal and particular doesn't demonstrate at all, in fact, that universal properties exist independently of particular properties. This last remark must not lead us to conclude that any reference to universality negates the difference, and that universal demands must be replaced by demands for respect of otherness or of particularity in moral philosophy. But we can nonetheless ask by what right universality could be opposed to demands for a recognition of the particular. That true universality should be understood from the perspective of the individual is a Hegelian principle (later turned against Hegel by Adorno)[19] that has not lost its relevance. From an epistemological point of view, what does the value of universality generally consist of, if not its capacity to take account of the particular content it subsumes? And in ethical and political matters, how can the values linked to universality be understood except as the possible unification of particular wants and needs?

It is enough that recognition of identity expresses a fundamental normative expectation, and that, therefore, it can claim a legitimacy recognized by all—a form of universality that can be called concrete because it is expressed in particular demands. It does not follow, for all that, that every identity deserves to be recognized, and even less that the idea of recognition of identity makes it possible to determine which identities deserve recognition and which do not. Finally, it is only within the framework of a criteriological way of thinking that a strict division between universals and particulars obtains. The fact that there aren't any criteria available to determine the specific legitimacy of identity-related demands is not enough to exclude these demands from the domain of justice, because the questions of scope and criteria are logically distinct, as we have already noted.

To argue for the integration of identity within the domain of justice from the perspective of a theory of recognition only ascribes a minimal form of legitimacy to identity-related demands. There are reasons to take these demands seriously, which does not mean either that they will always be legitimate or that they possess the highest level of legitimacy. This does not prohibit us from trying to provide arguments that would subject these demands to criticism. Following the logic of the argument developed above, identity-related demands ought to be compatible with recognition of dignity. That means that, ultimately, something must be kept of the idea of justice's priority over the good, while expanding the definition of justice in the direction of the good. When a cultural identity, for example, entails forms of racist, sexist, or xenophobic stigmatization, there is no doubt that it does not deserve to be defended as such, but ought rather to be abandoned or transformed. But it is also the case that experiences of injustice give birth to struggles for the recognition of identity that do not entail any denial of dignity. It does not follow, for all that, that these struggles are just. But because nothing prohibits us from acknowledging that they fall within the domain of social justice, and because there are no criteria for evaluating them (recognition of dignity is not enough to do so), the only solution is to go back to deliberation and collective confrontations in order to determine whether these struggles can or cannot lead to just social transformations.

If this expansion of the concept of justice is disturbing, that is because it clashes with the way in which we understand politics as a court of appeals against cultural particularism. This conception, common and reasonable, sometimes leads to the following argument: Because it is the function of politics to arbitrate disputes between social groups and between individuals and social groups, it cannot be based upon the acknowledgment of any rights except those that are based on our status as human beings. To integrate recognition of identity within a definition of social justice could lead to recognizing rights that contravene this demand. We are thus brought back to the debate between liberalism and communitarianism, but we can also see that this interpretation of the principle of politics as a court of appeals in fact turns the principle against itself. Liberalism maintains, in fact, that in the face of a diversity of shared conceptions of the good life, politics should restrict itself to topics that are neutral with respect to cultures and their fundamental values. It must therefore settle for an abstract construction of citizenship and turn politics into a space out of touch with everyday life where individuals always bring their commitments and strong evaluations. Recognized by political institutions as subjects of law, individuals see themselves misrecognized qua individuals endowed with an identity. Thus detached from some of their most fundamental aspirations, political principles lose their social validity in their eyes and sink into a political alienation already interpreted by Marx as the reduction of citizens to "pure, bare individuality," and as the denial of their membership in various social communities.[20] How, then, are political principles a court of appeals?

Communitarians maintain, on the contrary, that individuals must be recognized as actual individuals inserted within historically constituted traditional communities. This has the virtue of relocating justice within the complex network of normative expectations that structure our lives. In a certain sense, communitarians thus move in tandem with the Marxian critique of political alienation in condemning the illusory autonomy of politics and in connecting politics to conditions that are no longer material (as in Marx), but ethical and psychosocial. Nevertheless, whereas Marx maintained that material conditions only appear to be prepolitical but are truly political, communitarianism hopes to confirm this appearance concerning ethical and psychosocial conditions. If it is necessary to critique the view that reduces politics to an autonomous sphere governed by the simple demand for respect of rights, then it is also necessary, in order to fully plumb political questions,[21] to assert the political dimension of conditions for the political public sphere's social validity, even when those conditions have to do with identity. This raises the problem of what must be understood by the concept of a politics of identity, which will be taken up in the next chapter.

From the foregoing, however, it follows that social injustice is linked not only to nonrespect of some people's fundamental rights and the unequal distribution of wealth, but also to forms of inequality that come about through the recognition of group identities and personal identity. These forms of inequality must be taken into account in our conception of justice. This conception must be sufficiently broad to allow the ensemble of these inequalities to be publicly expressed and referred to in political debates in terms of injustice. Its definition must be broad enough for politics to be able to impact the potential for conflict borne by the various forms of denial of recognition (and thus to struggle against a narrowing of the space of institutionalized politics), while giving them a means for political expression (and thus giving them an alternative to unbridled violence). With the connection between justice and identity, the challenge is not so much to define principles of justice capable of determining which identity-related demands are just and which are not, but rather to propose a definition of justice that takes into account the right to an identity: If all identity-related demands are not inherently just, neither are they inherently unjust; if explicit recognition of identity is not always necessary, one nonetheless has a right to claim one's identity. Here is where normative reflection upon justice stops; what remains is a matter of political struggle and deliberation.

Chapter Five

A DEFENSE OF IDENTITY POLITICS

To understand justice starting from the experience of injustice means understanding justice from the perspective of practical and normative dynamics aimed at social transformation, and on that basis, in other words, it means connecting normative justifications with political objectives while showing that the practical dynamics that support these objectives are capable of transforming social logics that produce injustice. A complete justification for integrating references to identity within a definition of justice would entail wading into the full range of these problems. Until now, I only argued for the integration of references to identity within the domain of justice and injustice. However, the concept of identity is also connected to a whole set of more specific political challenges, some of which are linked to the aims pursued by identity-related demands, others to the social logics that structure identity. These challenges deserve consideration.

In sociological and philosophical literatures as well as in political discourse, the theme of identity is in vogue. The last fifty years have seen the development of struggles rooted in identity, which has led to a revitalization of political discourse. Clearly, identity has certainly become a simultaneously theoretical and practical problem. But do we have to take it seriously? That is what the preceding chapter tried to demonstrate through a defense of the idea that a pragmatist conception of identity makes it possible to answer a number of objections that can be raised against the very issue of identity; and moreover, that this conception makes it possible to analyze the specific features of identity-related experiences of injustice as well as the practical and cognitive dynamics that originate in these experiences. But this is not enough to demonstrate that identity-related demands can be the right response to these experiences of injustice. Such a demonstration is precisely the task of this chapter. To do so, I must begin by clarifying how we can understand struggles for identity by further developing the thesis, defended in chapter one, that struggles for identity constitute a specific type of social movement. I will then be able to examine the various possible critiques of the politics of identity—those that criticize its normative deficits, those that reduce identity to subjection, and those that oppose the politics of difference to the politics of identity.

STRUGGLES FOR IDENTITY—A SECOND KIND OF SOCIAL MOVEMENT?

Regarding the place of struggles for identity within collective struggles, there are three different, and opposed, approaches. The first maintains there are two kinds of social movements: class-related and redistributive social struggles ("traditional social movements"); and struggles for identity ("new social movements").[1] The second asserts that it is impossible to rigorously distinguish between these two types of social struggle and that the idea of new social movements is only the result of an erroneous interpretation of traditional social movements.[2] The third holds that the category of new social movements refers to a set of demands (feminist movements, religious movements, racist movements) that is too heterogeneous to be brought together in a single category.[3] I argued in chapter one that the theory of recognition is interesting notably because it offers a theory of the practical and cognitive dynamics that cut across the various forms of protest action in general, and the different types of social movements in particular. I also argued that the theory of recognition has the virtue of successfully rendering the specific features of different forms of protest action and different types of social movements, while still taking the full spectrum of protest action into account. Elaborating the idea that social struggles and struggles for identity indeed constitute two different and distinct types of social movement will make it possible to clarify the meaning of these various theses.

That struggles for identity can pursue very different aims is a fact that can lead to very divergent conclusions, depending on which aspect of their diversity one chooses to emphasize. A first kind of approach consists in underscoring that the term identity is not understood in the same way, depending on whether it is a matter of feminist or homosexual struggles, or struggles in defense of a minority culture. In the second of these two cases, struggles are linked to the defense of some specific feature that concerned individuals understand as identity-bearing, but this is not necessarily the case in the first, because it could then simply be linked to the refusal of a more or less degrading or stigmatizing label. Regardless, in both cases, these struggles draw their specific characteristics from the fact that they are directed against denials of recognition of identity, whether it is a question of an identity ascribed by others or an identity assumed by oneself. To be sure, these two kinds of struggles will aim at different objectives, which can be as diverse as recognition of a positive identity and struggling against a degrading or stigmatizing labeling, but in both cases, their specifics are connected to a set of characteristics that are dependent upon the logic of identity and the fact that personal identity can always, as a result of an institutional context, be transformed from a positive identity to a negative one.

A second kind of approach to the diversity of struggles for identity consists in stressing the conflicting political objectives that they can pursue, and the vast differences in their relative legitimacy. It is clear, in fact, that the legitimacy of struggles against gender discrimination is hardly comparable with that of movements that claim to defend a national identity in racist or xenophobic ways. Nonetheless, this assessment by itself is not enough to rule out that identity-related demands involve a particular form of legitimacy, one that is encompassed in a refusal of injustice. Here again, we must distinguish between the legitimacy of underlying motives and the legitimacy of objectives sought after and the means employed to realize them. There is no a priori reason, from the perspective of normative dynamics, why diverse struggles for identity could not find some coherence or common ground. In sum, therefore, the arguments that attempt to challenge the categorical unity of struggles for identity only lead to a distinction between different species of struggles for identity, without managing to show that they cannot share a number of common traits; whereas the existence of such generic traits does suffice to justify our use of this category.

Arguments that challenge the idea of a discontinuity between social struggles and struggles for identity are probably more convincing. We can recall on this point that modern political struggles have almost always pursued universal aims that are attached to particular identities—for example, struggles for liberation in the form of nationalist struggles, and internationalist struggles in the form of struggles for the working class.[4] Likewise, as I have already noted, when social struggles pursue objectives linked to redistribution, they often rely upon social identities (the working class[5]) or professional identities. These observations are probably enough to establish that struggles for identity cannot be assigned either to the category of "new social movements" (they aren't truly new, nor are they what the theoreticians of "new social movements" describe), or to the category of the "politics of recognition" (social struggles, too, are struggles for recognition). For all that, these observations do not allow us to conclude that social struggles and struggles for identity ought not be distinguished from one another. It is clear that there is a continuum between social struggles and struggles for identity, because redistributive struggles can have identity-laden elements, and struggles for identity can have redistributive elements. Struggles for recognition of the value of work provide an example of the former, for in many such cases it is the value associated with a professional identity that is recognized by one's wages. The struggles of Latin American indigenous peasants, for example, illustrate the latter, when a defense of the indigenous culture is carried out through a struggle against economic processes that exploit and victimize peasant agriculture, a constituent element of this culture. And so the leaders of the Ecuadorian revolt of January-February 2001 claimed to "see with two eyes, one for the poor and one for the indigenous."[6] Nonetheless, the existence of a continuity between the two poles of protest action does not at all constitute an argument against this polarity—on the contrary, it presupposes it. In the end, some redistributive demands have no connection to identity-related demands (for example, demands for a minimum wage or a guaranteed income), whereas some identity-related demands have absolutely no implications on directly redistributive demands (for example, the instruction of minority languages in public schools).

The strongest arguments against the specificity of struggles for identity are probably linked to the fact that recognition of identity can only be based upon a secondary or instrumental political objective. The majority of identity-related demands would serve as means to other ends.[7] Take, for example, struggles against denial of recognition of a group identity, such as racist disrespect and stigmatization. It can be doubted whether it portrays a realistic political objective insofar as racism occurs in customs and individual interactions upon which political and institutional decisions have no direct hold. On the other hand, it can be used to obtain different kinds of compensations. Now let's consider struggles for recognition of a culture (preservation of languages; preservation of social and religious practices). These may indeed lead to a set of institutional reforms, but it can be doubted whether they will effectively manage to maintain a living culture without a whole set of social conditions upon which political decisions have little grasp (the example of North American reservations provides a brutal illustration). Identity is anchored in customs whose permanence depends upon social conditions upon which demands in terms of identity have little grasp. Now, one might suspect that groups that call for recognition of their culture are pursuing a larger aim, the improvement of their place in society. To be sure, such an improvement comes about through identity, but it cannot be reduced to identity, because it also, and above all, is aimed at achieving easier access to power and wealth. Recognition of identity would not be the fundamental objective of social struggles that call for them, but only an element of a discursive strategy that would use symbolic means (the portrayal of one's own identity as being put in jeopardy) in order to achieve objectives that cannot be reduced to identity-related aims.

The principal limit of these arguments is tied to the facts that they only reflect a perspective external to the normative dynamics that carry identity struggles' demands; and that these arguments impose a foreign analytic framework upon the political discourse in which these demands are expressed. It is true that social movements are capable of seeking partially unrealizable aims—regardless of what sort of social movement—but this teaches us nothing about their own logics. That struggles for identity can also work for access to improved social status is, again, indisputable—but this hardly allows us to discount or derogate explicit demands (recognition of one's identity) in the name of a more basic demand. To justify such an interpretation of this kind of demand, it would have to be shown that the issues involved in recognition of identities and in access to more favorable social positions are heterogeneous with each other. And yet, the symbolic violence that occurs through the institutionalization of dominant groups' vision of the world is an essential facet of the process that keeps dominated and deprived groups in a subaltern position. It is rarely possible to escape from a subaltern social position without struggling against forms of the denial of recognition that take place through forms of devaluation and stigmatization of subaltern groups' identities (whether social or cultural, whether assumed or ascribed). If these groups struggle against forms of denial of recognition rooted in modes of identification (as status groups) rather than in modes of redistribution (as classes), nothing then forbids us from explaining the specificity of their struggles by using the category of struggles for identity.

Our examination of these various objections thus leads in fact to a confirmation that these struggles for identity exist, and that they have a twofold specificity: one is linked to social groups that take it on (status groups more so than classes); the other to the specific objectives that they pursue (struggle against a denial of recognition tied to deprecatory identities, rather than struggles against a denial of recognition tied to the distribution of wealth[8]). In any case, the concept of a struggle for identity remains an ideal-typical concept. There are many social struggles that pursue both kinds of objectives, many social groups that are victims of injustice simultaneously as status groups and as classes (for example, the Ecuadorian indigenous peoples, Native Americans and poor peasants, or the Dalits, stigmatized and exploited). There is in fact a continuum of social movements that is part of the continuum of collective protest action that I described in chapter three.

The objections that I have just examined thus carry little weight. But before assigning a political value to struggles for identity, we must still consider other arguments that are traditionally raised against them: a series of arguments tied to group identities' intrinsic normative deficit.

IDENTITY'S NORMATIVE DEFICIT

Experience shows, in fact, that identity-laden demands can sometimes lead to forms of radical denial of other human groups' value and of their members' individual liberty. Can we grant legitimacy to demands bearing on the cultural (cultures and religions), social (classes or professions), or anthropological (gender) specificity of certain groups? Mustn't we, on the contrary, acknowledge that the only politically legitimate demands are grounded in individuals' common humanity and their universal rights, or on the assertion of their equality?

Globalization gives a very particular intensity to this debate, which we have already seen in the last chapter. The convergence of inequalities and of cultural imperialism that go along with the spread of a very particular model of life and consumption produces an aggressive withdrawal by certain populations into collective identities in a fundamentalist mode. On the one hand, it is thus possible for certain thinkers to celebrate the fact that globalization finally makes all collective identities obsolete, so that individuals, finally rid of social and cultural constraints, are at last able to gain access to a melting pot and a liberating nomadism.[9] On the other hand, it can be replied that the fate of globalization is a "clash of civilizations."[10] The liberal position is in the middle. In the age of globalization and the interweaving of cultures, neutrality with respect to cultures and their fundamental values can seem to be the only way of assuring consensus and social cohesion within particular societies, and peace at the global level. When different processes have led to the simmering conflict of a fundamentalism against modernity, and the counterattack of a modernity that is transformed into a fundamentalism, it would be indisputably dangerous to simply abandon the modern demand for rational critique of cultures and morals in light of universal values. But the new fundamentalism of modernity shows that it is not enough to demand respect for universal rights in order to obtain peace and justice. The abstract universal of the United Nations' Universal Declaration of Human Rights has for a long time remained compatible with slavery, colonialism, and the exclusion of workers and women from political public spheres, and it is only by starting from the dynamics that emerged from specific experiences of injustice that it has become possible to reorient this abstract universal against its own limitations. Why wouldn't struggles for identity, in their turn, be able to make their own contributions toward the transformation of an abstract universal into a concrete universal?

As I have already noted, the fact that struggles for identity can pursue aims with differing levels of legitimacy is not enough to deny them all forms of legitimacy. Rather, it invites us to ask the question of their legitimacy from the perspective of the normative dynamics that traverse them. It must be stressed, on this point, that it is simply a fact that in order to evaluate and critique the world in which we live, we make reference first of all to the values that seem to us to be constitutive of *our* identity—and only then (and only perhaps) do we make reference to abstract norms that transcend our social and cultural context. In this sense, we could say, with Habermas, that it is within the lived world itself—that is, in our daily actions and in the beliefs that go along with it—that universal norms find their origins. We orient ourselves starting from values that we consider constitutive of our identity, but with reference to expectations of mutual recognition that contain within themselves a set of universal demands. These latter can remain implicit, but they can also be taken up in a dynamic of reflexive thematization in situations of conflict with others and with institutions, or in cases of upheaval of social or cultural worlds. This argument makes it possible to assign a genuine political relevance to identity-related demands, but these would be legitimate only if they have become problematic enough to be reflected from the point of view of universal norms: the fact that social developments disrupt the lived world and weaken or destabilize our attachments or strong evaluations would therefore not be inherently bad, but rather the occasion for these attachments and strong evaluations to no longer be valued as simple unquestioned convictions and to be raised up to the level of rational discussion and demands for universality.[11]

This position has the virtues of thinking of identity as a reflection on attachments and strong evaluations rooted in negative social experiences, and of capturing the normative dynamics that traverse struggles for identity. But this position rests upon a disputable characterization of the negative social experiences that give birth to these normative dynamics, and it also assumes unconvincingly that these normative dynamics should be articulated with reference to universality rather than to identity. Shouldn't we acknowledge instead that a life in conformity with our attachments and strong evaluations constitutes a fundamental demand, and that its negation produces a social suffering that is not so easily relativized in the name of reason and universality? Why shouldn't we acknowledge that in some cases, self-reflection on these attachments and strong evaluations in terms of identity is more relevant than self-reflection with reference to universality? The Habermasian approach runs up against a second problem: When he treats the destabilization of identities as the occasion for rational reflection upon their normative contents, doesn't he underestimate the fact that the denial of identity can lead to the negation of the positive relation to oneself, and thereby become an obstacle to rational examination?

Habermas does not seem to fully grasp what is at stake in experiences of injustice linked to the denial of recognition of identity, and he seems even less able to explain identity's role in the dynamics of struggle against injustice. Agents in struggles against social injustice are always social groups. Political philosophy ordinarily considers it unnecessary to articulate a concept of the social group, probably because it takes struggles for recognition of human rights and legal rights as the paradigm for politics.[12] Habermas joins this tradition when he understands the normative dynamics leading to struggle against injustice as a dynamic of dissolution of the identities that define social groups. A theory of struggle against injustice demands a concept of the social group, but the latter can be understood neither on the model of a grouping (an ensemble based upon objective characteristics) nor on the model of an association (an association based upon a voluntary act), but instead exclusively through reference to experience and social relations: the agents of struggles against injustice are groups (which may be classes or status groups) defined by social relations that structure their lives; by the negative social experiences that initiate their struggles; and by a consciousness of sharing the same experiences, attachments, and strong evaluations that allows their demands to take a collective form.[13] For Habermas, the disruption of identity is conceived as the occasion for a reflection upon its value, as an element of liberation. But identity also constitutes the framework that makes possible the creation of a public space internal to social movements (whether it takes the form of a professional identity in the context of a sector-specific struggle; the division between "us" and "them" in a more general class-based social struggle; or one's status and position in struggles for identity). If, for Habermas, identity's contribution is still understood in negative terms, this is probably because he reduces identities to background attachments and evaluations; that is, to a static and prereflexive background. Identities therefore can only achieve a political dimension once they have been activated by external disruptions, and then restructured by the communicative logic of their inscription into the public sphere. The opposite trap would be to consider identity as a mere political construction internal to a social struggle, a construction disconnected from the negative experiences that initiated the struggle.[14] The pragmatist conception of identity developed in the preceding chapter leads us, on the contrary, to see in identity a mode of reflexive thematization of background attachments and evaluations that are made problematic in these negative social experiences.

The static conception of identity is a presupposition largely shared in contemporary debates, where the issue of collective identities is most often reduced to its cultural dimension (the cultural element probably being the most stable and the most inert element of collective identities). However, as soon as identity becomes the object of a dynamic approach—as soon as it is understood as an instrument for reflexive resolution of the problematic aspects of certain negative social experiences—the aporias of struggles for identity cease to be insurmountable. What is generally not taken into account is that the normative dynamics lead identity-laden experiences of injustice to be transformed into struggles for identity that are accompanied by transformations of identity. The latter can follow opposite paths. There are cases in which the denial of recognition is so profound that there is nothing left of an individuality torn to shreds except the phantasmic assertion of its own value in the traits of an imaginary identity, or what Harbans Mukhia calls the "transmutation of identity." In individuals who fear seeing their lives entirely trampled over, the various elements of identity can come to merge together to constitute a monolithic, univocal, and exclusive identity. This can be observed in particular during community violence in which religious and national elements are mixed with sexual identity; for instance, through the politicization of rape, when collective and public rape is a symbolic form of territorial conquest and genealogical annihilation of the enemy (and recent decades provide too many examples, whether from India, the former Yugoslavia, or Chechnya).[15]

In return, struggles for identity provoked by an experience of injustice can contribute to the transformation of identity in light of norms of equality and freedom. The example of the Dalits in India offers an illustration. Their collective identification as "Untouchables" carries a religious legitimation of their absolute inferiority. When they struggle against this inequality, they do not settle for an assertion of equality in rejecting this identity. Such an assertion would constitute a mere proclamation, a demand without social validity or political effectiveness. They attempt, on the contrary, to develop a collective reflection on their place in society within the framework of a work on identity that comes about in particular through the replacement of the term "Untouchables" with "Dalits," stripped of religious connotations and incorporating other outcasts in the indigenous Indian populations. By starting with a collective identity, the Dalits' political movements are addressed to the ensemble of individuals who are subjected to this specific form of inequality, and they attempt to struggle against the forms of internalization of inequality in identity, by means of a work on identity that can take place in the public dramatization—the enactment—of their own identity.[16] They initiate struggles for equality through a collective identity.

This example offers another illustration of the fact that social critique cannot simply take publicly established demands as its only paradigm, but must also be applicable to all those forms of injustice that do not have a chance of rising up into a collective expression. Struggle against injustice itself takes two forms: the politics of established political and social movements; and all the approaches that have to be carried out on the forms of subjectivation that inhibit the struggle against injustice, all the politics that must first undertake a transformation of identity in order to be able to then lead to political and social movements.

As for the kind of legitimacy that can be attributed to struggles for identity, we must first distinguish between the legitimacy of motivations (that of struggling against injustice) and the legitimacy of the demands; and then between dynamics that transform identity either by turning it into an obstacle to any legitimate demand or, on the contrary, by making it a medium for legitimate demands. If struggles for identity can generally claim the first level of legitimacy, that of a refusal anchored in an experience of injustice, they can sometimes also claim the highest level of legitimacy, that related to the objectives sought and the means employed, when they are accompanied by emancipatory and egalitarian transformations of identity. More precisely, they can claim to have complete legitimacy if the four following conditions are met: (1) individuals take action against a long-standing (because socially established) denial of their identity; (2) they struggle against the institutional carriers of this denial of recognition; (3) the objectives sought and the means employed to that end do not lead to new forms of denial of recognition; and (4) the struggle imbues the collective identity with the values of freedom and equality.

A POLITICS AGAINST IDENTITY?

I have just argued that identities can be transformed through struggles for identity. But how must we understand these transformations of identities? If they ought to be transformed, isn't this precisely because they represent the internalization of relations of domination, of subjugating forms of subjectivation? And consequently, shouldn't we maintain that identity must be transformed through what should be conceived as a form of struggle against identity rather than as a struggle for identity? This was Michel Foucault's view, for whom the most significant struggles were precisely those directed against powers that routinely subjected individuals to social identifications.[17] In his view, power is political because it is the effect of a specific power relation; and genuine politics, that of struggles against subjection, fundamentally consists of a struggle *against* identity.

This view, which entails a rejection of the politics of identity in favor of a politics against identity, rests in part on a disputable reduction of identity to an effect of subjection. It certainly cannot be disputed that at the end of a long and relentless conditioning of the body and spirit (in the family, at school, in the various arenas of socialization), the individual incorporates a certain number of attachments and internalizes a certain number of values. In this respect, the process of individualization through socialization is a process of subjection. The relation that an individual consciously maintains with himself, when he comes to ask himself what he is and what he is worth, carries the marks of this subjection. Socialization and identity, for all that, cannot simply be reduced to subjection. In fact, in modern societies subject to powerful social differentiation, personal identity is not solely the result of a childhood immersion in a symbolic and cultural universe experienced as the only possible world. Primary socialization can already come about in heterogeneous social worlds; and added to that are a complex ensemble of identifications with roles that we fulfill in our adult social lives (parental roles, professional roles, leisure activities, etc.) in the course of secondary socialization.[18] The constitution of identity is never simply the result of primary socialization alone, but also of a secondary socialization whose logic is at least partially heterogeneous with the logic of primary socialization, as well as being mutually heteronomous.[19] This implies that identity is not simply the result of the internalization of institutional realms, but also of an "internal transaction"[20] in which various subjective effects of socialization interact with each other. This internal transaction is definitely not a case of an autonomous subject who would be free to interpret and to rearrange the various components of his identity as he might wish. We have already seen that it is conditioned by the unconscious and preconscious foundations of identity, and that it operates in the internal transactions of habits. When an individual comes to ask himself about his identity, the question's givens are imposed upon him and leave few margins for maneuver: habits, which delimit what is possible and what can be hoped for, are difficult to alter. Nonetheless, when the question of identity arises, there are various possible responses: in order for identity to constitute a problem, the answers best suited for the problematic situation must be unclear. It is then possible to try to rearrange the various components of one's identity, to attempt to reorient one's life plans, to try to experiment with new roles that could yield new capabilities, and to give up one's prior strong evaluations and commitments in order to find a more satisfying solution. When identity is conceived according to this pragmatist model, it can be understood as composed of moments of subjection, as well as of (and simultaneously with) autonomy.

It is useless to believe that individuals could extract themselves from the networks of power that are at work in the various processes of socialization. But it would be just as mistaken to think that individuals are, for all that, stripped of any form of autonomy. It follows that autonomy must not be conceived as the opposite of subjection, but as its transformation. Just as our analysis of processes of subjectivation leads to the idea that autonomy and subjection are inseparable and together define an "ambivalent constitution of the 'subject,'"[21] we can assert that identity—in the sense of a project to reflexively resolve problems in which the questions of who I am and what I am worth arise—participates in the ambivalent constitution of the subject. And if the term "autonomy" can only refer to a continuous transformation of subjection (a process of liberation, if you prefer), there are also reasons to hold that identity can play a role in this process (as is illustrated by the example of the Dalits discussed earlier). Now, if autonomy can only be understood as a transformation of subjection, and if identity can play a role in this transformation, then the idea that a politics against identity must take the place of a politics of identity loses its relevance.

THE POLITICS OF DIFFERENCE

There is another way, which could be called "postmodern," of rejecting the politics of identity. The category of the postmodern encompasses very diverse theoretical projects, all of which (in one way or another) consist of a critique of the Enlightenment (or of modernity), and of reason as the power of identification and of domination (or as the power of the universal). The ethical and political consequences of this theoretical position depend upon a theory of the irreducibility of the particular—whether it emphasizes the irreducibility of the other to a mere object of universal duties; or of particular cultures, knowledges, and social practices to a universal model of cultural and legal validity. On the side of cultural analysis, the postmodern position leads more precisely to a critique of the very idea of identity, understood as a new form of identification and of illusory mastery of difference. Then it is no longer a matter of defending collective identities against the universal (as in communitarianism), but rather of making the very idea of a collective identity appear as the form of a new universal that must be subject to critique. This critique tries to show that collective identities are never pure and univocal, but always inhabited by other identities; or rather, by irreducible differences. As a consequence, a defense of the irreducibility of knowledge and social practices should take the form of a "politics of difference," not of a "politics of identity."[22]

Against this line of reasoning, we can immediately raise a question having to do with its assumed historical diagnosis: Can postmodern critique successfully target the specific features of power relations and the injustices that characterize the present, as it claims it can? Politics of difference in the postmodern vein are especially directed against forms of domination proper to colonialism (the imposition of cultural codes on colonized countries) and to nation states (struggles against regional cultures) attempting to contain culturally dominated populations within stigmatizing identities in order to vindicate a more general oppression. But the forms of power that accompany globalization seem to rest upon different foundations. This is Negri and Hardt's suggestion in *Empire*, when they point out that postmodern and postcolonial concepts are quite close to the ideology of the global market, in promoting the dissolution of nations and national cultures, advocating cultural contact and exchange, and the like.[23] The argument that they develop specifically addresses the question of national and cultural identities, not the ensemble of collective identities, but it can also be applied to social and professional identities, and even to personal identity itself. In fact, in the most highly developed capitalist countries, we are witnessing the establishment of new work relationships and the development of a mode of justification that pits the individual against identity. The ideal worker is described as a perfectly flexible individual, sacrificing his own identity in order to be better able to adapt to the different positions and projects that are offered to him.[24] A critique of identity thus seems to lose all of its subversive force. Instead, it articulates the modes of legitimation of new forms of power. Shouldn't we conclude that a critical discourse adapted to the present should elaborate a critique of this kind of disqualification of identity?

The postmodern rejection of the politics of identity can also be challenged in a more immediately political way. The rejection then rests upon a binary opposition between an enclosed identity and openness to difference. It is true that collective identities are always based on processes of subjection and identification with institutions or groups, but struggles for the recognition of identities cannot therefore be reduced to an imprisonment in these identifications, on the one hand because identity is not reducible to subjection, and on the other because the struggles can entail an alteration of individuals' and groups' relations with the commitments and values that they embrace. They can lead to "an enlargement of personal identity for participants" as in the case of anti-racist struggles or struggles against various forms of stigmatization.[25] More generally, it can be maintained that this kind of enlargement is intrinsic to the politicization of identity entailed by the construction of a framework of injustice in social movements. The motivations for social struggles are always linked to a feeling of injustice that results either from a feeling of having one's general dignity as a human being negated, or an awareness that values that one takes as a facet of one's identity have been violated. However, the dynamic of these struggles entails the reexamination of one's own motivations by engaged individuals and groups, in order to justify these motivations in their own eyes and to answer the challenges raised against them. When an injury to identity is a protest's motivating spark, the reflexive self-examination that develops in the public space internal to these struggles constitutes a critical moment, because the question of what can be abandoned and what must be defended within an identity cannot fail to be asked (and this holds also for struggles for "minority peoples"[26]). The dynamic of the politicization of identity is thus also a dynamic of its opening—and indications of this opening can be found in the various sorts of coalitions and alliances that have been seen in recent decades: shared demands across different professions during the winter 1995 social movements in France; coalitions between different cultural and social groups in the antiglobalization movement's struggles, etc. It is significant that this critical recurrence has come about by starting from identity, and not by starting from the external perspective of universal rights or moral requirements (independent of identity). I have contended that the weakening of identity does not necessarily lead to a reflexivity that is open to universalization (it can impede reflexivity; or it can just as well give rise to a transmutation into an identity that assumes the form of racist, xenophobic, or even exterminating political movements). Conversely, we now see that the very possibility of such a process of universalization (or of "Marrano-ization")[27] can be rooted in identities that are not weakened. This is enough to demonstrate that the politics of identity cannot be conflated with an all-encompassing imprisonment.

The argument articulated here with respect to collective identities in general also holds for the most inflexible collective identities, such as cultural identities that are often the targets of arguments against the politics of identity. It is often claimed that any defense of a culture amounts to isolating oneself in an all-encompassing framework and losing sight of the demands of universality that must animate any emancipatory politics. This presupposes an inadequate vision of culture as an all-encompassing totality. We must challenge this interpretation that takes cultures to be closed entities irreducible to and incompatible with each other. On the contrary, we must remember that cultures are always caught up in a complex network of communication,[28] and that they never constitute univocal systems because they are always traversed by conflicts having to do with the interpretation of their fundamental values.[29] This does not mean that any cultural blending constitutes progress, or that cultures can "cross-pollinate" harmoniously and without limits. And so, in the context of contemporary globalization, communication between cultures mostly leads to cultural domination. But it can also become the vector for cultural resistance to oppression. If they are not entirely mutually exclusive, they are also not entirely homogenous. This is why contemporary globalization has had to confront "cultural disagreements" that emancipatory struggles (like anti-globalization struggles[30]) have seized upon for support, but which also sustain fundamentalist relapses. There are indeed two possible fates for cultural disagreements, and only a politics of identity can settle the problem of promoting the former rather than the latter.

The existence of such cultural disagreements presupposes a definition of culture neither as a coherent set of values and representations nor as a set of self-sufficient representations distinct from other cultures. It only presupposes the existence of cultural identities. An illustration of this can be found in the struggles in 2000–2002 in the Algerian region of Kabylia.

These struggles were particularly concerned with the status of the Berber language, and they were portrayed not so much as struggles for cultural survival as struggles against *Hogra*,[i] against contempt or disdain. The experience of *Hogra* transforms culture into a problem of identity. We can grant the anthropologists' point that the idea of culture in general (in the sense of a set of collective beliefs[31]), and that of the Berber culture in particular, are encompassed within an abstraction carried out upon a set of inconsistent representations and practices; but the critique of "culture" does not entail a critique of identity, if by identity we mean individuals' representations of their own value as individual members of socially determined groupings. In this sense, there is indeed a Berber identity that is made manifest in the commitment by a group of individuals to a set of values (which probably do not define a culture by themselves), values that are both threatened and embraced. If these values were to no longer be the object of an institutionalized contempt—if they were to be socially recognized—then the individuals would not have to thematize them reflectively, or would have the possibility of reinterpreting them reflectively in light of their own biographical problematic trajectories, rather than making them the object of collective demands and the stakes for their identity. In that case, those values would continue to be positively constitutive of who the individuals are.

IDENTITY AND RESISTANCE

If identity defines political perspectives, this is ultimately because it is the site for normative expectations' resistance to power relations, and to normative models that are at work in socialization. We can acknowledge, with Marx, that all social relations are subsumed in the mechanisms of social domination;[32] and, with Foucault, that bodies and subjectivities are always caught up in power relations. Nevertheless, the normative expectations that domination and power attempt to direct and exploit constitute sources for resistance to domination and power. Insofar as these normative expectations are always shaped in advance by socialization, they are expressed in a form always dependent upon strong evaluations and commitments that

i. Suzanne Ruta discusses this Algerian Arabic term in the blog post of February 4, 2011, "An Algerian Lexicon," on the site Words Without Borders, https://www.wordswithoutborders.org /dispatches/article/an-algerian-lexicon.

could be reflected in terms of identity. Consequently, the relation between identity and social contexts (themselves organized by institutions governed by power relations and social relations of domination) can be seen as one of the levers for the dynamics of social transformation.

Here again, it can be argued that the concept of identity is superfluous, for example because a theory of habits is enough to understand how individuals can resist institutional demands. Ultimately, this is Pierre Bourdieu's view, when he simultaneously asserts that resistance does not depend upon consciousness but rather upon dispositions,[33] and is based upon the discrepancy or gap between dispositions and social structures.[34] Such a view has the virtue of explaining the fact that resistance to social structures can take multiple forms, and that only a certain kind of resistance moves from a preconscious stage to a conscious stage—or even to a stage of explicit demands. It also has the disadvantage of being unable to explain the specificity of experiences of injustice—these phases of social experience in which the movement from implicit expectations to a stage of explicit elucidation takes place, and which prepare them to become explicit demands. In fact, in order that an experience of injustice obtain, a feeling that legitimate expectations have not been satisfied (a feeling that draws upon a diffuse or explicit representation of what makes my life valuable) must be added to the malaise that comes from a disturbance of one's habitus. But it is precisely this sort of representation that is constitutive of references to personal identity. Just as the majority of social struggles draw support from social or professional identities, in the same way, liberation movements have often been movements for national liberation, and revolutionary movements have often been class-based or religious movements. The norms for struggle against injustice are often mediated by collective identities.

Moreover, as I have already noted, even if we understand identity as a real fiction, we have to acknowledge that it produces effects by giving a specific hue to the practical logics that define habitus. In particular, it invests them with the normative content of these expectations experienced as legitimate, a content which necessarily impacts the ways in which socialization and resistance to power and domination take shape. The subjective effects of socialization blend together with the subjective work by which an individual tries to make the different elements of his identity compatible with his life. If, on the one hand, every institution imposes certain identities upon individuals, these identities must, on the other hand, be appropriated by each individual in such a way that individuals attempt to see their identities recognized within each institution. Hence, what we have in the end is not so much the imposed identity but its subjective reformulation, and the unification of various components of personal identity accompanied by a specific demand directed at institutions.[35] Socialization must not be understood as the imposition of an objective mold upon an unformed and infinitely malleable subjectivity (following the Durkheimian model of social facts as constraints, and of the opposition between the social and the psychological), but as a process in which the social's effects upon subjectivity are accompanied by resistance on the part of subjectivity[36] and by attempts at social transformation. This is a point that has been articulated in particular by the psychology of work.

A business as an institution exercises its control over bodies and subjectivities principally through prescriptions of the activity of work. But real work is irreducible to the work prescribed. This irreducibility is not attributable either to a failure of competence or to the intervention of an untamed subjectivity that would too liberally interpret the prescriptions; rather, it is due, on the one hand, to the fact that work must wrestle with the resistance of the real, and on the other hand, to the fact that individuals approach working situations already filled with concerns that stem from other areas of socialization. As Yves Clot has noted,

If real work is not in conformity with the prescribed work, this is because the women or men are not merely producers but also agents engaged in multiple worlds and times that are lived simultaneously, lived worlds and times that they try to make mutually compatible, whose contradictions they hope to overcome, shaping them to fit their own need for unity, even if the latter is merely an ideal.[37]

What is true for socialization within work also holds for socialization in general. The different phases of socialization should be understood simultaneously as a function of the self and a function of social worlds, functions through which the individual attempts to demand recognition (from one's employer, one's partner, etc.), of the specific meaning that he gives to the various facets of his own identity. This interaction between identity and institutions can take the form of (informal) "negotiation" in which individuals confronted by maladjusted or unsatisfying recognition simply try to obtain the right to apply the principles governing an institution's operation in conformity with their own subjective requirements, by taking advantage of the indeterminateness that characterizes norms, rules, and roles (this is what ordinarily happens in situations of paid labor through the transformation of prescribed work into real work). But there are cases in which such a negotiation fails because the institution itself, or the social world in general, cannot satisfy the subjective demand. In these situations where the demand for recognition of identity by the institution cannot be satisfied, the failure can be experienced as a wound to one's identity. If this wound is deep enough, the denial of recognition can be experienced as an injustice, and the subjectivity's resistance becomes transformed into a revolt, unleashing the practical and normative dynamics that lead from the weakening or collapse of identity to its politicization in the form of a social movement.

From the perspective of a theory of recognition of identity, the possibility that processes of social transformation are thus grounded in socialization itself—and no longer only in the failure of socialization (as in Marx, where it depends upon the formation of a proletarian mass that has been stripped of ideology because it is excluded from society;[38] or in Alain Touraine, for whom the failure of socialization is an occasion to free oneself from one's identity because "[a]n individual can become a subject . . . only if he resists the logic of social domination in the name of a logic of freedom and free self-production"[39]); or in the permanent restructuring of socialization through norms of interaction (as in Habermas, for whom the communicative norms of social interaction are what make possible a critique of culture and of the identities internalized in the course of socialization[40]); or in a theory of justification.[41] This sociological theory of resistance is the only one that can take seriously the normative motivations (those of a need for recognition) and the identity-laden components of some social struggles—because the other theories make resistance dependent upon either the absence of identity (the creation of a mass that is no longer defined by class, in Marx); or communicative norms or forms of consensual justification that, although present within them, transcend the forms of particular life whose value is reflected in terms of identity.

A POLITICS OF THE SELF

If every critical theory of society must sociologically account for the possibility of a social transformation, and if the possibility of such a transformation must make reference to actual struggles and not only to objective contradictions in the reproduction of social relations, then a critical theory must adopt a perspective that is not only sociological, but also psychosocial. To illustrate the relation between sociology and psychology that is implied here, it may be useful to recall Theodor Adorno's observations on this point.[42] For Adorno, it is self-evident that the "individual's powerlessness" in the modern world has social causes, and that this serves as evidence that the social cannot be reduced to the psychological. But an individual's powerlessness also makes clear that the disciplinary separation between sociology and psychology reflects the irrationality of a society that is unable to satisfy an individual's fundamental expectations; and this separation runs the risk of legitimizing this state of affairs by granting scientific status to the division between the social and the psychological. Adorno's perspective is thus particularly uncomfortable because it leads to a critique of this disciplinary division, while also being in opposition to attempts to reunify the two disciplines. The sociologization of psychoanalysis is to be avoided because it advocates an accommodation of the ego's fundamental needs that is just as dangerous as the naturalization of the disciplinary divide that leads to the view that the social could never satisfy the ego's needs. We must take account of the fact that an individual's expectations are always conditioned by the internalization of social models, while simultaneously irreducible to the social. Moreover, the reification of social relations makes it impossible to understand sociology as an applied psychology, even if the alienated society is otherwise characterized by the utilization of psychology as a technique of manipulation and suggestion. If we agree, with Robert Castel, Luc Boltanski, Ève Chiapello, Claude Dubar, and Alain Ehrenberg, that contemporary capitalism is accompanied by an even more advanced psychologization of social relations than existed in Adorno's time, we will probably also admit not only that the disciplinary divide is even harder to defend than Adorno thought, but also that a critical perspective on the forms of social instrumentalization of individual subjectivity (in the form of an appeal to autonomy and responsibility) must be maintained, which can be served by the principles of recognition of dignity and identity. If we further accept the theory of socialization as resistance that I have put forward, we will surely agree that a psychosociology of identity will make it possible to maintain psychology's irreducibility to the social (because the former poses resistance to the latter), while also preserving the demand (guiding this resistance) for recognition of identity—a matter with subversive import that defines the horizon for a reconciliation of the social and the psychological. But identity is only the submerged face of the psyche, and the instrumentalization of subjectivity—along with the motivations for resistance—also takes place in the foundations of identity, about which I have so far said virtually nothing. This claim will be confirmed when we turn to the question, itself politically decisive these days, of the politicization of social suffering.

PART III

Social Suffering

Chapter Six

SOCIAL CRITIQUE AS A VOICE FOR SUFFERING

Contemporary political philosophy, to its credit, has taken the new normative problems raised by identity as objects of study. The situation is different, however, with respect to social suffering, given that precarious and insecure work, long-term unemployment, homelessness, and vagrancy are almost never interrogated in a philosophical way. Are these lives too undeserving for the injustice of their situation to be taken into account? This silence is probably better explained by the specificity of the experiences of injustice at issue for them. We know that the experience of injustice can take three forms. It can correspond: (1) to an experience accompanied by a feeling of injustice based on an awareness of a violation of the established principles of justice; (2) to a feeling of injustice based upon the fact that fundamental expectations are not satisfied; but also (3) to a situation in which the feeling of injustice falls short. In that case, it is only from the perspective of social critique that this experience is an experience of injustice. The concept of social suffering is concerned precisely with this kind of experience in which, on the one hand, the injustice that is suffered can turn out to be so profound that the practical dynamics it unleashes could turn against the individual rather than against the injustice of the situation; and in which, on the other hand, the sufferer's cognitive resources can be insufficient for an awareness of the situation's injustice to develop.

Given both of these circumstances, it is rare for situations that produce this kind of experience of injustice to be the object of social struggles. When such struggles nevertheless do develop, they primarily take the form of what is sometimes called struggles of "those without" or struggles of "the deprived" [les "sans"].[i] I will thus begin by examining the characteristic traits of such struggles, and the ways in which they can be linked to the problem of social suffering. I will then attempt to show that the problem of social suffering illuminates several aspects of the "new social question." Finally, I will argue that the theory of recognition makes it possible to normatively justify an integration of social suffering within the definition of social justice.

THE STRUGGLES OF "THE DEPRIVED"

Most often understood by the phrase "struggles of the deprived" are the social movements of undocumented immigrants, the homeless (which is to say anyone without adequate housing), the unemployed, and the landless. If it is possible to see a certain homogeneity among these social movements, that is because they have two characteristic traits in common: the absence of a proper social basis of their own; and the objective of becoming integrated into generally accepted social and legal relations (recognition of rights, housing, factory or agricultural work). The fact that these movements lack a social basis of their own serves to underscore that diverse individuals join forces in these struggles on the basis of shared goals, and thus come to constitute a social group without prior membership in a shared class or shared status group. This is quite clear in the case of undocumented immigrants, whose cultural, social, and national origins are quite diverse and who are only united through their shared rejection of a social situation.[1] This is also the case for social actors engaged in struggles for housing and struggles of the unemployed. That these actors aim for integration into generally accepted social and legal relations means that their struggles are above all directed against injustices linked to being denied the enjoyment of rights recognized for others, and to being inserted into social relations that are unstable (such as work that is not protected by labor laws, or a

---

i. "The deprived" here captures the French term, "les 'sans,'" literally, "those without." See the translator's note for further discussion of "the deprived" and "les 'sans.'"

lack of access to social welfare) or degrading (such as poor or deteriorating housing, or stigmatizations linked to various types of social aid). These two situations are interconnected, because the denial of rights implies a loss of protection that contributes to or exasperates unstable and degrading social relations, while such social relations imply in turn a loss of the ability to exercise rights one had earlier enjoyed. Contrary to how it may appear, these struggles thus do not merely try to claim what ought to be accorded to a particular group and has already been granted to others (except in the case of undocumented immigrants[2]). They also articulate universal recognitive demands (recognition of a right to rights, of a right to housing, of a right to employment or a decent income) that broadly challenge a social order that restricts the application of these rights—a restriction endured not only by the "excluded" but also by many of the "included."

The social specifics of struggles of the deprived can be assessed in opposing ways: their lack of a social basis can be seen to offer either better possibilities than other social struggles for freedom and radical changes;[3] or, on the contrary, the risk of being imprisoned by practical powerlessness and desperate ways of making demands (as in hunger strikes[4]). Indeed, homelessness (for instance) is a calamity—and, to be sure, one has to adopt a very detached view to see opportunities for the opening of possibilities for freedom in experiences associated with such a form of disaffiliation. But it is nonetheless the case that struggles of the deprived have been able to effectively grow and achieve significant political effects.

At first glance, many factors seem aligned against mobilization of the deprived, the first among which is the wide diversity of individuals likely to engage in such struggles. In fact, the social struggle cannot be explained by the mobilization of social and cultural resources belonging to an already-constituted social group, such as a class or status group. This is why it is sometimes asserted that this kind of social movement is characterized by the important role played by "political entrepreneurs"; that is, individuals who do not share the experience at the root of the struggle, but who have the social and political capital—along with the political career—to be able to facilitate this struggle. Such an analysis can be illustrated by the fact that unemployed and (relatively) well-off college graduates are more easily enlisted than are less-educated and poor unemployed workers. This is further borne out in the case of struggles on behalf of undocumented immigrants, which are often organized by militant students and political refugees.[5] However, the category of "political entrepreneur" leads only to a partial view of how this sort of social movement develops. In fact, in order for a group of individuals to give validity to political demands, they would have to be able to recognize some issue or concern from their own experience in these demands. As a result, these demands should be viewed as a collective production, rather than simply as the result of influence exerted by political entrepreneurs; and the "leaders" of these struggles should be viewed as spokespersons (or "voices") rather than as political entrepreneurs. The idea of a political entrepreneur presupposes that the process of elaborating a political claim is quite independent of the experience of those for whom the claim is made. But such a presupposition just doesn't make sense as soon as we take into consideration not only the social and discursive skills required for the formation of such a claim, but also its normative contents and the conditions for its acceptance in the internal public sphere of these struggles. The framework of injustice that makes social movements possible must rather be understood as a set of shared meanings that are collectively articulated, even when not based upon an explication of the values contained in a shared collective identity.

Moreover, one characteristic of struggles for the deprived is that they assign a specific role to their *spokespersons*. It is thus appropriate to understand a "spokesperson" as someone who is not a mere political entrepreneur or a mere political representative. It is much rather the historical sense of the term that I am drawing upon here, that of the spokespersons or "voices" of the Republic, during the French Revolution, whose function was precisely to straddle the divide between political representation and the demands that burst forth from the social—the spokesperson thus being set against political representatives.[6] Spokespersons for the deprived undertake a project of elaborating an organization for—and giving form to—protests whose function is simultaneously to give political expression to demands adapted to a set of characteristics typical of certain experiences of injustice, and to open up a path to the political public sphere. It is worth noting that in the various movements of the deprived, those "without" (the homeless, the unemployed, undocumented immigrants) have recently developed practices typical of the spokesmen for the Republic.[7] We can even recall that the activities and the political discourses designated by the concept of a spokesperson can be understood as the "political production of exclusion" par excellence, precisely because the state of being marginalized or excluded does not allow any other means for achieving citizenship.[8] Another illustration can be found in the decisive role that struggles of indigenous peoples give to "word warriors."[ii] Their function is to fight against the closure of the political public sphere by articulating a number of "invisibilized" social experiences and demands that are spontaneously expressed in different idioms, in ways that can fit into the political space's frame of reference.[9]

The obstacles that struggles of the deprived run up against are due not only to a lack of social and cultural resources, but also to elements that obstruct or jam the dynamics of the experience of injustice. In the case of the unemployed especially, the lack of an adequate normative vocabulary can prevent individuals from being able to grasp the injustice of their situation. Most often, dynamics that could have led to the articulation of demands against an unjust situation, and to the will to transform it by employing the means appropriate to a politically relevant solution, are derailed. The practical dynamics of rejecting a painfully experienced situation can then turn against the individual himself, punishing him with the internalization of a devalued self-image. We can thus see that the movements of the unemployed do not come into being until volunteer work has managed to provide them with a framework of injustice[10] that allows them to stop seeing themselves as solely responsible for their circumstances, and to identify the latter as a form of social injustice. One of the aims of struggles for undocumented immigrants, too, is to allow them to escape from situations of silence and powerlessness by publicly coming forward and asserting that they are rights-bearing subjects who have been harmed by an injustice, and not "illegals," individuals in the wrong in the eyes of the law.[11] The impediments here are not only linked to a lack of social and cultural resources, but also to the effects of symbolic violence that traps individuals in unjust situations. But the lack of a social base creates different kinds of impediments to the construction of a framework of injustice: first, it isolates individuals by reducing them to silence and powerlessness; second, it does not allow the construction of a framework based upon the articulation of values constitutive of identity; and finally, it makes it more difficult for meanings elaborated together in the struggle to be disseminated.[12] Yet another impediment is added to these: the demands made by movements of the deprived are generally considered not to belong to the domain of justice.

---

ii. In English in the original.

It is striking that the problem of social suffering, as Pierre Bourdieu formulated it in *The Weight of the World*, was intended to serve as a response to some of these impediments. It was a matter not only of illuminating the many subjective difficulties entailed by a general deterioration of living conditions, but also of fighting against the guilt complexes that crush individuals through revealing the social causes of these subjective difficulties. For Bourdieu, the term "suffering" designates a set of subjective difficulties that are not publicly displayed—not because they are linked to partly inexpressible violations (such as those resulting result from extreme and traumatic forms of social violence), but because their partial, relative, and routinized character renders the social aspect of their causes barely perceptible. The problem of suffering is thus brought back, for Bourdieu, to different forms of positional suffering [*misère de position*] that are always less visible than material poverty [*misère de condition*] but just as real: "[the] suffering characteristic of a social order which, although it has undoubtedly reduced poverty overall . . . has also multiplied the social spaces . . . and set up the conditions for an unprecedented development of all kinds of ordinary suffering."[13] And because individuals are liable to blame themselves for their own suffering (the social character of which is hardly visible), sociology must bring the social causes to light and make it possible for "those who suffer to find out that their suffering can be imputed to social causes and thus to feel exonerated."[14]

Just as struggles of the deprived assume the intercession of spokespersons to formulate their language of protest, they also challenge the social sciences and political philosophy to devise a model of social critique adapted to their language of protest. For undocumented immigrants and the homeless, the injustice is obvious in the eyes of those who endure it. In these cases, the social sciences are needed mainly to show the social causes of their suffering; and philosophy mainly to legitimate their demands and the normative vocabulary in which these are articulated. But in the struggles of the unemployed—and, more generally, in any experiences of injustice that lead to the collapse of a positive relation to oneself and the possibility for protest action—injustice is not spontaneously experienced and expressed as an injustice. The social sciences can no longer be content, therefore, to merely identify the causes. They must also work specifically to fight against guilt complexes. The social sciences are not alone in pursuing this objective (as is demonstrated by the frameworks of injustice devised by associations representing the unemployed), and it certainly couldn't be achieved if they were the only ones to seek it, but they can play a role. As for philosophy, it is no longer enough for the discipline to enlarge its definitions of justice; it must also contribute to the articulation and the foundation of "frameworks of injustice" without which the voices that articulate differends cannot be expressed. In the absence of differends, the only possible way to contribute to this normative elaboration is to try to define justice from a perspective that, for the individuals themselves, seems to establish the fundamental stakes of experiences that they are unable to define as unjust, but which nonetheless seem to be typical of injustice. Rather than simply making explicit preexisting interests and claims, interests and claims must be elaborated directly from these experiences. Rather than simply portraying these experiences theoretically, we must fight against the cognitive obstacles and symbolic violence that oppose the ability of victims of injustice to find their voice and begin to speak; and we must thereby contribute to the articulation of a framework that will allow them to describe their own negative social experiences as unjust.

The term "social suffering" serves precisely to explain the principal characteristics of experiences of injustice that are difficult to express as such. Before we can take up the relation between social suffering and justice in itself, we must clarify the meaning of the concept of social suffering and indicate why a consideration of social suffering in a model of social critique seems useful.

THE CONCEPTS OF SOCIAL AND PSYCHIC SUFFERING

Today, the concept of social suffering seems endowed with an epistemological obviousness; looking back, one could be tempted to maintain that social suffering figures among sociology's most traditional objects.[15] If on this point it seems natural to make reference to texts such as Pierre Bourdieu's 1962 "Bachelorhood and the Peasant Condition" ["Célibat et condition paysanne"], or even Richard Hoggart's 1957 *The Uses of Literacy*,[iii] one would nevertheless be hard-pressed to find the term "social suffering"

---

iii. Pierre Bourdieu, "Bachelorhood and the Peasant Condition," Part I (pp. 7–130) in *The Bachelors' Ball: The Crisis of Peasant Society in Béarn*, trans. Richard Nice (Chicago: The University of Chicago Press, 2008); Richard Hoggart, *The Uses of Literacy: Aspects of Working-Class Life, with Special Reference to Publications and Entertainments* (New York: Oxford University Press, 1970).

(or even analyses explicitly grasping the social dimensions of suffering) in them. In France, the emergence of social suffering as an issue dates from the late 1980s and the early 1990s, in the proceedings from an interdisciplinary seminar organized by Christophe Dejours, *Pleasure and Suffering in Work* [*Plaisir et souffrance dans le travail*],[16] in Bourdieu's *The Weight of the World* [*La misère du monde*],[17] and Serge Paugam's *La Disqualification Sociale*, [*Social Exclusion*][18]; and in work done under the rubric of "clinical sociology."[19] However, it was not until the end of the 1990s that Christophe Dejours was able to generalize his analyses of suffering at work, in the 1998 monograph *Souffrance en France* [*Suffering in France*], and that Bourdieu and Paugam respectively, in *Pascalian Meditations* [*Méditations pascaliennes*][20] and *Le Salarié de la Precarité* [*Precarious Employment*],[21] were able to offer definitions of "social suffering" and have it included as an entry in the volumes' indexes. Ultimately, what seems to have been decisive in the establishment of the paradigm of social suffering was both the sociological problem of unearthing the social causes of suffering and investigations by public health authorities into the appearance of new psychological disorders linked to the effects of exclusion or disaffiliation. Within the context of this second approach, the critical milestone was Antoine Lazarus's report, produced in 1995 for the Délégation interministérielle à la ville and the Délégation interministérielle au revenu minimum d'insertion, entitled *Une Souffrance qu'on ne peut plus cacher* ["A suffering that can no longer be hidden"].[iv] Five years after this report, the concept of social suffering seems to have been well established as a paradigm—as, by the way, Antoine Lazarus himself and a group of theoreticians of psychosocial intervention with the homeless noted with concern in the July 2001 issue of the journal *Rhizome* entitled "La Souffrance psychique: un paradigme écran?" ["Psychic Suffering: A Screening Paradigm?"][22]

The Weight of the World appeared as a transitional text. If the notion of suffering was not included in its index, it is a central concern in the work itself, especially in the Postscript. There, in the course of a comparison between sociology and medicine, Bourdieu points out that a description is needed of what he terms "social malaise" in order for both fields to undertake an interpretation of symptoms and understanding of causes. Bourdieu portrays this "social malaise" as a kind of suffering when he notes

iv. Antoine Lazarus, ed., *Une Souffrance qu'on ne peut plus cacher* (Paris: DIV & DIRMI, 1995).

that the sociological message "can have [an effect] in allowing those who suffer to find out that their suffering can be imputed to social causes."[23] However, when it is a matter of specifying *The Weight of the World*'s subject matter and political import (as in the preface, "The Space of Points of View"), Bourdieu prefers to speak of poverty [misère] rather than suffering [souffrance].[v] The work's political aim is, in effect, simultaneously to emphasize the breadth and diversity of forms of social injustice (generally unacknowledged in policy discussions),[24] and to provide an account of their unity. From this perspective, the primary target was the then-current discourse that systematically put employees' demands in opposition to the condition of the unemployed and pitted public sector employees against those in the private sector, thus playing different forms of social injustice against one another. The concept of the value of poverty [misère] was especially linked to the possibility of articulating positional suffering [misère de position] and poverty [misère de condition], while maintaining that the former is also a kind of poverty. Bourdieu's book made significant waves, and it is undeniable that the themes he articulated in its preface and postscript, just like the text on the book's cover ("speak . . . (silence) suffering"), had much to do with the spread of the issue of social suffering. The work served almost immediately as the birth certificate for a sociological theory of social suffering.[25] But the concept was not created in this text. Bourdieu's task was to draw attention to phenomena that had been forgotten by political representatives rather than to put forward a veritable theory of it; and when he had to theorize, the sociological categories of malaise (maladjustment of the habitus with respect to situations) and poverty (as defined by the contrast between conditional and positional suffering) were preferable to the psychological term "suffering." Ultimately, for Bourdieu—as was true in many discussions of social suffering in the 1990s—the signifier "social suffering" remained a conceptless term, a term whose only meaning was in its polemical use, a term with an extension but without genuine intention, because it was applied to a set of objects that did not exclusively fall within the register of feelings and felt pain, even though the classic definition of suffering thus limited its scope.

---

v. Renault's distinction here is lost (though his larger point is aptly illustrated) in the English translation of *The Weight of the World*, where "misère" ("poverty," "misery," "woes") is translated as "suffering" (French p. 11, English p. 4) and "souffrances" ("suffering") as "distress" (French p. 10, English p. 4).

In conformity with a rather classic conception of the disciplinary divide between sociology and psychology, Bourdieu's interest was directed more toward the causes of suffering rather than the suffering itself. To find a first attempt to conceptualize social suffering, we must leave sociology for a while, turning instead to Antoine Lazarus's public health report *Une souffrance qu'on ne peut plus cacher*. In this report, it appears clearly that the concept of social suffering is very directly linked to a short-term fact that is quite unique and relatively independent of the issues Bourdieu had raised: the major changes to welfare policy entailed by the creation of a guaranteed minimum income for the long-term unemployed (revenu minimum d'insertion, or RMI). The establishment of this system entailed individualized monitoring of its beneficiaries in order to offer them "actions and activities . . . necessary for one's social and professional integration" (article 2) and to verify that they really undertook said activities. This system was thus accompanied by a new kind of relationship between social workers and the recipients of public welfare: it was no longer simply a matter of providing temporary assistance (access to emergency funds; access to medical care, to housing, to education), but also of taking responsibility for the individual's biographical trajectory and requiring a commitment from him to reintegrate into society, a commitment which he can hardly meet precisely because of his biographical trajectory. Social workers, thus directly confronted by the absurdity of this legal requirement, were also the recipients of complaints in which the beneficiaries of the RMI expressed their inability to meet this requirement. The suffering that can no longer be hidden was, first of all, the malaise of social workers, who were just as unable as doctors or psychiatrists to accept what made the system of reintegration unenforceable: the malaise of socially alienated or disaffiliated individuals.

What became clear with this report was that poverty cannot be reduced to a strictly economic definition—that is, to an objective condition for which an income is an adequate solution—but that it also contains an irreducible subjective aspect that the systems of reintegration must acknowledge. This subjective aspect is that which what we designate by the category of "psychic suffering" understood as a particular type of psychological suffering. Is psychic suffering a mental illness or a social suffering? This question delineates the concept of psychic suffering as a nonpathological kind of suffering with social origins, which presupposes a distinction between two kinds of psychological problems: illness, and serious but nonpathological psychological problems. Psychological suffering thus ceases to be understood as a strictly individual phenomenon and acquires a social dimension; and this social dimension does not refer to the fact that the psyche is always socially conditioned, but rather to particular psychological effects of specific social processes (increasing precariousness and social disaffiliation).

Defining psychic suffering as a subjectively felt suffering with social origins raised a challenge to both sociology and psychoanalysis. Sociology typically refers questions about subjective experience of social conditions to psychology, and it studies the subjective effects of the social principally insofar as they are dependent upon collective representations or behaviors acquired through socialization. It is ill-equipped to describe the subjective effects of negative social experiences in terms of suffering. Psychoanalysis is no better able to do so. Freud, in *Civilization and its Discontents*, did indeed speak of a "social source of suffering,"[26] but the latter is connected to his theory of the relation between superego and ego, whereas psychic suffering is connected to different forms of precariousness and social disaffiliation. Freud is examining a source of suffering that refers to society as a global symbolic institution, not the suffering produced by specific social causes.

The inadequacies of these approaches will become quite clear if we consider the example of a typical kind of severe psychological problem produced by a social situation: the extreme social disaffiliation of life on the street. It is quite clear that classic psychoanalytic theory is unable to explain the experiences of those sometimes called "vagrants" or "bums," even if it is true that social accidents like the loss of one's job, spouse, or home could lead to such an extreme state only given rather particular biographical circumstances. And the definition of social suffering in dispositional terms proposed by Bourdieu in *Pascalian Meditations*,[27] which ultimately reduces social suffering to the maladjustment produced by a loss of social position, is thus just as unable to explain the fact that the victims of extreme social disaffiliation are in a situation that is better described as the radical loss of a set of fundamental conditions for habitus than as a difficult change of habitus. The model of a suffering produced by a torn habitus or mutually incompatible habitus,[28] also employed by Bourdieu, is no more applicable. The problem is not the modification of a second nature and its incompatibility with institutional contexts, nor is it the contradictions that traverse a second nature; the problem is the destruction of an intersubjectively constituted nature, the deinstitutionalization of life, or dehumanization.[29]

Concerning Bourdieu's approach, we probably have to recognize the inadequacy of the dispositional conception of social suffering as an indication of the more general inadequacy of a theory that understands social conflict as a form of struggle for position, or for a better integration, and for this reason is unsuitable when it is a matter of describing the pathologies of extreme social disaffiliation and of social and personal disintegration.

In this way, an approach in terms of recognition, based upon the theory that a positive relation to oneself is vulnerable, seems better suited. Applied to psychic suffering, this theoretical model of recognition plays a dual role: it makes it possible to explain, first, the phenomenon of narcissistic collapse (characteristic of cases of extreme social disaffiliation—a point that will be taken up in the next chapter); and, second, the fact that the suffering of extreme social disaffiliation is not simply tied to a loss of intersubjective supports for individual lives, but also to integration within disparaging social relations. The loss of rewarding social relations and integration within disparaging social relations are two faces of the denial of recognition that, if we accept the theory of recognition, can end in the destruction of the positive relation to oneself that constitutes an essential aspect of subjective life. The value of the concept of recognition resides, moreover, in its capacity to merge a descriptive perspective with a normative perspective on psychic suffering—it provides a theoretical model that makes it possible to combine a representation of psychic suffering with a critique of the social relations that produce it.

POLITICAL OBJECTIONS

But do the concepts of psychic suffering and social suffering, as they have just been defined, have political relevance? The question is constantly raised. A first sort of objection has to do with the risks entailed by collaboration between medicine and politics, as it happens, through the medicalization of the social question. However, psychic suffering is immediately defined as a socially produced suffering. It thus designates a social pathology rather than an individual pathology; the kinds of responses that it calls for have less to do with individual therapy than the transformation of socially produced conditions of suffering. This is the view that Dejours supported, for example, in the seminar *Plaisir et Souffrance dans le Travail*, when he maintained that the psychopathology of work tries to describe the various forms of suffering at work not in order to define an appropriate therapeutic procedure, but rather to identify the pathogenic conditions of work that should be transformed.[30] The concept of social suffering does not so much lead to a medicalization of the social question as to a concern with transforming the social conditions creating injustice and guilt complexes that stand in the way of a struggle against injustice. One could always reply that the very issue of social pathology inherently presupposes a medical model hardly compatible with a social critique that would be mindful of its contributions to a transformation of society. To conceive of social injustice as a social pathology would be to settle for the interpretation of symptoms and the establishment of diagnoses—while passing over in silence both the social actors' aspirations and the relations of domination in which they are caught—thereby running the risk of locking them into the role of powerless victims. That would amount to adopting the approach of an expert who turns a deaf ear to basic and general questions in order to better isolate some specific social problems without really offering any means for their transformation. It would amount to presupposing an analogy between the social and the biological that implies, on the one hand, that societies are organisms that are always potentially healthy, such that radical transformation would never be advisable; and, on the other hand, that social problems should be entrusted to experts of social normalcy, just as questions about illness and health are left to medical authorities.

These Foucauldian suspicions are only partially justified. The concept of social pathology does not have a univocal meaning, and it is possible to make use of it to designate an approach that consists in identifying specific social problems (diagnostics), decisive social causes (etiology), and desirable social transformations (therapeutics).[31] These social problems, for their part, can be identified starting from the effects produced by institutions on individuals' health without subjecting the analysis of desirable social transformations to medical norms. This has been the case at least since Marx, who used the concept of "industrial pathology"[32] to describe the morbid effects of lengthening the workday and of inhuman working conditions. Studies of public health[33] made it possible for him to underscore that poverty cannot be reduced to its economic definition in terms of income levels, because it also encompasses a general alteration in the conditions of life and vital capacities (accelerated loss of height and weight; a decrease in life expectancy; an increase in infant mortality; and death from overwork)[34]—an alteration captured in terms and phrases like "suffering," "degeneration of the industrial population," and physical and intellectual "decay."[35]

It can be added that the concept of psychic suffering does not presuppose any sort of strict distinction between the normal and the pathological, but rather a dissolution of this distinction. Taking inspiration from Nietzsche and Georges Canguilhem, Dejours argues that health is not a stable state but rather a goal, whereas suffering is the domain that separates health from illness.[36] Suffering always exists in society, and the latter generally forms a part of individuals' health. There are a vast number of social means to make the suffering produced by society tolerable, just as there are many biological and psychological means for bringing a state of suffering back to a state of health. However, we can speak of a social pathology when a given society is incapable of providing the means to make the suffering it produces tolerable; in other words, when it imprisons individuals in an intolerable situation. To claim that suffering is the domain separating health from illness amounts to claiming that there are no criteria by which to distinguish "healthy" from "unhealthy" suffering, but rather that it is always legitimate to demand a transformation of situations producing this kind of imprisonment in suffering.

Then, the claim can be made that these situations should be described in terms of social suffering so that struggles against these situations will be effective. We have already grasped the implications of such descriptions: whereas suffering tends to psychologize social injustice, by leading individuals to take responsibility for their own suffering, the description of injustice in terms of social suffering makes it possible to "sociologize," and thereby to politicize, suffering. Producing such a politization of suffering had been Bourdieu's aim in *The Weight of the World*, as well as Dejours's in *Souffrance en France*. The latter work notably sought to struggle against a discourse aiming to juxtapose unemployed workers' suffering with the conditions of wage earners. Dejours analyzed the process by which attention brought by politicians and unions to issues of unemployment led many wage earners to feel guilty for feeling and expressing their own suffering at work, and thus produced various ways of banalizing suffering. The problem of social suffering thus made it possible to explain the specific nature of the injustice victimizing workers who were made to feel guilty about having gainful employment and thereby led to accept ever more degraded working conditions. Social suffering thus offered an explanation for the atrophying of social struggles over work sites, at the same time as it suggested that by taking account politically of the injustice of suffering at work, the dynamics of formulating demands could be unblocked.

These analyses lead to the idea that Bourdieu's project—aimed at explaining the different forms of social injustice and their unity, while also providing individuals with a political representation of the injustice of their condition—could only succeed if social injustice were described in terms of social suffering. But we must not conclude therefrom that all forms of social injustice are forms of suffering, or that we can safely equate a struggle against injustice with a struggle against suffering. Richard Rorty provides an illustration of the impasse that such a short circuit can create. In *Contingency, Irony, Solidarity*, he equates justice with the struggle against suffering, pain, and humiliation. This definition encompasses two primary theses. The first begins from the critical import of the concept of justice— an abolitionist concept, for its substantive content is inseparable from a struggle against injustice. The second presupposes a prioritarian definition of justice as a struggle that should be directed, above all, against the worst forms of injustice: suffering being the worst evil that a society could produce, justice must be understood above all as a demand for the abolition of suffering. We have already highlighted the general problems with prioritarianism and the creation of a hierarchy of injustices that it entails. Because it is impossible to claim that all forms of injustice are also forms of suffering (the denial of political rights is not generally experienced as suffering), some injustices appear to be less important than others. Prioritarianism leads to pitting injustices against each other rather than connecting them. Moreover, it is difficult to claim that all the forms of injustice accompanied by suffering should be primarily presented as forms of suffering. Even if the violation of political rights entailed an experience of suffering, it would be dangerous to suggest that it is only appropriate to assert one's rights in order to reduce suffering (this would effectively renew the reactionary argument that struggles for rights are merely the expression of resentment by the poor; it would rubber-stamp a trivially utilitarian view that politics is only concerned with the administration of punishments and rewards).

SUFFERING AND THE DEFINITION OF JUSTICE

If the concept of justice designates socially produced inequalities, and if the concepts of psychic suffering and social suffering designate inequalities that are characteristic of certain contemporary forms of the social question, it seems reasonable to attempt to integrate a reference to suffering into the definition of justice. The problem is then to establish the legitimacy of a new project to enlarge the definition of justice.

It is indeed a matter of enlarging the definition, because it is hard to see how a reference to suffering could be integrated within current definitions of justice. Does justice consist in giving to each the suffering that he is due? Should we speak of an allocation of suffering in proportion to each one's needs or virtues? Or again, should suffering be distributed in proportion to rights? None of these questions makes any sense. Nor is it enough, here, to draw upon the utilitarian tradition to resolve the problem: suffering can hardly be compared to disutility, and the quantification of pleasures and pains is only a new way of misrecognizing the qualitative dimensions and the irreducibility of various forms of psychic suffering. But one could take these challenges as an indication that questions of justice are on a different level than those of suffering.

Again, the principal argument against any attempt to take suffering into account in discussions about social justice is connected to the demands for universality associated with the idea of justice. Suffering would be linked with individuals' particular expectations and the social uses of the body that distinguish groups and peoples, while justice would consist of the rules that make it possible to determine the universal conditions for the value of institutions, regardless of their ability to satisfy individual or collective idiosyncrasies. It is the very variety of psychological, social, and cultural conditions in combination that entail whether a hardship or a violence will be felt and expressed as suffering. Moreover, the refusal of suffering seems to be related to the particular conditions that make for a good life—and not the conditions that make institutions just. All this seems to exclude suffering from the domain of justice. Once again, we are encountering arguments that have already been shown to be inadequate. First of all, the idea of a life without intolerable suffering is a general expectation. To be sure, there are neither objective nor subjective criteria that would allow us to determine in a universal way what constitutes intolerable suffering. But that is not enough to conclude that inequalities concerning the conditions in which this general expectation could be met do not fall within the domain of justice. As I have already argued, questions concerning the *domain* of justice are logically independent of questions concerning *criteria* for justice, and the latter presuppose the former. Secondly, if expectations define what constitutes a good life in general, that gives us no reason to conclude that they cannot also relate to justice (as I have also already noted). The opposition between justice and the good is not absolute.

When justice is understood in the sense of social justice, and when suffering is understood in the sense of social suffering, the arguments against taking suffering into consideration as belonging to the domain of justice are even weaker. These arguments can be expressed as follows: Suffering cannot provide a relevant guide for the transformation of institutions—on the one hand, because we cannot logically move from subjective suffering to the objective value of institutions; and on the other, because individual experiences are categorically different from that which defines universal validity. But this claim—that suffering is only a subjective and individual phenomenon, disconnected from institutional objectivity and generality—can no longer be accepted with respect to social suffering; that is, suffering produced in specific social contexts and affecting groups of individuals. The opposition between the particularity of experience and the universality of validity is no longer relevant. As I have already noted, universal validity claims function to explain the particular realities subsumed within them. What could principles of justice be worth that would legitimate institutions playing a decisive role in experiences of intolerable suffering? And yet, it is precisely this sort of relation between suffering and institutions that the idea of social suffering designates. We must at least be suspicious about the validity claims of such principles of justice, not only because they assert a false universality by legitimating what ought to be seen as an injustice, but also because they assert that any demand on the part of those who endure these injustices would be illegitimate, and in so doing, contribute to their silencing. Adorno articulated this kind of critique when he noted that ideology is an identitarian discourse that only wants to see those parts of the world that fit with abstract principles of legitimation. This is how suffering, in its particularity and subjectivity, thus comes to play a polemical and demystifying role: "The smallest trace of senseless suffering in the empirical world belies all the identitarian philosophy that would talk us out of that suffering . . . The physical moment tells our knowledge that suffering ought not to be, that things should be different . . . Hence the convergence of specific materialism with criticism, with social change in practice."[37]

If we can accept, first, that the kind of universality required for a definition is not the same as what is required for a criterion; second, that the question of the domain circumscribed by a definition (the extension associated with the intension of a concept) has priority with respect to questions of criteria; and finally, that what is at stake in social suffering is the value of social contexts and institutional settings, then the objections lose all strength. But indeed, asserting that socially produced suffering can *generally* be considered as an injustice does not mean that all suffering linked to specific social situations should be considered an injustice. We need not assert that the concept of justice analytically contains that of social suffering, nor that suffering should be the criterion for social injustice. We need only understand that the concept of social suffering must be viewed as the concept of some types of injustice, and that these injustices must be taken seriously in deliberations and debates concerned with social justice.

All the arguments I have just made in favor of integrating suffering within the domain of social justice and injustice have been negative in character (they are principally responses to objections), and do not seem to be able to be supported by the kind of analysis that the preceding chapters called for—namely, an analysis of the general connections between experiences of injustice and the denial of recognition. To this point, I have justified expanding our definitions of justice on the grounds that what is at stake in experiences of injustice is recognition. But, as we have just noted, the idea of social suffering designates situations that are not necessarily experienced as injustices, and that could even stand in the way of this kind of experience. Even if denial of recognition is a powerful source of social suffering, it would be absurd to assert that the stakes involved in this sort of experience are, for those who live them, matters of recognition. Thus, it is not by starting from the issue of what is at stake in recognition that we will be able to identify the traits common to different forms of these new types of injustice. And hence, in order to discuss these particular types of injustice, we began neither with recognition nor with a feeling of injustice, but rather with a question about the universality of expectations (of avoiding intolerable suffering), and about inequalities concerning the satisfaction of these expectations.

But even so, the theory of recognition is not without resources here, because the problem of the vulnerability of one's positive relation to oneself explains some of the fundamental stakes of these experiences of injustice without a feeling of injustice. In fact, the idea of social suffering designates different ways in which a positive relation to oneself can be weakened, reversed, or even broken; and it does so not only at the level of identity (doubts about one's identity, a loss of reference points, a negative identity) but also at the level of psyche (problems such as narcissistic collapse or the loss of the reality principle). I have emphasized in the preceding chapters that the intersubjective constitution of one's relation to oneself is the basis for recognitive expectations that, when unsatisfied, can give rise to experiences of injustice (accompanied by a feeling of injustice). It is true that we must first expect to be recognized in order to find situations unjust in which one is subject to a denial of recognition. We now have a demonstration that this claim can be linked with the idea of a decisive relation between the intersubjective constitution and confirmation of a positive relation to oneself (through recognitive expectations). In cases of social suffering in which the relation to oneself is reversed or destroyed, there are no longer any recognitive expectations or a feeling of injustice. Justice and injustice cease to be dimensions of the experience. The social conditions that, for an individual, enable one to maintain a positive relation to oneself thus also function as the conditions that make justice and injustice available as dimensions of one's experience. In this way, we can say that the theory of recognition develops a transcendental argument (if we understand "transcendental" as having to do with conditions of possibility) in favor of the consideration of social suffering in discussions about social justice. What justifies this new expansion of our definitions of justice is not, as in the preceding chapters, the fact that the various issues at stake in our experiences of justice carry a number of similarities, but rather the fact that the conditions for a positive relation to oneself are also the conditions for experiences of injustice accompanied by a feeling of injustice, and that in experiences of social suffering, it is precisely these conditions that are at stake.

THE VACILLATIONS OF SOCIAL JUSTICE

Insofar as it offers a method for reconstructing a definition of justice that starts from experiences of injustice, while simultaneously showing that the question of the confirmation of a positive relation to oneself is an issue of fundamental justice, the theory of recognition justifies the intuition that social suffering is a matter of injustice. It thus makes it possible to spell out the definition of justice presupposed by the "frames of injustice" called for by critical analysis of some of our societies' most characteristic social pathologies: suffering at work, the suffering of the unemployed, the suffering unique to extreme social disaffiliation. It thus articulates a model for social critique that allows us to explain both the specificity of the struggles of the deprived, and situations in which individuals suffer an injustice specifically tied to the fact that the inequalities they endure do not rise to the level of being the objects of social struggle, such that nothing seems to be able to bring them to the attention of the political public sphere.

Integrating these questions within its model of social critique, the theory of recognition provides a new illustration of the principle that the conceptual problems of political philosophy are simultaneously logical and political problems. Can the concept of justice be associated only with a definition of justice, or should it also require criteria of justice and of injustice? This conceptual question will receive different answers, depending upon whether one takes the central issue to be the improvement of a relatively just situation (the optimistic view implied by Habermas's and Honneth's philosophies of history); the correction of the worst injustices (the prioritarian view of Rawls and Rorty); or rather, the undoing of a vast set of intolerable injustices. The theory of recognition that I am proposing here takes the third perspective. It puts situations that are judged to be intolerable by those who live them at the center of its model of social critique. It chooses to serve as the spokesperson and voice for all those who suffer these injustices, arguing on their behalf and dismantling arguments that would either justify other models of social critique or attempt to justify the existing social order. By serving as a spokesperson, it does not reduce philosophy to a mere ideological weapon, nor does it abandon the task of investigating the normative claims of definitions of justice; rather, it tries to explicitly connect this normative investigation with its political presuppositions and consequences. As this entails an abandonment (which could be deemed disappointing, from a speculative point of view) of the search for criteria, it is probably worthwhile to conclude this chapter by recalling Max Horkheimer, one of the few philosophers (probably because of his taste for Schopenhauer) who was able to overcome a reluctance provoked by the subjective dimension of suffering and to take account of the latter in his descriptions of injustice.[38] In particular, this enabled him to assert that "the concept of justice epitomizes the demands of the oppressed at any given moment, and it is therefore as changeable as those demands themselves."[39] These demands are "changeable"—they vacillate—precisely because they make reference to experiences that are as ambiguous as they are diverse: ambiguous, because as soon as an experience of injustice is accompanied by suffering, it tends to be seen as an experience of suffering rather than as an experience of injustice—for reasons that are as much phenomenological (suffering monopolizes one's attention) as psychodynamic (suffering can invert or shatter a positive relation to oneself); diverse, because there are many forms of social suffering, and because the suffering that goes along with some of them serves to pit them against one another rather than uniting them—as much from a speculative point of view (because it is counterintuitive to integrate references to suffering in the domain of justice) as from a political one (because the suffering that one endures naturally appears more important than the injustices that others suffer). Must we then conclude that the "demands of the oppressed" should be described from a more general, more stable, and less ambiguous point of view—that of the principles of justice—or from that of structures of oppression? It is certainly possible to maintain, for example, that two forms of macrosocial domination—capital and male domination—cut across all social fields and overdetermine all forms of domination,[40] but it is a safe bet that explanations of particular injustices and sufferings in terms of capitalist relations or gendered social relations will not be enough to convince many individuals that their particular sufferings are signs of a generally unjust society. Likewise, it is difficult to see how abstract principles of justice could get groups that suffer ever-particular injustices to understand that common concerns run through their demands, and that this is one of the conditions of possibility for a counterhegemonic politics. Only a social critique that consciously assumes the role of a spokesperson for different experiences of injustice can make it possible for the dominated and the deprived to recognize their particular situations as both unjust and analogous to those of other dominated and deprived groups. Only this sort of social critique can simultaneously carry out both an expansion of justice that legitimates the "frames of injustice" required by their particular situations, and a reformulation of justice that can offer a sounding board for the voices that condemn these unjust situations.

Chapter Seven

RECOGNITION AND PSYCHIC SUFFERING

One of the advantages of the concept of recognition is that it offers a model that makes it possible to connect an understanding of social suffering as injustice with a resolution of social suffering's conceptual and political aporias. Up to this point, I have been interested in psychic suffering as the psychological flip side of social suffering without becoming immersed in a detailed analysis of the meaning that should be given here to the ideas and the social genesis of suffering. To be sure, the theory of recognition cannot take the place of social psychology and clinical psychiatry in order to elaborate a theory of psychological suffering, but it can begin to outline a model that would allow us to grasp some of the characteristic traits of psychic suffering and to attempt to answer some of the epistemological suspicions concerning the concept of psychic suffering in particular—and, more generally, the descriptive and explanatory relevance of an approach in terms of social suffering.

In the pages that follow, I will delineate different forms of psychic suffering and I will explain how an approach in terms of recognition can explain the continuum of psychic suffering by connecting the social processes giving rise to the devaluation and increasing hardship of life with those producing a complete dismantling of an individual's psychic life. At the same time, I will try to spell out the relationship between social suffering and the experience of injustice. Insofar as it is socially produced, yet experienced only by particular individuals, psychic suffering can be seen as the worst debasement of an individual's life conditions, and thus as the worst form of injustice, even though it is rarely taken into consideration by prioritarian definitions of justice. However, insofar as psychic suffering is sometimes accompanied by identification with these life conditions and an apparent disappearance of all normative expectations, it seems difficult to portray as an experience of injustice. We saw in the last chapter why this paradox leads to an argument for the expansion of the domain of justice. We can add that that it brings us to the fuzzy edges of the domain of justice. It would of course be quite convenient to use this opacity as a reason to avoid these issues, but the presupposition that the world is naturally governed in accordance with our logical categories is too naïve to be accepted as such. As the world has not been created by a divine intellect that wishes the best for us, it doesn't necessarily conform to our categories. And if there is much that is fuzzy or gray in our experience, why shouldn't there also be gray areas in the experience of injustice? Why should we expect matters of injustice to be easily divided between the just and the unjust? Why should something essential for justice be excluded therefrom, simply because the limits of injustice are unclear?

MENTAL ILLNESS AND NONPATHOLOGICAL PSYCHIC SUFFERING

Until now, the concept of psychic suffering has been articulated primarily from a public health perspective. When the Lazarus Report identified psychic suffering as a socially originated "symptom of severe psychic distress," it delineated a sort of threat to the psychic elements of health—according to a broad definition of the latter—that would make it possible to distinguish between a lack of health, and mental illness. Since 1948, the World Health Organization (WHO) has defined health as "a state of complete physical, mental and social well-being and not merely the absence of disease or infirmity."[i] In line with this definition, a reference to the social can be integrated into the concept of psychic suffering to designate not only the general social conditions for health (housing, diet and nutrition, medical

---

i. World Health Organization, "Constitution of the World Health Organization," from the Preamble. Available at http://apps.who.int/gb/bd/PDF/bd47/EN/constitution-en.pdf?ua=1 (accessed March 19, 2018).

access, etc.), but also the psychological effects of specific social processes. Hence, the particularities of severe but nonpathological psychic problems can be designated within the category of "malaise" ["mal-être"].[1] The inadequacies of this approach to psychic suffering are easily seen. The concept of "malaise" includes a vast ensemble of phenomena that do not have any clear coherence: suffering at work, welfare recipients' negative self-images, and the dismantling of the psyche in extremely disaffiliated homeless persons—all constitute distinct psychological problems that are far from being identical. Moreover, it is not enough to mention specific social processes' effects, or even to consider them in discussions of insecurity and precariousness, in order to give consistency to the second element of psychic suffering—namely, the idea of similar social processes generating similar psychological problems. It seems doubtful that psychological problems related to working conditions, stigmatization, or extreme disaffiliation would have similar social origins. Ultimately, insofar as it is articulated within a public health paradigm, the concept of psychic suffering remains defined in a negative way, by stating what it is not: it is not pathological, and it is linked to social conditions apart from the general conditions of health. This says nothing positive about what psychic suffering is. [And] these difficulties are, at least in part, irreducible insofar as the concept of psychic suffering really encompasses situations that are themselves at least partially irreducible: suffering at work, subjective problems tied to long-term unemployment, and the sufferings of homelessness are defined by unique psychological problems and unique social relations. It does not follow, for all that, that the concept of psychic suffering has no object. It is indeed possible to positively determine that content, by specifying that the suffering in question is an expressed suffering, and that its social origins depend upon social supports that make it possible for individuals to alleviate the sufferings produced by various forms of social violence.[2] Psychic suffering then designates nonpathological problems expressed as suffering that originate, on the one hand, from insertion within symbolically or physically violent social relations (disaffiliation as devaluation); and on the other, from the failure of social supports (disaffiliation as increasing precariousness). An approach in terms of recognition makes it possible to explain the impact of these two kinds of subjective relations on subjective life. It then makes it possible to assign a common structure to the different psychological problems and social processes designated by the category of psychic suffering.

But the concept of psychic suffering has not been elaborated exclusively within the framework of public health, and it is officially recognized as an object not only in this field but also in psychiatry—where, too, it is a contested concept. As a psychiatric concept, it presupposes not only the definition of *symptoms* proper to populations targeted by psychosocial intervention (symptoms of suffering rather than a simple expression of suffering), but also the definition of specific *processes*. At the moment when psychiatry has to respond to calls for psychosocial intervention (especially with homeless people in situations of extreme disaffiliation), it can no longer consider mental illness to be its sole concern—it must also carefully distinguish mental illness from nonpathological psychic suffering, a distinction which supposes a more narrowly construed use of the term "psychic suffering" than in public health contexts (in what follows, I will speak of *psychic suffering in the narrow sense* to denote this). In any case, the distinction between mental illness and nonpathological psychic suffering is not immediately self-evident, because it can be admitted that all mental illness is accompanied by some suffering, and that there are no more breaks in continuity between the different kinds of psychic problems than there are between the sufferings that accompany them. The entire legitimacy of the distinction—and, in the same way, that of the concept of psychic suffering—thus depends upon a terminological convention. The concept of psychic suffering appears, in fact, as a new nosographic category that aims to explain psychic problems distinguished *both* by their symptoms *and* by specific processes. Nor is this double specification any more self-evident. The idea of symptoms and specific processes must not be understood too strictly, because the origins of psychic suffering are not exclusively social and, moreover, could also become pathological. In the case of psychic suffering linked to extreme disaffiliation, the interweaving of the psychological and the social is complex. As Olivier Douville has noted, three facts are clear here: (1) social conditions have specific subjective ramifications that can be very serious; (2) "exclusion can also be the behavioral form of an insecure stabilization in the social of particular psychotic economic situations"; and (3) "private madness and socially linked illness can find themselves mutually overdetermined in certain cases of exclusion. And we can see here just how many demands are made upon psychiatry by the various professionals concerned with exclusion."[3] Even while acknowledging these reservations, the concept of nonpathological psychic suffering can nonetheless claim relevance, as long as it could be established [first,] that the term "suffering" adequately describes these specific symptoms, and as long as the manner can be specified by which social factors can intervene in processes that create suffering. But the term "suffering" is problematic from these two perspectives.

It is problematic from the symptomatological perspective, first of all, because—in the strict sense of the term—the notion of suffering designates an affect rather than a symptom; whereas the symptoms of psychic suffering also carry the traces of a mobilization of psychic defenses against suffering, defenses that can cause suffering to disappear from conscious awareness or transform it into an exclusively unconscious suffering. From a psychodynamic perspective, the concept of psychic suffering designates the consequences of the mobilization of defenses rather than a lived suffering. This problem does not truly constitute an objection. If suffering must be understood as an ongoing failure to satisfy the ego's needs (a failure to satisfy that does not destroy the expectations rooted in these needs), it must be admitted that what is at stake here is too deeply rooted in the psyche to be contained within the sphere of conscious life: the ego's needs are themselves irreducible to the ways in which they are consciously expressed in the form of expectations. As a consequence, it becomes possible to assert that the specific problems designated by the concept of psychic suffering remain connected to suffering in two ways: first, because the existence of suffering is evidenced by the mobilization of defenses (against suffering, or at least against the effects of the nonsatisfaction of some of the ego's needs); and second, because letting those defenses down, in the wake of a change in social context or a psychotherapeutic intervention, runs the risk of subjecting the individual to a resurgence of extremely violent suffering.[4] In a word, even if it is unconscious, suffering is still present and decisive.

From the perspective of processes, too, the term "psychic suffering" is problematic. Suffering is, in fact, something that falls within the scope of individual psychology, whereas the concept of psychic suffering makes reference to a social origin of suffering. The idea of psychic suffering thus supposes that it would be possible to disentangle the elements within each individual's experience that have to do only with the individual's life history, and those that are explained only by reference to the social. Such an operation, in itself problematic, supposes, moreover, that we have the theoretical tools to be able to carry it out: as it so happens, models for understanding the social's influence upon the psychological. But a vast uncertainty prevails over these models.

These two kinds of problems are of a conceptual order because it is a matter of determining, first, if the term "suffering" can designate something that that does not fall within conscious affective life while still being connected to a social process; and, second, which concepts would make it possible to understand the social's influence upon the psychological. Because it is a matter of conceptual problems, it may be useful to take a detour through the philosophical modeling of suffering.

PHILOSOPHICAL MODELS OF SUFFERING

We can begin our presentation of these problems by examining the debate between two opposed philosophies of suffering. For Schopenhauer, the concept of suffering was the object of an unprecedented philosophical promotion, one that is still unequaled. We know that he distinguished between the world as representation and the world as will.[5] As representation, the world is the set of all phenomena; it is the world as it is given to external and internal consciousness. But if the phenomena are the objects of a consciousness, they are also the result of a fundamental dynamism that transcends the laws of our consciousness and that conditions our consciousness itself (which explains how one could try to bring Schopenhauer into a genealogy of psychoanalysis[6]). Schopenhauer designates this fundamental dynamism with the term "will," which he employs in a sense that is neither psychological nor anthropological, but physical or ontological in that it refers back to a fundamental force or drive, a striving (*Streben*) from which all things draw their reality. Everything is will, even inert objects. In living beings, will takes the particular form of a "will to life" (*Wille zum Leben*) that is a striving simultaneously to preserve the individual and the species.[7] This "will to life" is not subject to any of the laws that give representation its coherence— and this leads to an endless conflict between individuals, and to permanent dissatisfaction. Whence the thesis that suffering is the foundation of every life.[8] We see here, on the one hand, that suffering is explained by this conflict; and on the other hand, that suffering is the object of a metaphysical conceptualization whose psychological repercussions are relatively undefined. The Schopenhauerian concept of suffering belongs in fact to two distinct analytical levels: it is realized both from the perspective of the world as will (insofar as it is explained by the conflict between blind drives that governs our lives); and from the perspective of the world as representation (it designates the affect that is part of the conflict between the effects of [blind] drives on our conscious life). Schopenhauer is content to assert that suffering qua internal conflict of the will (suffering as will) is at the origin of suffering qua affect (suffering as representation), without explaining how this conflict produces this affect. What we have here is the ontologization of a psychological concept rather than the ontological explanation of a psychological phenomenon. To posit suffering as belonging to the unconscious world (the world as will), and thus as something other than an affect, is simultaneously the virtue and the limit of his project: the virtue, because it thus emphasizes that what is at play in suffering always exceeds what is explicit in an individual consciousness; the limit, for in no longer being able to see the link that weds ontological suffering and affective suffering, it is no longer possible to see why ontological suffering can still be called suffering.[9] All this anticipates the paradox of unconscious suffering.

If these Schopenhauerian reflections are useful in the context of reflections upon psychic suffering, it is above all because they propose to interpret suffering according to the paradigm of conflict[10]—struggle, domination, and dissatisfaction are many of the forms of this conflict setting the fundamental striving that inhabits all beings against the world in which this striving unfolds. Is suffering explained in general by the constraints imposed upon a life understood as a fundamental dynamism? Must we distinguish, among the various kinds of suffering, a specifically social suffering in the sense that it would be produced by specifically social constraints? This is sometimes asserted on occasion even now, by those who suggest applying a Schopenhauerian model to certain forms of psychic suffering.[11]

It can appear surprising to turn to Marx immediately after Schopenhauer, but the young Marx does indeed give decisive importance to suffering, while elaborating an alternative paradigm to that of conflict. The theme of suffering only comes to the foreground in a number of texts that appeared in *Les Annales franco-allemandes*, published in Paris in early 1844. But it plays a critical role. In fact, the theme of suffering makes it possible to clarify the status of the critical philosophy Marx is trying to elaborate, and which presupposes, according to Marx, a connection between the perspective of left-Hegelian critical philosophy and that of the nascent workers' movement. This connection is then understood as an alliance between theoretical critique, which is the task of philosophy, and practical critique, which would be the mission of the proletariat: critique must be based upon an alliance between "thinking humanity" (critical philosophy) and "suffering mankind" (the proletariat).[12] This formulation could seem to be a simple rhetorical trick, but the model of social critique that Marx articulated at the time was indeed based upon it. He maintained that the proletariat is a universal class because their sufferings are universal.[13] If an alliance between philosophy and the proletariat is possible, that is because the proletariat is a philosophical class insofar as it is universal. Being composed of all individuals who are excluded from the advantages of social life, it is no longer linked to any particular interest, but only to the universal interest in ceasing to lead an inhuman life. And so it must be viewed as the medium for the historical realization of the universality that philosophy aims at. Here, the genesis of suffering is no longer ontological, but rather social. Marx suggests that the stakes of suffering are larger than their psychological or conscious appearances because they are social, but he offers no theory of the passage from social processes to their psychological effects. Ultimately, he offers a simple sociological extrapolation of suffering, whereas Schopenhauer proposed a metaphysical extrapolation. The primary value of Marx's elaboration lies elsewhere—it lies in the alternative paradigm to that of conflict, the paradigm of alienation. Whereas Schopenhauer connected suffering to the constraints exercised upon a life conceived as a dynamism anterior to the social, Marx links it to the loss of social supports for life, which in turn supposes that human life is posited from the beginning as fully social. Conflict, or alienation?[14] The implications of this dichotomy for the status of psychic suffering are twofold. They are linked, on the one hand, to the characterization of the distresses specific to psychic suffering, and to the critique of social conditions that produce them: Should these problems be understood as impediments to action or rather as forms of a loss of self (becoming part of what one does not wish to be: the loss of a positive self-image)? Must society be critiqued only because it exercises constraints, or also because it is established within a pathological context where the social supports for life (and the constraints linked to them) are lacking and where this lack undermines the horizons of expectation—and, even more generally, psychic life itself? On the other hand, the implications of this dichotomy are linked to the interpretation of what kinds of processes produce psychic suffering: Is psychic suffering socially originated only because of the social constraints exercised upon a life governed by a dynamism that, in itself, could be equally social or presocial; or is psychic suffering social in a stronger sense, because it results from the nonsatisfaction of a demand that is, in itself, fundamentally intersubjective? Is suffering social because the constraints encountered by life are of social provenance, or because life cannot manage to satisfy something that is, in itself, fundamentally intersubjective and communicative?

Conflict, or alienation? The question arises on at least three levels: that of the psychosocial clinic; that of the description of pathogenic social processes; and that of the metapsychological description of intrapsychic mechanisms that transmit social processes. The psychosocial clinic, by paying particular attention to extreme cases such as "self-exclusion syndrome,"[15] indeed offers a description in terms of alienation. It seems quite clear, moreover, that the homeless and the long-term unemployed do not suffer only from their integration into social relations of domination (institutional stigmatization for the latter; and for the former, extremely devaluing interactions with the "included" and insertion in social relations in which extreme forms of violence can prevail[16]), but also from the loss of social support. If we admit the existence of an essential link between social precariousness and psychic suffering, we will have to conclude that psychic suffering is better explained by a loss of social supports for life than by processes of domination. And then, the whole issue will be to determine whether it is better to understand this loss according to the logic of "exclusion" or that of "disaffiliation," understanding by the latter a multiform process of desocialization that traverses the entirety of social life.[17] The loss of social supports is the progenitor of psychic problems precisely because it makes individuals more vulnerable to the violence of the social situations in which they are inserted, in such a way that the models of alienation and of conflict must ultimately be completed by each other. The metapsychological problem is thus to determine if psychic suffering can be understood without making reference to the Freudian paradigm of conflict[18] and how his theory of the psychic apparatus can explain the communicative dimension of psychic suffering, a dimension evidenced by the mirrored relations between the more-or-less expressed suffering of the excluded, and the suffering explicitly formulated by psychosocial therapists and social workers. These problems are engaged by specific clinical, sociological, and psychoanalytic forms of expertise that seem to shield themselves from philosophical

interrogation. It is nonetheless possible to ask ourselves whether a philosophical model exists that could grasp what seems to be demanded by the
problem of psychic suffering; namely, the causal effects of devaluing social
contexts and loss of social support upon a vulnerable subjective life.

DISAFFILIATION AND A POSITIVE RELATION TO ONESELF

If it is appropriate to make use of the model of recognition, that is because
the issue of the fragility of a positive relation to oneself, and the issue of
social relations' repercussions on the positive relation to oneself, seem to be
at the heart of the problematic of psychic suffering. Many writers acknowledge that the forms of suffering most characteristic of the extended economic and social crisis we are experiencing are linked to different ways in
which a positive relation to oneself can collapse (loss of self-esteem, shame,
depression, suicidal thoughts[19]), phenomena that can be designated notably with the categories of "narcissistic problems"[20] and "identity crises."[21]
The theory of recognition makes it possible to specify the nature of the
relation that the transformations of social relations have with the collapse
of a positive relation to oneself.

To speak of a positive self-image is to speak of the ways in which a
self-image is established through primary identifications with "significant
others" such as one's parents and other role models; of the ways in which
narcissism feeds off of one's relation to others; and of the ways in which
various assumed social roles come to constitute the image we have of our
own worth. As a positive relation to oneself is subjectively established in
recognitive relations, it is characterized by a form of vulnerability to intersubjective relations that give rise to the denial of recognition. This theme,
which makes up the heart of the theory of recognition, can be applied just as
well to psychic suffering in the broad sense (socially originated "malaise")
as in the narrow sense (symptoms specific to nonpathological psychic suffering in situations of extreme disaffiliation).

Analyzed in terms of recognition, psychic suffering in the narrow sense
will appear as the most extreme form of the negation of a positive relation to
oneself—a form in which, since a positive image can no longer be maintained
by any rewarding relation with an other, the ego loses the possibility to view
itself as the bearer of value and to draw positively upon its own resources to
compensate for the present and past sorrows of one's life. One can then be

led to flee any contact with oneself, or with the reality that forces one to confront oneself, whether through voluntary behaviors (such as alcoholism and drug abuse[22]) or through the establishment of specific psychic dispositions. Interpreted in terms of recognition, psychic suffering appears simultaneously as the effect of a failure to meet expectations oriented toward the social, and as a situation in which one's relations to others take a form that no longer allows the individual to maintain a relation to himself—in other words, in an intersubjective situation structured as alienation. Indeed, specialists in psychosocial intervention describe psychic suffering in the narrow sense in terms of an intersubjectivist concept of alienation: "It happens that certain patients, at certain moments, as a result of such disappointments in their encounters [with others], or even of the concrete, real risks of an encounter, can entirely believe that having a psychic life is simply not worth it."[23]

The specificity of this kind of effect that intersubjective relations have upon subjective life will become clearer if we compare the different *types* of *social genesis* of suffering. When the denial of recognition is produced by the action of a particular individual, or as a result of a degrading situation that remains exceptional and nontraumatic, the denial of recognition creates a narcissistic wound that can be called moral suffering. In adulthood, this kind of suffering is more normal than pathological, and it expresses part of the dynamism of a life that includes the struggle against suffering as an essential dimension (it is on the basis of this hardly disputable evidence that Nietzsche, for example, grounds his positive evaluation of suffering). But one's positive relation to oneself can be more profoundly affected, either by traumas that can themselves be "intrapsychic" (to the extent that they characterize one's most private psychic history) or "exogenous" (insofar as they are part of the violence of a situation that is experienced as an event that seems to shatter an individual's life history).[24] In this latter case, the violence can be produced either by events that are not directly impacted by social conditions (such as rape, or the disappearance of a loved one), or by events that are directly impacted by social conditions (the economic causes of ecological catastrophes like Bhopal; the political or ethnic causes of genocides, civil wars, etc.). Socially originated traumatic violence defines a first form of *"social suffering."*[25] [ii] This form, which refers

ii. Note also that here (and in quotations and italicized in Table 7.1)—and only in these two instances—Renault uses the phrase "social suffering" in English, in the French text.

back to the model of conflict, does not have any necessary connection with the issue of recognition, and does not correspond either to what is indicated by the concept of psychic suffering or to what is meant by "social suffering" in France.

Moreover, the positive relation to oneself can be profoundly affected by a violence whose effects are linked to routinization rather than the power of a traumatic event. This kind of suffering most often depends upon the institutionalization of symbolic forms of violence—endlessly repeated because they are embodied in institutions; routinized because what belongs to the symbolic order most often remains, at least partially, invisible. Insofar as it is tied to the institutionalization of violence, this kind of suffering must be called social; and insofar as it is connected to symbolic violence, it finds its social genesis in the denial of recognition.

The kind of violence that characterizes social suffering (the lower right box in the table) can take different forms: devaluing forms of recognition, which prohibit the ego from valuing its existence and in this way increases the weight of past and present sorrows, even to the point of making life extremely onerous (this is the case par excellence in suffering at work); disqualifying social relations, which lead to a negative relation to oneself and the internalization of shame (this is the case par excellence for the long-term unemployed and the recipients of the RMI [guaranteed minimum income],[26] for whom suffering takes the form of depreciative feelings rather than onerousness); and finally, [forms of] nonrecognition which seem to lead not only to the weakening of a positive relation to oneself (onerousness), or to the establishment of a negative relation to oneself (internalization of shame), but [also] to the destruction of one's relation to oneself. This third

TABLE 7.1

	Individual causes	*Social causes*
Normal violence	Individual difficulties	Social difficulties
Intrapsychic traumatic violence	Neuroses and psychoses	Neuroses and psychoses
Exogenous traumatic violence	Trauma	*"Social suffering"* (the first form, i.e., socially originated traumatic violence)
Routinized (institutionalized) violence		Social suffering

type of suffering characterizes psychic suffering in the narrow sense. In the case of the institutionalization of forms of extreme symbolic violence—such as the type that homeless "bums" inflict upon each other, and suffer from passersby and institutions—networks of sociability no longer offer any support. The only escape is a permanent enlistment of various defense mechanisms and a denial of reality, whose methods include adaptation and an alienating identification with the situation—and thus with suffering[27]—which can be called "self-exclusion syndrome."[28] In these situations of extreme disaffiliation, it is sometimes the narcissistic mirror itself which is shattered, as is shown, for instance, in situations where shame gives way to a complete absence of inhibitions:

With the destruction of all inhibitions—and this is what is demonstrated by individuals who will relieve and evacuate themselves in full view of everyone—exclusion reinforces, in terrifying fashion, its psychotic effects. It produces a subject whose libidinal investment not only in his image, but also in his earliest oral and anal eroticism has been destroyed, a subject denied any privacy or modesty, a subject denied at both the anthropological and the psychic levels any hope of sharing.[29]

It will be noted, however, that alienation is never total, and that it is sometimes enough, for example, to establish a relationship of trust with an extremely desocialized homeless person in order for an assertion that he is homeless by choice—or for a declaration of shamelessness—to appear as mere bravado. Here again, this is because alienation is never so complete a voiding of the self that no reestablishment would be possible:[30] even in pieces, something of the relation to oneself remains.

We see, in this way, that a typology of the forms of denial of recognition—those forms of denial of recognition that are associated with different kinds of injury to a positive relation to oneself—manages simultaneously to explain the general connection between psychic suffering and disaffiliation, some of the specificities of psychic suffering in the strict sense, and a structure common to different ideal types of psychic suffering in the broad

TABLE 7.2

Relation to oneself	Positive and weakened	Inverted	Broken
Psychic suffering	Onerousness (malaise)	Internalization of shame (malaise)	Psychic suffering in the narrow sense

sense. To be sure, the kind of denial of recognition indicated by the concept of disaffiliation seems to be different in nature from the kind maintained in extreme situations of massive desocialization—to the extent that it entails the weakening of intersubjective supports for life, rather than the radical failure of social supports; and the loss of rewarding social relations, rather than insertion in extremely devaluing and violent social relations. But as the concept of disaffiliation indicates a general dynamic of degradation of stable and rewarding social relations, it makes it possible to locate the social relations typical of radical desocialization on a continuum for which they represent only the most extreme forms. By modeling this continuum in terms of recognition, we can successfully distinguish certain typical effects of disaffiliation on subjective life, while also explaining their formal unity: between (a) the psychic suffering of the worker in a precarious position or in degraded working conditions (onerousness linked to the weakening of one's positive relation to oneself), (b) that of the long-term unemployed (shame and internalization of shame linked to the *inversion* from a positive relation to oneself to a negative relation to oneself), and (c) that of victims of the most extreme forms of desocialization (shamelessness, and a sacrifice of the psyche indicating a form of *rupture* of the relation to oneself), there is no real break in continuity.

Moreover, this typology of forms of recognition makes it possible to distinguish different forms of socially originated suffering from a perspective that is not only concerned with the form of this suffering (onerousness, devaluation, sacrifice of the psyche), but also its very object: (a) the destroyed *self-confidence* in homeless people who no longer manage to find a feeling of their own corporal and affective integrity in the relations they maintain with people in their world and people in the other world (ours)—a situation so paradoxical that it can lead to an absence of suffering due to an "affective-cognitive inhibition"[31] such that self-mutilation can constitute the only available means for reestablishing contact with the bodily ego; (b) the damaged *self-respect* in suburban youths[iii] for whom school, center-city and downtown business districts, paid work, and nightclubs all communicate an image of failure and inferiority; (c) the weakened *self-esteem* in employees who no longer manage to work in conditions that would allow them to impart a minimum of value to their activity, such that they are no

---

iii. Suburban youths, in a French context; inner-city youths, in an American context.

longer allowed to transform the suffering of work into satisfaction; and (d) the damaged *self-respect* and destroyed *self-esteem* of the long-term unemployed who so often experience the loss of rewarding social relations accompanying the loss of work not only as a negation of the social value of their lives, but also as a humiliation and a general deprivation.[32]

The hypothesis that I have just presented makes it possible to explain the unity of different forms of psychic suffering, and to locate the many phenomena that can be encompassed within the problematic of social suffering, on a continuum. If the social question today warrants being characterized as much in terms of social injustice as of social pathology, this is because the transformations of the institutional structure of society and of social relations—the traditional objects of a characterization in terms of justice—are accompanied by effects of serious subjective disorganization, one of the repercussions of which is violence. It is difficult not to diagnose a weakening of a positive relation to oneself in certain forms of violence that are expressed in areas of social relegation. Social spaces that remain intact or relatively intact (schools, downtowns, etc.) can only offer a devaluing socialization to many individuals—one that, rather than contributing to their insertion into larger social circles, pushes them off into spaces of relegation and can lead them to a general rejection of the external social order. The denial of recognition and the symbolic violence that one can encounter upon stepping beyond the boundaries of the "projects" (academic failure, racial profiling in upscale neighborhoods, etc.) can lead one to withdraw back into the projects, and to view them as the only place where one can obtain recognition and validation.[33] Whence come these acts of violence based in a defense of the only value (honor tied to one's neighborhood) proving that one is not a "nothing."

We have just considered examples of forms of social suffering typically linked to clearly identifiable denials of recognition. The denial of recognition suffered by the homeless and by youths in neglected neighborhoods corresponds to a violence that, despite being routinized, is at least partially visible and can be expressed by the individuals who are victimized by it (as is testified, for example, by the transformation of shame into hate on the part of some homeless individuals,[34] or the combination of a demand for "respect" and a declaration that "I am full of hatred" on the part of some "suburban youths"). The same does not hold for those forms of routinized symbolic violence that can be produced by familial environments or certain forms of contemporary organization of work—as described, for example, in a striking article in *Actes de la Recherche en Sciences Sociales*,[35] where the authors argue that the concomitant requirement for physical and mental conformity to a corporate image, on the one hand; and working in an open office plan, on the other, can subject employees to psychic pressure such that, once entirely internalized, the medical office is the only place where personal expression is possible. The symbolic violence of a denial of recognition is all that much worse, given that the suffering it engenders is unable to be recognized or acknowledged, masked as it is by the institution's operation and its own self-justification.

THE CONSEQUENCES OF DENIAL OF RECOGNITION

When the injury to a positive relation to oneself is not so profound as to lead to a state of "shamelessness" (as the homeless are, often misleadingly, described), or to an "absence of demands" (in the psychoanalytic sense),[36] it manifests precisely as a demand for recognition—whether it comes in homeless individuals' social fantasies (that is, in the mythologized tales of their past life, their defiance of authority, and their grandiose plans),[37] in suburban youths' demands for "respect" (or even by the dramatization of their own individual worth in rappers' "ego trips"), or in the articulated demand for recognition of the reality and the value of one's work. But not every denial of recognition ends in a demand for recognition, whether directly expressed in demands for recognition of a social function (as in the social struggles of nurses and teachers), or indirectly through a demand for respect. What follows from the denial of recognition is more complex. We can distinguish at least five major outcomes that can result from a denial of recognition.

The first form corresponds to situations of the most extreme desocialization, where the destruction of a positive relation to oneself leads to the loss of inhibitions and an identification of life exclusively with the satisfaction of needs: "An identification that has given up on any ideal points that the narcissistic mirror might present will aim instead for a desperate collaboration with scum."[38] The second form corresponds to cases where the positive relation to oneself is inverted—is no longer present except as the instrument of the worst devaluing of the self, as in the case of internalized shame (for example, the negative self-image of the long-term unemployed individual who identifies himself as a "good for nothing" and a socially useless creature). In both of these cases, we are dealing with an internalization of a degraded image of oneself as communicated by an other or, more generally, by the modalities of social interaction—an internalization that is accompanied by a loss of the capacity to react against violent situations experienced in the past and that the individual is still victimized by. Only psychosocial intervention and the modification of one's social context will thus be able to awaken a desire to reestablish a positive relation to oneself.

But the individual is still capable of reacting: even shame can be reactive.[39] Three kinds of reaction to social contempt can be distinguished. The first form is a self-destructive reaction in which violence is not directed against the violent situation itself, but against the ego which becomes an object of hate by virtue of its nonconformity with the ego-ideal. Suicidal violence— and perhaps more generally (if we believe Patrick Baudry) also the various forms of risk-taking behavior[40]—are examples of this first kind of reaction. The second form of reaction corresponds to what Donald W. Winnicott called "the antisocial tendency." Here it is a matter of violence that is directed against the violent situation itself (against the physical and symbolic environment), and which can be interpreted as an attempt aimed at the reestablishment of a lost environment that would be likely to satisfy the ego's needs.[41] A third form of reaction to a denial of recognition corresponds to claims consciously directed against a violent situation, whether through a discursive assertion of certain demands (for respect or for recognition) or through protest action, ranging from social movements that occur within a legal framework to various forms of illegal violence against purported or presumed sources of social violence.

These are not the only possible results of a denial of recognition. Specialists in adolescent violence insist on the fact that violence is always an expression of suffering, and that a lack of recognition of violent behavior by one's family and friends is worse than the denial of recognition that produced the initial suffering. The lack of recognition of a reactive violence by one's family and friends can take two forms: it can occur when family and friends do not want to see that the violence has meaning, that it has at least some legitimacy; or, still more radically, when they don't even want to see that this violence exists. In both cases, it constitutes a way of refusing to recognize that something of an individual's value is being expressed through this violent behavior. The authors of the report *Violence et souffrance à l'adolescence* insist upon the fact that adolescents' relations with their family and friends are thereby lastingly compromised.[42] That a denial of recognition would be even worse once it has been thus raised to a second power—or that in any case it would engender new forms of suffering—can be observed, it seems, in phenomena related to social suffering. It is possible, in fact, to interpret Christophe Dejours's analyses in *Souffrance en France*[43] according to this logic of denial of recognition taken to the second power. In the context of a degradation of working conditions, what is broken first of all are the means for having one's work recognized by management and one's work collective; this makes it impossible to transmute suffering at work into satisfaction at work; that is, it leads to an increase in suffering. Now, in a context of high unemployment, those who have employment are deemed to be in an enviable position, in such a way that public recognition of their own suffering is henceforth rendered impossible. This is misrecognition of the effects of a first misrecognition; and this denial of recognition to the second power deepens the suffering that is experienced. It is likely that the working conditions of hospital staff in psychiatric institutions—and even of social workers, given that they are always in the presence of individuals who clearly suffer much more than they do—leads to an analogous kind of denial of recognition that generates a similar type of suffering.[44]

CAN SUFFERING BE DEINSTITUTIONALIZED?

The theory of recognition is not only useful for the etiology of suffering. It also identifies the ego's fundamental needs that may or may not be satisfied in the framework of intersubjective relations. Degrading or devaluing intersubjective relations produces social suffering when these degraded relations are socially established. This brings us back to the political problem of the transformation of institutions that structurally produce a degraded or devalued image of individuals who are socialized within them; that is, institutions that destroy their relation to themselves. Insofar as this suffering is produced in determinate social contexts, and insofar as it is (in the same way) limited to certain groups of individuals, it merits being considered a socially originated inequality in life conditions—or as a form of social injustice. However, it is clear that this kind of injustice greatly exceeds the parameters within which debates about justice are usually confined.

Asked from the perspective of a theory of recognition, the question of social justice greatly exceeds the sphere to which political problems tend to be restricted: [a traditional sphere defined by] respect for formal rights; the distribution of honors and wealth; and social rights (in the traditional sense of rights) to a set of goods (income), transactions (employment), and services (housing, education, etc.). Not only does the question [of social justice as] raised by the theory of recognition exceed this sphere, but it [also] requires that this sphere be enlarged. From the perspective of the theory of recognition, political problems are concerned with the entirety of our lives, in our capacity as social beings whose lives are always lived within institutions—lives, however, that can never be reduced to an institutionalized life, for they can be brought to the point of suffering from these institutions and [hence] rejecting them. The theory of recognition that I have been presenting demands that we ask political questions within the framework of an interrogation of our relations to all institutions. It brings us to believe that "the real political task in a society such as ours is to criticize the workings of institutions."[45]

As a general rule, it is not easy to know how we ought to live with our institutions. If the latter cannot be reduced to frameworks of oppression, the political question becomes not how to destroy them, but how to transform them—and according to which principles? The traditional political questions of equitable distribution of wealth, or respect for universal rights, can be resolved virtually a priori, because it is possible to make use, on this point, of the most widely accepted representations of justice and dignity. But this kind of social critique is not enough to identify the injustices produced by institutions. On the one hand, these institutions are specific social settings governed by particular [systems of] social logic, and a first difficulty derives from not automatically knowing which supplemental principles should be applied in order to take these specificities into account and to determine how the institutions ought to be transformed. To resolve this problem, we would need to make reference to an expanded definition of justice: one that, starting from a constitutive concept of recognition, would manage to describe from an immanent perspective the injustices produced by these institutions, as well as the practical and normative dynamics that would make it possible to struggle against them. A second difficulty consists in the fact that our lives are always determined by those institutions that we must transform, in such a way that we are stakeholders in the transformation that we would have the exterior world undergo, and in such a way that it is thus difficult for us to judge in advance the legitimacy of our expectations for this transformation. Because the expanded definition of justice in recognitive terms is only qualitative, and because we are dependent on institutions, the solution can only come about through some kind of institutional bricolage; that is, a gradual and experimental process of reciprocal transformation of the institutional presuppositions of our lives and also of our expectations with regard to institutions—a process whose normative resources I have tried to describe by highlighting personal identity and suffering as critical elements immanent to the process of socialization.

The problematic of suffering is essential for a social critique that is attentive to the fact that life is always both lived within institutions, and yet also irreducible to this "institutionalization," precisely because suffering is the index for a misalignment between the needs of the ego and its institutional contexts. This is quite likely the most fundamental rationale for an expansion of a definition of social justice that would take suffering into account. If, for example, one wanted to subject those monstrous edifices of institutionalized injustice—prisons—to critique, it would probably be necessary to condemn all their human rights violations and all of their various modes of contempt for prisoners' moral and physical integrity. But this classic approach to injustice is not enough, for it is also necessary to take into account the fact that prisons impose power relations upon the prisoners as well as their guards, power relations that make prisoners lose any sense of the various modes of communication they could maintain with each other, and that coerce prisoners into completely distorted intersubjective relations to which they are able to adapt only at the price of heavy subjective difficulties—a price so high it can hardly be expressed.[46] Here again, the injustice of the situation is tied to a denial of recognition raised to the second power; here again, suffering is both a symptom and an element: it is both suffering linked to the practical nonrecognition of the ego's needs, and a denial of this suffering because linguistic communication has no meaning except when integrated within a network of recognitive relations that are lacking here. But what is true for penal institutions is also true, albeit to a lesser degree, for other institutions in which injustice comes about through suffering and through the denial of recognition of suffering—to be sure, not because communication is completely distorted in them, but because communication is structured by principles of justification (as well as by definitions of justice) that often preclude it from being fully expressed and taken into account. The organization of contemporary workplaces gives an illustration of this, as I have already noted.

The problematic of suffering fulfills another crucial function for a social critique marked by attentiveness to the fact that life is always both lived within institutions and irreducible to this "institutionalization." In fact, there can also be a deinstitutionalization of individuals' lives (or a dynamics of deinstitutionalization), at which point suffering no longer serves as the index of a maladjustment with the ego's needs, but rather as the index of the impossibility of satisfying them. In such a case, the injustice of the situation is wholly encompassed in psychic suffering in the strict sense, even if we run up here against the limits of the domain of justice. In situations of extreme desocialization, the degradation of conditions of life should be analyzed with reference to at least two kinds of social processes, which are to be understood as dynamics of deinstitutionalization (and not merely as forms of social relegation): looking back [to identify] the social processes that have played a role in one's personal trajectory (and the concept of disaffiliation will probably find an immediate applicability here); looking forward [to identify] social processes in which the denial of recognition is so extreme that nothing is left for the individual to do but either identify with the denial of recognition or abandon any sense of oneself. This explains why it is difficult to describe the situation as a social injustice: on the one hand, because catastrophic social trajectories have biographical or idiosyncratic conditions and not only social conditions; on the other, because it is difficult to characterize a situation as an injustice when the individuals concerned seem entirely unable to comprehend it as unjust, even when they are provided with an adequate framework of [the idea of] injustice. Up to this point, I have described the experience of injustice as the nonsatisfaction of fundamental normative expectations. But what could the very idea of normative expectations mean for a homeless individual who tends to define his life in terms of the satisfaction of basic physical needs while also identifying with the situation? The problem is clearer still in cases of mental illness. How can a demand for recognition of the value of one's psychophysical life, of freedom, of social life, and of identity retain any meaning when the psyche is totally broken down by psychosis?

Olivier Douville notes, regarding psychosocial intervention, that a "psychologization of the social runs the risk of introducing additional exclusions and segregations."[47] Psychosocial intervention has generally been shown to be aware of the risks of imprisoning twice over, through identification as someone who is "mentally ill," a subject who is already imprisoned by the socially denigrated identification of "bum".[48] On this point, Sylvie Quesemand Zucca insists on the fact that a psychiatrist must become aware that "in a given interaction with one of the excluded, there are not two (the caregiver and the excluded) but three (the caregiver, the excluded, and a third, represented here as the social)."[49] The psychiatrist represents social contempt itself—not as a psychiatrist representing a particular social function and endowed with a specific expertise, but as a positively socialized individual—even though he is working toward resolving the suffering of a desocialized individual, a suffering that results, at least in part, from a negative socialization. How could he not raise social contempt to a second power, in implicitly stating that "you are a bum, and now, thanks to me, you will be a madman as well"? A similar question arises with respect to mental illness: How could we avoid imprisoning individuals who suffer from psychoses in the "mentally ill identity" that the rest of the social world throws at them, that of senseless speech and complete irresponsibility? Even when institutional responses are unable to focus on the social factors that have produced a denial of recognition, as in psychiatry, the requirement that we avoid raising the denial of recognition to the second power clearly remains a principle of justice.

CONCLUSION

Critique as a Voice Against Injustice

I argued in the introduction that the model of "taking sides" is the only one that will allow political philosophy to adequately grasp and to explicitly assume its own political dimension. I have also suggested that it is only when social critique is understood as an *instrument* engaged in political struggles that the critical function of theory can be truly understood as taking sides. In a certain respect, the concept of a spokesperson or voice serves to summarize this instrumentalist conception of critique, while also adding three specifications: first, to be effective as such an instrument, theoretical social critique should try to express as much as possible what is at stake in the experiences of injustice of those whose concerns are taken up by social critique (voice then means *expressivity*); second, it also should subject to criticism forms of social injustice that are associated with silenced or muted experiences of injustice (voice then means *giving voice* to muted persons); thirdly, whatever form it may take, the discourse of theoretical critique will be subject to other norms than those of the discourse of individuals who experience injustice or who participate in a social struggle (voice then means *the voice of an other*, at best that of a spokesperson).[1] The concept of a spokesperson is part of an instrumentalist model of social critique that can itself take two distinct forms—forms that are not mutually exclusive (they should be connected to each other)—depending on whether the theoretical contribution to critique is conceived as the *transfer point* or *relay* for already constituted political practices, or as the *creation* of a voice that ought to be a constitutive element of political practices.

When Marx states, in the postface to the second edition of *Capital*, that the critique of political economy represents the proletariat; when Antonio Gramsci conceives the critical function in terms of a model of the "organic intellectual"; or when feminist critique presents itself as the theoretical expression of a "different voice,"[2] theory is always in a relation of *reflection* upon that for which it takes sides. It is the transfer point for political practices that have already found their own discourse, or for ethical discourses that have not yet found their politics, but it always postulates an established discourse (which, moreover, can speak for itself[3]) to which it is content to give theoretical form by reflecting upon its presuppositions and implications. But it is also possible to conceive of theoretical critique as the transfer point for political practices without presupposing any such reflective relation. This was, for example, the aim of Michel Foucault and Gilles Deleuze, who rejected this conception of theory as reflection. While still keeping the model of social critique as a transfer point, they wanted to make theoretical critique the *expression* of innovative political practices rather than a (self-) reflection upon those discourses and practices.[4] [In this context,] theoretical critique was thus still conceived as a spokesperson or voice, but what is spoken was no longer necessarily an already established political or ethical discourse, although it could be a form of speech trying to find itself in existing political practices. For Foucault or Deleuze, the theoretician would not hesitate to suggest new concepts to the actors in these practices.

Regardless of how the model of a voice is elaborated when conceived as a transfer point, theoretical critique understands itself here as the theoretical extension of practical and normative dynamics that are independently established—dynamics that, ultimately, theoretical critique serves only to amplify and reformulate. These dynamics could emerge from the contradictions of the social world, as in Marx. Theoretical critique would then display these contradictions while also showing that they undermine the justification for the present system, and that the only possible solution is a radical transformation of the existing state of things. These dynamics could also take the forms of deterritorialization and exodus, as in Deleuze and Negri. Theoretical critique would then be able to show off creative or revolutionary powers. In all of these cases, theoretical critique will be understood as the transfer point for largely self-sufficient political dynamics—and this is what demarcates the limits of this model. Today, in fact, social critique seems to face different challenges: on the one hand, those stemming from various forms of social injustice that, while visible, are nevertheless not taken up as concerns by powerful political movements; on the other hand, challenges stemming from various forms of social injustice that remain invisible. At the same time, it is no longer possible to rely solely upon the contradictions of the social world in order to envisage its possible transformation. And if forms of "escapism" (escape from paid work, the rejection of traditional modes of political participation, "temporary autonomous zones," etc.) have had an undeniable subversive impact, they are only available to those who still have the freedom to escape from forms of domination supported by powerful justificatory discourses; that is, those who are not fighting against the fear of becoming excluded from stable social relations, and those who are not stuck in social relations marked by violence and a failure of social supports. Social critique cannot merely adopt the perspective of structural contradictions and class struggle (the perspective of exploitation), nor that of margins defined by lines of flight (the perspective of minorities); it must also articulate a view "from below" in order to demystify the justifications that perpetuate injustice (the perspective of the dominated) and a view "from the side" to account for all the invisible injustices (the perspective of the deprived).

It is for these reasons that the spokesperson must also be a stakeholder in the *creation* of political discourses and practices, and not simply a transfer point. The very object of social critique is defined today by situations in which a number of cognitive (or symbolic—or ideological, if you prefer) obstacles prevent individuals from grasping the injustice of their situations and from enlisting in a conscious political struggle, in such a way that the theoretical instrument must not so much relay a discourse or practices as contribute to their creation. This model of a spokesperson conceived as productive or creative has already been articulated by Étienne de La Boétie in his *Discourse on Voluntary Servitude*. And it is to La Boétie, as it happens, that Bourdieu alludes when he interprets sociology's critical function through the concept of a spokesperson.[5] To be sure, it would be difficult to incorporate everything that Bourdieu says about the political function of the social sciences within the concept of a spokesperson. Recall, in fact, that his opposition between science and *doxa*, as well as his conception of the authentic intellectual as a representative of the universal, bring him rather close to a rationalist model of social critique—even if, quite often, his political activity leads him toward the instrumentalist model upon which the idea of a spokesperson indeed depends. Recall as well that Bourdieu's model of social critique, when it is instrumentalist and not rationalist, should be viewed as a fusing of two conceptions of the spokesperson. Bourdieu, who remains trapped by a definition of politics as "struggles about classification" in an integrated social order, tends in fact to understand the critical function in terms of *legitimation* of dominated social groups' vision of the world, according to a relation that thus remains in the mode of *reflection* rather than *creation.*

Theoretical critique as a voice actively working toward the creation of demands—this is the model I have wanted to employ in attempting to rebuild (more precisely, in attempting *both* to rearticulate *and* to enlarge or expand) the definitions of justice by starting from the experience of injustice. With respect to the reformulation of definitions of justice, I have argued for adopting a perspective from below, so that the normative discourse could rediscover social struggles directed against those injustices that the definitions of justice allow to be identified. With respect to the expansion of these definitions, I have argued for adopting a perspective "from the side," in order to integrate into the normative discourse various forms of injustice that it has been unable to identify as such. But in both respects, I have tried to overcome obstacles that, in the established normative vocabulary, interfere with the development of political practices and discourses directed against injustice. My aim was not simply to effect a theoretical transmission or relay of these struggles, but to demonstrate the possibility of contributing, by means of theoretical instruments, to the development of struggles and practices against injustice.

If such a conception of the spokesperson is vital for social critique today, this is doubtless because a number of social struggles have caused this political figure to emerge. The concepts of exclusion and of social suffering, however we may assess their analytical relevance and their descriptive fruitfulness, designate social transformations that bring new forms of injustice to light and new social struggles to the surface—struggles such as those of the deprived. These struggles, as we have seen, have a very direct connection to the spokesperson's political function. But of course, the concept of a spokesperson or voice as a model of theoretical critique cannot be reduced to the political function of a spokesperson or to the crucial role this function plays in some social movements. It also designates a kind of theoretical critique that can embrace the perspective of other kinds of social movements (social struggles as well as struggles for identity). With respect to the struggles of the deprived, theoretical critique is likely to intervene as a theoretical spokesperson in the articulation of "frames of injustice" (which does not mean that philosophy is able to create these frames by itself, or to guide—or even give rise to—these social movements). With respect to social struggles and struggles for identity, theoretical critique extends these struggles: as a theoretical voice for social movements whose political claims are articulated independently of a political spokesperson, and even more independently of a theoretical spokesperson. In that case, the theoretical spokesperson is a voice understood not as creative, but as a relay for a social struggle—a relay that is simultaneously its expression and its reflection, because it extends the imperfect hermeneutic (both expressive and reflective) at the heart of the struggle's normative dynamics. The theoretical model of a spokesperson thus only has general relevance by virtue of its equivocation. It makes it possible to give an account, in theoretical critique, of the problems posed by new forms of injustice, and of the particularities of struggles that are oriented against them, without for all that taking something new as the only object of social critique and thereby dismissing all those who still suffer from more traditional forms of injustice. It makes it possible to rethink social critique in general—the theoretical critique of different forms of injustice, and the practical critique of different kinds of social movements—by bringing its attention to the entire spectrum of social injustice.

To understand theoretical critique as a spokesperson or voice is also to take into account the necessity of a struggle against the forms of ideology that mask the experience of injustice today. One of the specific tasks of the voice of the spokesperson, be it as a transfer point for existing struggles or as a contributor to the emergence of some struggles, is to struggle with theoretical means against the existing forms of public justification of contemporary social injustice. In the introduction, I noted the paradoxical fact that an increase in injustices has not been accompanied by a strengthening of discourses of legitimation. The inequalities have not yet disappeared, but their justifications follow different paths. They come about through justificatory discourses immanent in certain practices of injustice, and by the erasure or "invisibilization" of other forms of injustice.

Of course, social action has always presupposed a need for justifications— at least in order to provide individuals the means to resolve those conflicts liable to give rise to interaction—but in contemporary societies, the function of principles of justification seem to be of a different nature. Social differentiation and the individualization of social relations imply that the problem of how to adjust one's plans of action has become ever more crucial, and the possibility of conflict in interaction has become ever greater. Moreover, the development of various forms of social injustice, no longer exclusively in the margins of society or in social spheres hidden from the view of the vast majority (such as in prisons, factories, and mines), implies that individuals would have ever more need for principles of justification to strengthen their resolve to act, despite the visibility of their at least passive participation in injustice. The need to justify oneself in the eyes of others and in one's own eyes will continue to grow, and will thus make routinized justification a powerful contributor to the banalization of social injustice. And this gives rise to a new challenge for the characterization of typical forms of injustice: how to make visible all those injustices covered over by the discourse of justification in order to invalidate them—and thus to show them to be injustices that are indefensible.

Moreover, there is a kind of justification by means of "invisibilization," in the twin forms of dissimulation (or concealment) and understatement (or euphemism). The most intolerable injustices are difficult to portray in their full truth, whence the automatic tendency to conceal them or to understate them, which can be reinforced by social interests that encourage some social groups to mask the reality of social injustice in the actual world, and to minimize the reality and the gravity of its effects. Certain kinds of injustice are, more than others, the object of these sorts of dissimulations and euphemisms. It is typically the case for injustices connected to massive degradations of living conditions, even the debasement of life itself, and to the creation of vast populations living in slums and sometimes pushed to the extremity of selling their body or their organs to survive (the creation of "throw-away people").[6] Such injustices can no longer be legitimated, nor cloaked in discourses of justification. They have no other justification except the negative and indirect justification of "invisibilization." Something similar can be said concerning the understatement of, and euphemisms for, the living and working conditions of the dominated and deprived in our societies. This is evident in the masking of and dissimulation about the extreme conditions to which entire populations are reduced by the "structural adjustments" required by the International Monetary Fund.

Many nongovernmental organizations (NGOs) do try to raise the political problem of such injustices' visibility [or lack thereof]. But most of the time, they only bring a dramatic but brief spotlight to these problems, and this dramatization implies a form of depolitization that ultimately serves only to reinforce their invisibility—the only remedy for which is a description of these experiences of injustice in their full negativity. And this gives rise to another new challenge for the characterization of typical forms of injustice: to bring to light the disruptive reality of injustices—injustices that are excluded from our view when the social world is described as desirable and likely to satisfy us—in order to undermine the modalities of our identification with the world and to bring out what is, quite simply, intolerable.

NOTES

TRANSLATOR'S NOTE

1. Christophe Dejours, Jean-Philippe Deranty, Emmanuel Renault, and Nicholas H. Smith, *The Return of Work in Critical Theory: Self, Society, Politics* (New York: Columbia University Press, 2018), esp. chap. 4, quoted at p. 94.
2. Emmanuel Renault, *Social Suffering: Sociology, Psychology, Politics*, trans. Maude Dews (New York: Rowman & Littlefield, 2017), esp. chap. 3.
3. For example, Pierre Vergniaud was called "the voice [*porte-parole*] of the Revolution."

PREFACE

1. See for example Axel Honneth, "The Social Dynamics of Disrespect: On the Location of Critical Theory Today" and "Moral Consciousness and Class Domination: Some Problems in the Analysis of Hidden Morality," both in *Disrespect: The Normative Foundations of Critical Theory* (Malden, MA: Polity, 2007).
2. See Axel Honneth, "Critical Theory," in *The Fragmented World of the Social: Essays in Social and Political Philosophy* (Albany: SUNY Press, 1995), as well as the essays collected in *Pathologies of Reason: On the Legacy of Critical Theory* (New York: Columbia University Press, 2009).
3. Emmanuel Renault, "Philosophie politique et critique de la politique," *Actuel Marx*, no. 28 (August 2000): 97–114.
4. Pierre Bourdieu, *The Weight of the World: Social Suffering in Contemporary Society* (Stanford, CA: Stanford University Press, 1999); *Pascalian Meditations* (Stanford, CA: Stanford University Press, 2000).
5. Luc Boltanski and Eve Chiapello, *The New Spirit of Capitalism* (New York: Verso, 2007).

6. Christophe Dejours, *Souffrance en France: la banalisation de l'injustice sociale* (Paris: Seuil, 1998).

7. See Franck Fischbach, *Fichte et Hegel: la reconnaissance* (Paris: Presses Universitaires de France, 1999); Emmanuel Renault, *Mépris social: éthique et politique de la reconnaissance*, (Bègles, France: Éditions du Passant, 2000).

8. See Paul Ricoeur, *The Course of Recognition* (Cambridge, MA: Harvard University Press, 2005), 247–49, where he rejects the tendency to overestimate the phenomena of stigmatization in contemporary approaches to recognition. [This book was initially published in French as *Parcours de la reconnaissance* (Paris: Stock, 2004).]

9. See Axel Honneth, "A Fragmented World: On the Implicit Relevance of Lukács' Early Work" and "Foucault and Adorno: Two Forms of the Critique of Modernity," both in *Fragmented World*; "The Possibility of a Disclosing Critique of Society: The *Dialectic of Enlightenment* in Light of Current Debates in Social Criticism," in *Disrespect*; and "A Physiognomy of the Capitalist Form of Life: A Sketch of Adorno's Social Theory" and "Performing Justice: Adorno's Introduction to *Negative Dialectics*," both in *Pathologies*.

10. Axel Honneth, *Reification: A New Look at an Old Idea* (Oxford: Oxford University Press, 2008).

11. Axel Honneth, "Recognition as Ideology," in *The I in We: Studies in the Theory of Recognition* (Malden, MA: Polity, 2012); also in *Recognition and Power: Axel Honneth and the Tradition of Critical Social Theory*, ed. Bert van den Brink and David Owen (Cambridge: Cambridge University Press, 2007), 323–47.

12. Axel Honneth with Martin Hartmann, "Paradoxes of Capitalist Modernization: A Research Programme," in *The I in We*. See also Axel Honneth, ed., *Befreiung aus der Mündigkeit: Paradoxien des gegenwärtigen Kapitalismus* (New York: Campus Verlag, 2002).

13. Axel Honneth, "The Limits of Liberalism: On the Political-Ethical Discussion Concerning Communitarianism," in *Fragmented World*.

14. Axel Honneth, "The Social Dynamics of Disrespect: On the Location of Critical Theory Today" in *Disrespect*.

15. Axel Honneth, "Pathologies of the Social: The Past and Present of Social Philosophy" in *Disrespect*; also in D. M. Rasmussen, ed., *The Handbook of Critical Theory* (Oxford: Blackwell, 1996), 369–96.

16. Axel Honneth, *Desintegration: Bruchstücke einer soziologischen Zeitdiagnose* (Frankfurt am Main, Germany: Fischer, 1994).

17. See also the project begun in 2004 that led to the recent publication: Axel Honneth, Ophelia Lindemann, and Stephan Voswinkel, eds., *Strukturwandel der Anerkennung: Paradoxien sozialer Integration in der Gegenwart* (New York: Campus Verlag, 2013).

18. See Jean-Philippe Deranty, *Beyond Communication: A Critical Study of Axel Honneth's Social Philosophy* (Leiden, The Netherlands: Brill, 2009), 138–47, 208–210.

19. "Conflicting Publics," a series of six one-hour interviews on contemporary political thought with Arne Naess, Axel Honneth, Ernesto Laclau and Chantal Mouffe, George McRobie, Jean Bethke Elshtain, and John O'Neill; first broadcast on *The Knowledge Network*, Fall 1998. I cite from an uncorrected transcription that was once, but no longer, available on the internet. [A video recording of this interview is available at the Institute for the Humanities at Simon Fraser University in Vancouver, Canada.]

20. "Conflicting Publics," 3.

21. "Conflicting Publics," 7; transcription modified.

22. "Conflicting Publics," 3, 4.

23. "Conflicting Publics," 4. A bit later, Honneth compares the importance that he has given to the description of ordinary experiences to the way that Ernst Bloch had tried to identify utopian aspirations in ordinary practices and feelings, in a kind of "phenomenology of everyday experiences" (6).

24. If Honneth takes from Habermas the idea of an "internal rationality in communication" (3), he seeks to discover it beginning with negative experiences in which the normative presuppositions of the interaction are made known in a negative manner, precisely where Habermas had tried to identify those presuppositions through their positive expression in linguistic practices (3).

25. "Conflicting Publics," 6.

26. "Conflicting Publics," 3.

27. "Conflicting Publics," 6.

28. "Conflicting Publics," 6.

29. Emmanuel Renault, "Adorno: de la philosophie sociale à la théorie sociale," *Recherches sur la philosophie et le langage*, no. 28 (2012) : 229–58.

30. Emmanuel Renault, *Social Suffering: Sociology, Psychology, Politics*, trans. Maude Dews (Lanham, MD: Rowman & Littlefield, 2017).

31. Michael Walzer has underscored the abolitionist dimension of political concepts, with regard to equality, in the preface of *Spheres of Justice* (New York: Basic Books, 1983), xii.

32. See Walter Bryce Gallie, "Essentially contested concepts," *Proceedings of the Aristotelian Society* 56 (1955–1956): 167–98; republished in Walter Bryce Gallie, *Philosophy and the Historical Understanding* (New York: Schocken, 1968), 157–91). I will make use of his analysis, although limiting its domain of real pertinence to the political and disregarding its teleological aspects.

33. This reorientation is at the heart of his responses to Nancy Fraser in *Redistribution or Recognition?: A Political-Philosophical Exchange* (New York: Verso, 2003).

34. See the Afterword [Nachwort] to the 2003 revised German edition of *The Struggle for Recognition: Kampf um Anerkennung*, erw. ausg. (Frankfurt am Main, Germany: Suhrkamp, 2003).

35. I discuss the history of this distinction and how it is employed in contemporary debates in Emmanuel Renault, "Théorie critique et critique immanente," *Illusio*, no. 10/11 (2013): 257–78.

36. Axel Honneth, *Freedom's Right: The Social Foundations of Democratic Life* (New York: Columbia University Press, 2014).

37. Jean-Philippe Deranty, *Beyond Communication*; Jean-Philippe Deranty, "The Loss of Nature in Axel Honneth's Theory of Recognition. Rereading Mead with Merleau-Ponty," *Critical Horizons* 6 (2005): 153–81.

38. See for instance Heikki Ikäheimo and Arto Laitinen, eds., *Recognition and Social Ontology* (Dordrecht, The Netherlands: Brill, 2011).

39. On my debate with Honneth on this point, see Emmanuel Renault, "The Theory of Recognition and Critique of Institutions," and Axel Honneth's "Rejoinder" in Danielle Petherbridge, ed., *Axel Honneth: Critical Essays. With a Reply by Axel Honneth* (Dordrecht, The Netherlands: Brill, 2011), 207–31, 391–421.

40. See Emmanuel Renault, *Social Suffering*, chap. 3.

41. On these questions, see esp. Emmanuel Renault, "What is the Use of the Notion of Recognition?" *Revista de Ciencia Politica* 27, no. 2 (2007): 195–205.

42. See, for example, models developed in different forms by Jacques Rancière, Chantal Mouffe and Étienne Balibar.

43. See Emmanuel Renault, *Marx et la Philosophie* (Paris: Presses Universitaires de France, 2014).

44. Jean-Philippe Deranty and Emmanuel Renault, "Politicizing Honneth's Ethics of Recognition," *Thesis Eleven*, no. 88 (February 2007): 92–111. See also Jean-Philippe Deranty and Emmanuel Renault, "Democratic Agon: Striving for Distinction or Struggle against Domination and Injustice?," in Andrew Schaap, ed., *Law and Agonistic Politics* (Burlington, VT: Ashgate, 2009), 43–56.

45. This is a project that I have tried to develop in several texts: "Le discours du respect," in A. Caillé, ed., *La quête de reconnaissance: un nouveau phénomène social total* (Paris: La Découverte, 2007); with Djemila Zeneidi-Henry in "Formes de reconnaissance conflictuelle: relations sociales, appropriation de territoire, culture et politique dans un groupe de Punks squatters," in *La reconnaissance à l'épreuve: explorations socio-anthropologiques*, ed. Jean-Paul Payet and Alain Battegay, (Villeneuve d'Ascq, France: Presses Universitaires du Septentrion, 2008); "Violence and Disrespect in the French Revolt of November 2005," in *Violence in France and Australia: Disorder in the Postcolonial Welfare State*, ed. Craig Browne and Justine McGill (Sydney: Sydney University Press, 2010), 169–80. The first two texts are also available in *Reconnaissance, Conflit, Domination* (Paris: CNRS, 2017).

46. See the special issue of *Actuel Marx* on "Populism/Counter-Populism" (no. 54, 2013), edited by Étienne Balibar and Emmanuel Renault.

47. It may seem that the very object of this book is still too narrow, since social struggles sometimes seem to be incited by the experience of domination rather than of injustice. However, following Max Weber, we can recall that all domination is accompanied by forms of justification, such that domination cannot take the form of an experience of domination unless it also appears as unjustified, or unjust, domination.

48. And all of these methodological orientations seem to me to be in conformity with Adorno's understanding of the project of a social philosophy; see Emmanuel Renault, "Adorno: de la philosophie sociale à la théorie sociale."

INTRODUCTION: POLITICAL PHILOSOPHY AND THE CLINIC OF INJUSTICE

1. See Max Horkheimer, "Traditional and Critical Theory," in *Critical Theory: Selected Essays*, trans. Matthew J. O'Connell (New York: Continuum, 1989), 188–243.

2. John Rawls, "The Idea of an Overlapping Consensus" (1987), in *Collected Papers*, ed. Samuel Freeman (Cambridge, MA: Harvard University Press, 1999), 429; see also 436: "by avoiding comprehensive doctrines we try to bypass religion and philosophy's profoundest controversies so as to have some hope of uncovering a basis of a stable overlapping consensus."

3. Rawls, "Overlapping Consensus," 437.

4. Walter Bryce Gallie, "Essentially contested concepts," *Proceedings of the Aristotelian Society for the Systematic Study of Philosophy* 56 (1955–56): 167–98. Republished in Gallie, *Philosophy and the Historical Understanding* (New York: Schocken, 1968), 157–91.

5. For an application of the idea of "essentially contested concepts" to the question of utopia, see Nestor Capdevila, "Utopie ou idéologie?," *L'Homme et la société*, no. 136–137 (April-September 2000): 77–93.

6. John Rawls, in *A Theory of Justice* (Cambridge, MA: Harvard University Press, 1970), chap. 1, §§1–3, tried to circumvent this difficulty by distinguishing between a "concept of justice" that we all share and "conceptions of justice" (based upon different "principles of justice"), which are the objects of disagreements. That we all share a "concept of justice" that is specific enough to identify principles acceptable to all, and not merely the impression that we are all talking about the same thing (in this case, "justice") when we disagree—this is precisely what Gallie makes it possible to challenge.

7. Jacques Rancière, *Disagreement: Politics and Philosophy*, trans. Julie Rose (Minneapolis: University of Minnesota Press, 1999), ix: "Philosophy becomes 'political' when it embraces aporia or the quandary proper to politics."

8. Note that Charles Taylor also adopts this perspective when he tries to distance himself from Rawls; on this point see "The Nature and Scope of Distributive Justice," *Philosophy and the Human Sciences: Philosophical Papers* 2 (Cambridge: Cambridge University Press, 1985), 289–317.

9. John Dewey, "The Need for a Recovery of Philosophy," in *Essays on Philosophy and Education, 1916–1917*, vol. 10 of *The Middle Works of John Dewey, 1899–1924* (Carbondale: Southern Illinois University Press, 1980), 46: "Philosophy recovers itself when it ceases to be a device for dealing with the problems of philosophers and becomes a method, cultivated by philosophers, for dealing with the problems of men."

10. Michael Walzer, *Interpretation and Social Criticism*, The Tanner Lectures on Human Values, 1985 (Cambridge, MA: Harvard University Press, 1987).

11. These questions were posed by Axel Honneth in "Formen der Gesellschaftskritik," in *Desintegration: Bruchstücke einer soziologischen Zeitdiagnose* (Frankfort am Main, Germany: Fischer, 1994), 71–79.

12. Adorno clearly claims a "clinical" approach in his conception of social research, for example in "Scientific Experiences of a European Scholar in America," in *Critical Models: Interventions and Catchwords*, trans. Henry W. Pickford (New York: Columbia University Press, 1998), 215–42. More generally, we can regard the "micrological" perspective that he adopts to be connected to a "clinical" orientation. On the connection between the *Deutung* of experience and the " physiognomy of the social world," see his "Introduction," in *The Positivist Dispute in German Sociology*, trans. Glyn Adey and David Frisby (London: Heinemann, 1976), 1–67.

13. Michel Legrand, *L'Approche biographique: théorie, clinique* (Paris: Desclée de Brouwer, 1993).

14. Hilary Putnam, "Fact and Value," in *Reason, Truth and History* (Cambridge: Cambridge University Press, 1981), 127–49.

15. Thus Luc Boltanski maintains that social critique must take the form of a "sociology of translation": *Love and Justice as Competences: Three Essays on the Sociology of Action* (Cambridge, MA: Polity, 2012), 29.

16. Theodor W. Adorno, "Cultural Criticism and Society," in *Prisms: Essays in Cultural Criticism and Society*, trans. Shierry Weber Nicholsen and Samuel Weber (Cambridge, MA: The MIT Press, 1983), 31: "Today, ideology means society as appearance."

17. This is an objection often raised against any attempt to consider experience as a political starting point; see for instance Joan W. Scott, " 'Experience," in *Feminists Theorize the Political*, ed. Judith Butler and Joan W. Scott (New York: Routledge, 1992), 22–40.

18. On this point see Sandra Laugier, "Pourquoi des théories morales? L'ordinaire contre la norme," *Cités* 1, no. 5 (2001): 93–112.

19. Another Adornian theme, inscribed at the heart of *Dialectic of Enlightenment*, as Axel Honneth has pointed out in "The Possibility of a Disclosing Critique of Society: The *Dialectic of Enlightenment* in Light of Current Debates in Social Criticism," in *Disrespect: The Normative Foundations of Critical Theory* (Cambridge, MA: Polity, 2007), 49–62.

20. Judith N. Shklar, *The Faces of Injustice* (New Haven, NJ: Yale University Press, 1990), 16.

21. Shklar, *The Faces of Injustice*, 20–28 (the section entitled "Doubts about Justice in the Empire of Injustice").

22. Hans Joas, *The Creativity of Action*, trans. Jeremy Gaines and Paul Keast (Chicago: University of Chicago Press, 1996).

23. Jacques Rancière, *Disagreement: Politics and Philosophy*, trans. Julie Rose (Minneapolis: University of Minnesota Press, 1999), xi: "Disagreement occurs wherever contention over what speaking means constitutes the very rationality of the speech situation."

24. Michel Foucault, *"Society Must Be Defended": Lectures at the Collège de France, 1975–1976*, trans. David Macey (New York: Picador, 2003), 7. Giving an explicitly political form to an experience is indeed one of the central aspects of the kind of social critique that Foucault attempted to define beginning with the work of the Groupe d'information sur les prisons [GIP; Prison Information Group]: "These experiences, these isolated revolts must be transformed into common knowledge and coordinated practice." "(On Prisons)," in *Intolerable: Writings from Michel Foucault and the Prisons Information Group (1970–1980)*, ed. Kevin Thompson and Perry Zurn, trans. Perry Zurn and Erik Beranek (Minneapolis: University of Minnesota Press, forthcoming) ["(Sur les prisons)," in *Dits et Écrits, 1954–1988* (Paris: Gallimard, 1994), vol. 2 (1970–1975), no. 87, 176]. But Foucault started from the principle that experience was accompanied by an adequate political knowledge and that all that remained was to give a public form to this knowledge: "And when the prisoners began to speak, they themselves possessed a theory of prisons, the penal system, and justice. It is this form of discourse which ultimately matters, a discourse against power, the counter-discourse of prisoners and those we call delinquents—and not a theory *about* delinquency." "Intellectuals and Power: A Conversation between Michel Foucault and Gilles Deleuze," in *Language, Counter-Memory, Practice: Selected Essays and Interviews*, ed. Donald F. Bouchard, trans. Donald F. Bouchard and Sherry Simon (Ithaca, NY: Cornell University Press, 1977), 209; translation modified. Victims of injustice themselves probably do have a theory of oppression, but the experience of injustice is not so easily accompanied by a theory of injustice.

25. For the contrast between a diurnal and a nocturnal politics, see Marina Garcés, "Pirater la vie. Politique diurne, politique nocturne," *Le Passant ordinaire*, no. 49 (June–September 2004), http://www.passant-ordinaire.org/revue/49-651.asp.

26. Véronique Guienne, "Du sentiment d'injustice à la justice sociale," *Cahiers internationaux de sociologie* 110, no. 1 (January–June 2001): 131–42.

27. Jean-François Lyotard, *The Differend: Phrases in Dispute*, trans. Georges Van Den Abbeele (Minneapolis: University of Minnesota Press, 1988), xi.

28. Lyotard, *The Differend*, 5: "This is what a wrong [*tort*] would be: a damage [*dommage*] accompanied by the loss of the means to prove the damage. This is the case if the victim is deprived of life, or of all his or her liberties, or of the freedom to make his or her ideas or opinions public, or simply of the right to testify to the damage, or even more simply if the testifying phrase is itself deprived of authority."

29. Lyotard, *Differend*, 9–10.

30. Lyotard, *Differend*, 13.

31. The concept of the experience of consciousness was articulated by Hegel in the "Introduction" of the *Phenomenology of Spirit*, trans. A. V. Miller (Oxford: Oxford University Press, 1977), see esp. 56, para. 88. See the commentaries by Adorno, "The Experiential Content of Hegel's Philosophy," in *Hegel: Three Studies*, trans. Shierry Weber Nicholsen (Cambridge, MA: The MIT Press, 1993), 53–88; and by Jürgen Habermas, "Hegel's Critique of Kant: Radicalization or Abolition of the Theory of Knowledge," in *Knowledge and Human Interests*, trans. Jeremy J. Shapiro (Boston: Beacon Press, 1971), 7–24.

32. On the meaning of this concept, see Rancière, *Disagreement*, x-xii.

33. On this point, see Carol Gilligan, *In a Different Voice: Psychological Theory and Women's Development* (Cambridge, MA: Harvard University Press, 1982).

34. Gayatri Chakravorty Spivak, "Can the Subaltern Speak?," in Cary Nelson and Lawrence Grossberg, eds., *Marxism and the Interpretation of Culture* (Urbana: University of Illinois Press, 1988), 271–313.

35. Luc Boltanski and Laurent Thévenot, *On Justification: Economies of Worth*, trans. Catherine Porter (Princeton, NJ: Princeton University Press, 2006).

36. This distinction between injustice and misfortune constitutes the principal subject of Judith Shklar's *The Faces of Injustice*. In a certain sense, the neoliberal challenge to the concept of social justice, in Friedrich Hayek, is nothing more than the systematic substitution of misfortune for injustice.

37. Shklar, *The Faces of Injustice*, 1–4.

38. On this point, see Léo Thiers-Vidal, "De la masculinité à l'anti-masculinisme: penser les rapports sociaux de sexe à partir d'une position sociale oppressive," *Nouvelles Questions Féministes* 21, no. 3 (December 2002): 71–83.

39. Karl Marx, *Economic and Philosophical Manuscripts of 1844*, ed. Dirk J. Struik, trans. Martin Milligan (New York: International Publishers, 1964), 152–53: "The meaning which production has in relation to the rich is seen *revealed* in the meaning which it has for the poor. At the top the manifestation is always refined, veiled, ambiguous—a sham; lower, it is rough, straightforward, frank—the real thing."

40. Marx, "The German Ideology," in *The Marx-Engels Reader*, 2nd ed., ed. Robert C. Tucker (New York: Norton, 1978), 166: "For the mass of men, i.e., the proletariat, these theoretical notions [constituent elements of ideology] do not exist and hence do not require to be dissolved, and if this mass ever had any theoretical notions, e.g., religion, etc., these have now long been dissolved by circumstances."

41. As Michael Walzer notes with respect to equality, in the preface to *Spheres of Justice: A Defense of Pluralism and Equality* (New York: Basic Books, 1984).

42. John S. Adams, "Towards an Understanding of Inequity," *Journal of Abnormal and Social Psychology* 67, no. 5 (November 1963): 422–36.

43. See Christian Baudelot and Michel Gollac, *Travailler pour être heureux?: le bonheur et le travail en France* (Paris: Fayard, 2003), 277ff.

44. The concept of moral hypocrisy stems from Marx (see on this point Emmanuel Renault, "La justice entre critique du droit et critique de la morale," *Skepsis* (Delagrave), no. 1 (2002) , but the idea of a moral priority for the standpoint of injustice has also been developed in other forms, by Adorno, Shklar, and Avishai Margalit, for example.

45. To clarify the direction of this project, it can be compared with Avishai Margalit's, which is similar in many respects. In the introduction to *The Decent Society* (Cambridge, MA: Harvard University Press, 1996), Margalit makes three arguments to justify the negative definition of the concept of justice that is encompassed in the phrase "the decent society": first, an argument for the moral priority of the struggle against injustice; second, an argument that the demand for respect can be satisfied by institutions in all sorts of ways, while only its denial constitutes a criterion applicable to societies; and third, an argument that only through a study of its denial can we arrive at an understanding of the essential characteristics of respect. I take up the first two arguments myself, but I apply them to the question of justice rather than limiting them to that of respect. I rearticulate the third argument, because the negative definition that I am proposing does not only serve to *reformulate* an established principle of justice (the definition of justice in terms of respect), but also to *enlarge* and to *transform* the definition of the concept of justice. Margalit's first argument is moral, his second is logical, and the third epistemological. I will add an epistemological argument, a political argument, and a conceptual argument that specifically address the point of view of the experience of injustice: (1) the experience of injustice contains the cognitive resources that enable an enlargement of the established definitions of justice, for it at least implicitly entails the demand for new definitions of justice; (2) the social and political problems associated with injustice cannot be adequately characterized and accounted for, except by adopting the standpoint of those who suffer injustice; and (3), the political significance of the concept of justice can only be made explicit if the meaning of this concept is articulated beginning with the three characteristics of the experience of injustice, which are also characteristics of political action.

46. Paul Ricoeur, *The Course of Recognition*, trans. David Pellauer (Cambridge, MA: Harvard University Press, 2005), 247; translation modified.

47. Emmanuel Renault, "Identité et reconnaissance chez Hegel," *Kairos* 17 (2001), 173–97.

48. For a study of the stages of this tradition, see Franck Fischbach, *Fichte et Hegel: la reconnaissance* (Paris: Presses Universitaires de France, 1999), and Axel Honneth, *The Struggle for Recognition: The Moral Grammar of Social Conflicts*, trans. Joel Anderson (Cambridge, MA: Polity, 1995), chapter 7.

49. Axel Honneth, *The Critique of Power: Reflective Stages in a Critical Social Theory*, trans. Kenneth Baynes (Cambridge, MA: The MIT Press, 1991).

50. Axel Honneth, "The Social Dynamics of Disrespect: On the Location of Critical Theory Today," in *Disrespect: The Normative Foundations of Critical Theory* (Cambridge, MA: Polity, 2007), 255–67.

51. Axel Honneth, *The Struggle for Recognition: The Moral Grammar of Social Conflicts*, trans. Joel Anderson (Cambridge, MA: Polity, 1995).

52. On this point, compare the Lacanian opposition between "empty" and "full" speech: Jacques Lacan, *The Seminar of Jacques Lacan, Book 1: Freud's Papers on Technique, 1953–1954*, trans. John Forrester (New York: Norton, 1988), 51; and Jacques Lacan, "The Function and Field of Speech and Language in Psychoanalysis," in *Écrits: A Selection*, trans. Alan Sheridan (New York: Norton, 1977), 30–113.

53. On the concept of distorted communication, see Jürgen Habermas, "On systematically distorted communication," *Inquiry* 13, nos. 1–4 (1970): 205–18.

1. SOCIAL MOVEMENTS AND CRITIQUE OF POLITICS

1. Jacques Rancière, *Disagreement: Politics and Philosophy*, trans. Julie Rose (Minneapolis: University of Minnesota Press, 1999), viii. [*La Mésentente* (Paris: Galilée, 1995).]

2. On this question, see Pierre Bourdieu, *Propos sur le champ politique* (Lyon: Presses Universitaires de Lyon, 2000).

3. Erik Neveu, *Sociologie des mouvements sociaux* (Paris: La Découverte, 2002), 17–20.

4. Albert O. Hirschman, "Social Conflicts as Pillars of Democratic Market Society," *Political Theory* 22, no. 2 (May 1994): 203–18; also available in Albert O. Hirschman, *A Propensity to Self-Subversion* (Cambridge, MA: Harvard University Press, 1995), 231–48.

5. John Holloway, *Change the World Without Taking Power: The Meaning of Revolution Today*, new edition (New York: Pluto Press, 2010). Holloway is not satisfied with the idea of besieging power; he aims rather to define a project of struggle against established power in the name of constituent power. For a critical presentation of this point of view, see Daniel Bensaïd, *Un monde à changer: mouvements et stratégies* (Paris: Textuel, 2003), 131ff.

6. For a comparison of Rawls and Habermas on this point, see Yves Sintomer, *La démocratie impossible? : politique et modernité chez Weber et Habermas* (Paris: La Découverte, 1999), 261–64.

7. John Rawls, *Political Liberalism*, expanded ed. (New York: Columbia University Press, 2005), 6.

8. Jürgen Habermas, *Between Facts and Norms: Contributions to a Discourse Theory of Law and Democracy*, trans. William Rehg (Cambridge, MA: The MIT Press, 1996), 9, 82.

9. Habermas, *Facts and Norms*, 157–62.

10. Axel Honneth, *The Struggle for Recognition: The Moral Grammar of Social Conflicts*, trans. Joel Anderson (Cambridge, MA: Polity, 1995), esp. chaps. 5 and 6; Honneth, "Reconnaissance," in *Dictionnaire d'Éthique et de Philosophie Morale*, ed. Monique Canto-Sperber (Paris: Presses Universitaires de France, 1996), 1272–78; Honneth, "Redistribution as Recognition: A Response to Nancy Fraser," in Nancy Fraser and Axel Honneth, *Redistribution or Recognition?: A Political-Philosophical Exchange* (New York: Verso, 2003), 110–97, esp. 125–34.

11. This dimension of the experience of denial of recognition guides Sartre's analysis of the relation between "the look," "recognition," and "alienation" in *Being and Nothingness*, trans. Hazel Barnes (New York: Washington Square Books, 1956), 326–27.

12. The term "alienation" here designates the experience of the world as one that has become foreign and hostile, "alienated" or "estranged" in the sense that Marx gave to the concept of "*Emtfremdung*" in *The Economic and Philosophic Manuscripts of 1844*. I make use of this concept here without taking up the metaphysics of the "species-being" that is associated with it in this text. Marx had already employed the distinction between being alienated from oneself and being estranged from the world.

13. John Rawls, *A Theory of Justice* (Cambridge, MA: Harvard University Press, 1971), § 11, 62.

14. Rawls, *A Theory of Justice*, 62.

15. Rawls, *A Theory of Justice*, 60.

16. John Rawls, *Political Liberalism*, 291.

17. Rawls, *Political Liberalism*, 295.

18. Rawls, *Political Liberalism*, 297.

19. Rawls, *A Theory of Justice*, §67.

20. For a critical examination of this point, see Christian Lazzeri, "Le problème de la reconnaissance dans le libéralisme déontologique de John Rawls," *Revue du MAUSS* 23, no. 1 (2004): 165–79.

21. Rawls, *A Theory of Justice*, 442.

22. It is only supported by the naïve theory of recognition as reciprocal emulation [the "companion effect"] developed in §65.

23. Rawls, *A Theory of Justice*, § 37, 234.

24. Habermas, *Between Facts and Norms*, 104–11, 157–62.

25. Jürgen Habermas, "Moral Consciousness and Communicative Action," in *Moral Consciousness and Communicative Action*, trans. Christian Lenhardt and Shierry Weber Nicholsen (Cambridge, MA: MIT Press, 1990), 122. For a discussion of the debate between Rawls and Habermas, see Sintomer, *La démocratie impossible?*, 264–73; and Stéphane Haber, *Jürgen Habermas: une introduction* (Paris: La Découverte, 2001), 291–306.

26. Habermas, *Between Facts and Norms*, 120–23.

27. Habermas, *Between Facts and Norms*, 123.

28. I am thinking in particular of Joan C. Tronto, *Moral Boundaries: A Political Argument for an Ethic of Care* (New York: Routledge, 1993).

29. On this point, see Sintomer, *La démocratie impossible?*, 272–74.

30. Rawls, *A Theory of Justice*, 250.

31. On this point, see §42 of *A Theory of Justice*, and especially §§41ff of Rawls, *Justice as Fairness: A Restatement* (Cambridge: Harvard University Press, 2001). In the latter work, Rawls tried to respond to arguments that the model of property-owning democracy is not outlined precisely enough to pave the way for radical social transformations.

32. This is the principle of the view defended by Jacques Bidet, *Théorie générale: théorie du droit, de l'économie et de la politique* (Paris: Presses Universitaires de France, 1999).

33. Rancière, *Disagreement*, p. 123.

34. Christophe Dejours, *Souffrance en France: la banalisation de l'injustice sociale* (Paris: Seuil, 1998).

35. Nancy Fraser uses this sort of a principle to reject an approach that begins from the experience of a denial of recognition rather than from properly political formulations of

demands for justice. See Nancy Fraser, "Distorted Beyond All Recognition: A Rejoinder to Axel Honneth," in Fraser and Honneth, *Redistribution or Recognition?*, esp. 203–7.

36. Unlike Charles Tilly ["Social Movements and National Politics," in *Statemaking and Social Movements: Essays in History and Theory*, ed. Charles Bright and Susan Harding (Ann Arbor: University of Michigan Press, 1984), 297–317], I do not think it is legitimate to make confrontation with public authorities one of the criteria for social movements—for example, a strike could aim only for goals internal to a specific business. This is why I will speak only of a kind of conflict that challenges society in general or some particular institutions, the state among them.

37. In distinguishing between these two types of social struggle, I am following Nancy Fraser, "Social Justice in the Age of Identity Politics: Redistribution, Recognition, and Participation," in *The Tanner Lectures on Human Values*, vol. 19, ed. Grethe B. Peterson (Salt Lake City: University of Utah Press, 1998), 1–67.

38. [Axel Honneth, "Afterword to the Second German Edition (1988)", *The Critique of Power*, p. xiv.]

39. Ted Robert Gurr, *Why Men Rebel* (New York: Paradigm, 2010; orig. Princeton, NJ: Princeton University Press, 1970); Mancur Olson, Jr., *The Logic of Collective Action: Public Goods and the Theory of Groups* (Cambridge, MA: Harvard University Press, 1965); for a summary, see Erik Neveu, *Sociologie des mouvements sociaux*, 40–51.

40. Michel Vakaloulis, "Mouvement social et analyse politique," in *Faire mouvement: novembre-décembre 1995*, ed. Claude Leneveu and Michel Vakaloulis (Paris: Presses Universitaires de France, 1998), 27–28.

41. Barrington Moore, Jr., *Injustice: The Social Bases of Obedience and Revolt* (White Plains, NY: M.E. Sharpe, Inc., 1978).

42. For a critique of this orientation, see for example William A. Gamson "The Social Psychology of Collective Action" in *Frontiers in Social Movement Theory*, ed. Aldon D. Morris and Carol McClurg Mueller (New Haven: Yale University Press, 1992), 53–76.

43. For an overview of "frame analysis" research and its relation to approaches in terms of opportunity and mobilization, see Doug McAdam, John D. McCarthy, and Mayer N. Zald, "Introduction: Opportunities, Mobilizing Structures and Framing Processes—Toward a Synthetic, Comparative Perspective on Social Movements," in *Comparative Perspectives on Social Movements: Political Opportunities, Mobilizing Structures, and Cultural Framings*, ed. Doug McAdam, John D. McCarthy, and Mayer N. Zald (New York: Cambridge University Press, 1996), 1–20, quoted at page 5.

44. For a summary of these questions, see David A. Snow and Robert D. Benford, "Master Frames and Cycles of Protest," in Morris and Mueller, *Frontiers in Social Movement Theory*, 133–55, and in particular 135–38.

45. Honneth, *The Struggle for Recognition*, 168.

46. John Dewey, *Human Nature and Conduct* (1922), The Middle Works of John Dewey, 1899–1924, vol. 14, ed. Jo Ann Boydston (Carbondale: Southern Illinois Press, 1988).

47. Honneth, *Struggle*, 137.

48. Honneth, *Struggle*, 138.

49. Gamson, "The Social Psychology of Collective Action," 67–71. The idea of an experience structured by social frames but capable, through its internal dynamics, of transforming these frames, is at the heart of Erving Goffman's *Frame Analysis: An Essay on the Organization of Experience* (Cambridge: Harvard University Press, 1974), the work that inspired the "frame analysis" movement.

50. Lyotard, *The Differend*, 13: "The differend is the unstable state and instant of language wherein something which must be able to be put into phrases cannot yet be. This state includes silence, which is a negative phrase, but it also calls upon phrases which are in principle possible. This state is signaled by what one ordinarily calls a feeling."

51. Avishai Margalit, *The Decent Society*, trans. Naomi Goldblum (Cambridge: Harvard University Press, 1998), 9–10.

52. Richard Rorty, *Contingency, Irony, and Solidarity* (Cambridge: Cambridge University Press, 1989).

53. Theodor W. Adorno, *Negative Dialectics*, trans. Ernst B. Ashton (New York: Seabury Press, 1973), 5: "Dialectics is the consistent sense of nonidentity."

54. David A. Snow and Robert D. Benford, "Master Frames and Cycles of Protest," 136.

55. Snow and Benford, "Master Frames," 136.

56. I take this distinction from Albert O. Hirschman, "Social Conflicts as Pillars of Democratic Market Society."

57. In this sense, one could say that it is in the nature of a strike to never be finished, as Vincent Houillon maintains in "La grève n'est pas finie," *Le Passant Ordinaire* 48 (April–June 2004), http://www.passant-ordinaire.org/revue/48-615.asp#.

58. Social movements should be considered as reactions anchored in disrupted forms of life and as "collective enterprises to establish a new order of life," following the classic definition given by Blumer in "Collective Behavior," in *Principles of Sociology*, ed. Alfred McLung Lee (New York: Barnes & Noble, 1951), 199.

59. Albert O. Hirschman, *Exit, Voice, and Loyalty: Responses to Decline in Firms, Organizations, and States* (Cambridge: Harvard University Press, 1970).

60. Charles Tilly, *The Contentious French* (Cambridge: Belknap Press, 1986).

61. Arlette Farge and Jacques Revel, *The Vanishing Children of Paris: Rumor and Politics Before the French Revolution*, trans. Claudia Mieville (Cambridge: Harvard University Press, 1991), 52; also available as *The Rules of Rebellion: Child Abductions in Paris in 1750* (Cambridge: Polity Press, 1991).

62. Farge and Revel, *Vanishing Children*, 57.

63. On this point see McAdam, McCarthy, and Zald, "Introduction: Opportunities, Mobilizing Structures and Framing Processes," 16–17.

64. Hans Joas, *The Creativity of Action*, trans. Jeremy Gaines and Paul Keast (Chicago: University of Chicago Press, 1996), 163: "We must establish in concrete action-situations what satisfies our aspirations and what accords with our values. Both the concretization of values and the satisfaction of needs depend on exercising powers of creativity."

65. Joas, *The Creativity of Action*, chap. 4.1, "Creativity and Collective Action," 199–209.

66. Stéphane Beaud and Michel Pialoux, *Violences urbaines, violence sociale: genèse des nouvelles classes dangereuses* (Paris: Fayard, 2003), 21–22: "In the case of immigrants' children, a motif has become omnipresent—'we don't have any place here,' 'we feel degraded'—fueling a profound resentment."

67. Beaud and Pialoux, *Violences urbaines*, 337ff.

68. Hans Magnus Enzensberger, *Civil Wars: From L.A. to Bosnia* (New York: The New Press, 1994); also available as *Civil War*, trans. Piers Spence and Martin Chalmers (London: Granta Books, 1994).

69. Beaud and Pialoux, *Violences urbaines*, 341: "Through these attitudes . . . we cannot avoid seeing a ferocious will to concretely take control of the 'neighborhood's' area,

to hold onto what is still their own, in this area where they are and feel themselves to be safe. The search for control over places and the dispossession of 'others,' perceived as established in life, appears to be the spatial retranslation and the other side of their economic and social dispossession."

70. See, for example, Sophie Body-Gendrot, "Violence urbaine: recherche de sens (France et U.S.A.)," *Lignes* 25 (1995): 70–85, quoted here at p. 72: "Vandalism, graffiti, looting: [these are] so many responses given by residents to the symbolic violence that is exercised upon them and to the disparaging image of themselves that city planners present to them, whether in soulless highrises or lowrise housing."

71. This is illustrated by the action of associations like the Mouvement pour l'Immigration et la Banlieue [MIB, the Movement for Immigration and Suburbs], which, in the 1990s and 2000s, through the elaboration of weak (though always difficult to establish) organizational frameworks, attempted to convert violent protests into politicized protest, into a social movement working toward political ends.

2. THE APORIAS OF SOCIAL JUSTICE

1. Paul Ricoeur, *The Just*, trans. David Pellauer (Chicago: University of Chicago Press, 2000), x.

2. Michael Walzer, *Spheres of Justice* (New York: Basic Books, 1983), xii.

3. Friedrich A. Hayek, *Law, Legislation and Liberty: Volume 2, The Mirage of Social Justice* (Chicago: University of Chicago Press, 1976), 62–67.

4. Hayek, *Law, Legislation and Liberty*, 66–67.

5. John Rawls, *A Theory of Justice* (Cambridge, MA: Harvard University Press, 1971), §§ 31, 36.

6. Otfried Höffe, "Justice," in *Dictionnaire de philosophie politique*, ed. Philippe Raynaud and Stéphane Rials (Paris: Presses Universitaires de France, 1996), 314–19.

7. Iris Marion Young, "Displacing the Distributive Paradigm," in *Justice and the Politics of Difference* (Princeton, NJ: Princeton University Press, 1990), 15–38.

8. John Stuart Mill, *Utilitarianism*, 2nd ed. (Indianapolis, IN: Hackett, 2001), 61–62; italics in original.

9. William D. Ross, *Aristotle* (London: Methuen, 1949), 210.

10. See for example Ronald Dworkin, "Liberalism," in *A Matter of Principle* (Cambridge, MA: Harvard University Press, 1985), 193–95.

11. Albert Michel, *Autour du "modernisme social," la "justice sociale" et la "doctrine catholique"* (Lille, France: Questions Ecclésiastiques, 1912).

12. The problem itself had not only already been recognized by a few, but also incorporated into their political philosophy. See on this point Jean-Claude Bourdin, "Hegel et la 'question sociale': société civile, vie et détresse," *Revue germanique internationale* 15 (2001): 145–76.

13. Robert Castel, *From Manual Workers to Wage Laborers: Transformation of the Social Question*, trans. Richard Boyd (New Brunswick, NJ: Transaction Publishers, 2003), xx.

14. On this point see Jacques Donzelot, *L'Invention du social: essai sur le déclin des passions politiques* (Paris: Seuil, 1994); and Castel, *From Manual Workers to Wage Laborers*, chap. 6.

15. Léon Bourgeois, *Solidarité* (Paris: A. Colin, 1896).
16. Karl Marx, "Critical Marginal Notes on the Article 'The King of Prussia and Social Reform. By a Prussian,'" in *Marx: Early Political Writings*, ed. and trans. Joseph O'Malley with Richard A. Davis (Cambridge: Cambridge University Press, 1994), 97–114.
17. Marx, "Critical Marginal Notes," 102.
18. Marx, "Critical Marginal Notes," 103–4.
19. Max Weber, *Economy and Society: An Outline of Interpretive Sociology*, 2 vols., ed. Guenther Roth and Claus Wittich, (Berkeley: University of California Press, 1978), chap. 1, § 8 ("Conflict, Competition, Selection").
20. Weber, *Economy and* Society, chap. 1, § 3, 27: "Hence, the definition [of 'social relationship'] does not specify whether the relation of the actors is co-operative [in the French translation: "is one of solidarity"] or the opposite."
21. Rawls, *A Theory of Justice*, 9–10.
22. Rawls, *A Theory of Justice*, 5.
23. Rawls, *A Theory of Justice*, 15.
24. Rawls, *A Theory of Justice*, § 32, 204.
25. Rawls, *A Theory of Justice*, § 11, 62.
26. John Rawls, "Justice as Fairness: Political not Metaphysical," (1985), in *John Rawls: Collected Papers*, ed. Samuel R. Freeman (Cambridge, MA: Harvard University Press, 1999), 400n19: "I prefer not to think of justice as fairness as a right-based view." He makes this point in response to Ronald Dworkin's interpretation of his theory.
27. Rawls, *A Theory of Justice*, 62.
28. For a general presentation of how this conflict has developed in contemporary debates, see the introduction of Jean-Christophe Merle, *Justice et progrès: contributionà une doctrine du droit économique et social* (Paris: Presses Universitaires de France, 1997).
29. Rawls, *A Theory of Justice*, 61.
30. Immanuel Kant, "The Doctrine of Right," Part 1 of *The Metaphysics of Morals*, trans. Mary Gregor (Cambridge: Cambridge University Press, 1996), §49, C, 100–102.
31. G. W. F. Hegel, *Hegel's Philosophy of Right*, trans. Thomas M. Knox (London: Oxford University Press, 1967), §29, 33. [The two earlier quotations come from a different translation: G. W. F. Hegel, *Elements of the Philosophy of Right*, ed. Allen Wood, trans. H. B. Nisbet (Cambridge: Cambridge University Press, 1991), respectively §23, 54 and §29, 58. The Nisbet translation of this passage reads in full: "*Right* is any existence [Dasein] in general which is the *existence* of the *free will*."]
32. Hegel, *Elements of the Philosophy of Right*, §230, 260.
33. Habermas, *Between Facts and Norms*, trans. William Rehg (Malden, MA: Polity Press, 1997), 123.
34. Charles Taylor, "What's Wrong with Negative Liberty," in *Philosophy and the Human Sciences: Philosophical Papers*, vol. 2 (Cambridge: Cambridge University Press, 1985), 211–29.
35. Rawls, *A Theory of Justice*, 3, 4.
36. Rawls, *A Theory of Justice*, 9.
37. Rawls, *A Theory of Justice*, 6.
38. Alasdair MacIntyre, *After Virtue: A Study in Moral Theory* (Notre Dame, IN: University of Notre Dame Press, 1984).

39. Friedrich A. Hayek, *Law, Legislation and Liberty*, 2 vols. (Chicago: University of Chicago Press, 1976).

40. John Rawls, "The Domain of the Political and Overlapping Consensus" (1989), in *Collected Papers*, 479.

41. Charles Taylor, "La conduite de la vie et le moment du bien," in *La Liberté des Modernes*, ed. Philippe de Lara (Paris: Presses Universitaires de France, 1997), 294. I won't dwell on the fact that this contrast seems at least to have been poorly chosen, and that exploitation can also occur (to be sure, in a form that is more insidious than brutal) in the division of household work.

42. Charles Taylor, "Atomism," in *Philosophy and the Human Sciences*, 199. [The sentence continues, "and thus in accepting certain standards by which a life may be judged full or truncated."]

43. Charles Taylor, "Le Juste et le bien," *Revue de Métaphysique et de Morale* 93, no. 1 (January-March 1988), 33–56.

44. Taylor, "Le Juste et le bien," 33: "[I]t would be impossible to define a just distribution without taking account of the culture, the traditions, and the way of life of the society in question."

45. Charles Taylor, "The nature and scope of distributive justice," in *Philosophy and the Human Sciences*, 289–317.

46. Charles Taylor, *Multiculturalism and "The Politics of Recognition": An Essay* (Princeton, NJ: Princeton University Press, 1992).

47. Nancy Fraser criticizes the theory of recognition from these two perspectives in her debate with Axel Honneth, in Nancy Fraser and Axel Honneth, *Redistribution or Recognition?: A Political-Philosophical Exchange* (New York: Verso, 2003).

48. Fraser and Honneth, *Redistribution or Recognition?*, 262–64.

3. THE INSTITUTIONS OF INJUSTICE

1. Max Weber, *Economy and Society: An Outline of Interpretive Sociology*, 2 vols., ed. Guenther Roth and Claus Wittich (Berkeley: University of California Press, 1978), 1.4, § 1.

2. Ludwig Wittgenstein, *Philosophical Investigations*, trans. Gertrude E. M. Anscombe (New York: MacMillan, 1968), §§ 23, 199; 11, 81.

3. Vincent Descombes, *The Institutions of Meaning: A Defense of Anthropological Holism*, trans. Stephen Adam Schwartz (Cambridge, MA: Harvard University Press, 2014), § 10.4, 303–313.

4. Marcel Mauss and Paul Fauconnet, "Sociologie" (1901), in Marcel Mauss, *Oeuvres*, Vol. 3, *Cohésion Sociale et Divisions de la Sociologie* (Paris: Minuit, 1969), 150.

5. Weber, *Economy and Society*, chap. 1, § 4.

6. Weber, *Economy and Society*, chap. 1, § 5.

7. Weber, *Economy and Society*, chap. 1, §§ 12–15; see also Max Weber, "Some Categories of Interpretive Sociology," *The Sociological Quarterly* 22, no. 2 (Spring 1981): 151–80, esp. § 7. By "compulsory organization" ["institution" in the French translation] in this narrow sense, Weber thus means organizations for which neither internal and administrative organization nor membership depend upon a voluntary declaration, by which these institutions (for example, schools, prisons, or the state)

are differentiated from simple organizations based upon agreement (the family, for example), as well as from voluntary associations and "enterprises" (administrative organizations with voluntary membership and defined by continuous rational activity of a specified kind).

8. Weber, *Economy and Society*, chap. 1, § 16.
9. Weber, *Economy and Society*, chap. 1, § 7.
10. Weber, *Economy and Society*, chap. 1, § 16, and chap. 3.
11. Luc Boltanski and Laurent Thévenot, *On Justification: Economies of Worth*, trans. Catherine Porter (Princeton, NJ: Princeton University Press, 2006).
12. Boltanski and Thévenot, *On Justification: Economies of Worth*. For an extensive analysis of this conception of social critique, see Claude Gautier, "The Renewal of Critique in Neo-Capitalism," *Critical Horizons :A Journal of Philosophy and Social Theory* 8, no. 1 (August 2007): 116–29.
13. Axel Honneth, *The Critique of Power: Reflective Stages in a Critical Social Theory*, trans. Kenneth Baynes (Cambridge, MA: The MIT Press, 1991), "Afterword to the Second German Edition (1988)" and chap. 9.
14. This is an observation rather than a normative statement: For example, it is a fact that in the majority of cases, recognition of one's spouse's freedom, or the value of spousal labor, is secondary to a demand for love in a romantic relationship, but each couple is the site of a negotiation between these two elements of recognition.
15. An effort undertaken for example by Husserl, which was criticized for this reason by Habermas, for example, in "Reflections on the Linguistic Foundation of Sociology: The Christian Gauss Lecture [sic] (Princeton University, February-March 1971)," in *On the Pragmatics of Social Interaction: Preliminary Studies in the Theory of Communicative Action*, trans. Barbara Fultner (Cambridge, MA: The MIT Press, 2001), 1–104.
16. John Dewey, *Human Nature and Conduct (1922)*, vol. 14 of The Middle Works of John Dewey, 1899-1924 (Carbondale, IL: Southern Illinois University Press, 1988), Part 2.
17. John Dewey, "Psychology and Work," in *The Later Works, 1925–1953: Volume 5, 1929–1930* (Carbondale: Southern Illinois University Press, 1984), 239.
18. Pierre Bourdieu, *Pascalian Meditations*, trans. Richard Nice (Stanford, CA: Stanford University Press, 2000), 166.
19. Dewey, *Human Nature and Conduct (1922)*, Part 1.
20. See in particular Bourdieu, *Pascalian Meditations*, chap. 5.
21. On this point see Descombes, *The Institutions of Meaning*, §10.3, p. 302, from whom I've taken this claim and its illustrative example.
22. Djemila Zeneidi-Henry, *Les SDF et la ville: géographie du savoir-survivre* (Paris: Bréal, 2002), 265–68.
23. Bernard Lahire, *The Plural Actor*, trans. David Fernbach (Cambridge: Polity, 2001), pp. 42ff.
24. Richard Sennett, *The Corrosion of Character: The Personal Consequences of Work in the New Capitalism* (New York: W.W. Norton & Company, 1998), 26–27
25. Sennett, *The Corrosion of Character*, 31.
26. Bourdieu, *Pascalian Meditations*, 160.
27. Abdelmalek Sayad, *The Suffering of the Immigrant*, trans. David Macey (Cambridge: Polity Press, 2004). [The French text was entitled *La Double absence*, the phrase Renault quotes here. It makes reference to one's "absence" both as an émigré and an immigrant.]

28. Nancy Fraser, "Social Justice in the Age of Identity Politics: Redistribution, Recognition and Participation," in Fraser and Axel Honneth, *Redistribution or Recognition?*, 16–22.

29. Dejours, "Les rapports domestiques entre amour et domination," *Travailler* no. 8 (2002), 27–43.

30. Carol Gilligan, *In a Different Voice: Psychological Theory and Women's Development* (Cambridge, MA: Harvard University Press, 1982).

31. Dejours, "Les rapports domestiques entre amour et domination."

32. See for example, Jean-Marie Vincent, *Abstract Labor: A Critique*, trans. Jim Cohen (New York: St. Martin's Press, 1991); and Moishe Postone, *Time, Labor, and Social Domination: A Reinterpretation of Marx's Critical Theory* (Cambridge: Cambridge University Press, 1993), chap. 6.

33. Nancy Fraser, "Distorted Beyond All Recognition: A Rejoinder to Axel Honneth," in Fraser and Honneth, *Redistribution or Recognition?*, 211–22.

34. Christian Baudelot and Michel Gollac, *Travailler pour être heureux?: le bonheur et le travail en France* (Paris: Fayard, 2003).

35. Marx writes, in *Capital*, that "the labor of the private individual manifests itself as an element of the total labor of society, only through the relations which the act of exchange establishes between the products, and, through their mediation, between the producers." Karl Marx, *Capital*, trans. Ben Fowkes (London: Penguin Books, 1990), Book 1, chap. 1, § 4, 165. And, a bit further, "it [the labor of the individual producer] must, as a definite useful kind of labor, satisfy a definite social need, and thus maintain its position as an element of the total labor, as a branch of the social division of labor, which originally sprang up spontaneously" (1, § 4, 166). For an examination of this conception of the market as validation, see Carlo Benetti and Jean Cartelier, *Marchands, salariat, et capitalistes* (Paris: Librairie François Maspero, 1980), esp. note 1.

36. Henceforth, the term "value" does not designate an economic measure, but is taken in the sense that work is simultaneously the vehicle for recognition of a life's social value (one tries to be recognized through work), and its object (it is through recognition of the value of one's work that the social value of one's life is recognized).

37. On the various forms of a feeling of injustice in work, see Baudelot and Gollac, *Travailler pour être heureux?*, 277–96. The argument is often made that understanding struggles for higher wages as struggles for recognition poses the following political risk: one is thereby calling for purely symbolic compensation for economic demands. However, if we take the example of nurses or teachers who have made these kinds of demands in France, we clearly see that their demand for recognition is about recognizing the social utility of their work and changing the fact that they no longer have the material resources needed to accomplish their work. Thus no purely symbolic compensation is possible.

38. On this point see Emmanuel Renault, "Identité et reconnaissance chez Hegel," *Kairos* 17 (2001).

39. Antonio Negri and Michael Hardt, *Empire* (Cambridge, MA: Harvard University Press, 2000), § 1.2 and § 3.4, 22ff., 280ff.

40. André Gorz, *Reclaiming Work: Beyond the Wage-Based Society*, trans. Chris Turner (Cambridge, MA: Polity Press, 1999), 27ff.

41. A more thorough critique of the sociology applied here to new forms of organizing work can be found in Claude Gautier, "The Renewal of Critique in Neo-Capitalism."

42. Danièle Linhart, *La Modernisation des entreprises* (Paris: La Découverte: 2010), 30–32.

43. Yves Schwartz, *Expérience et connaissance du travail* (Paris: Messidor: 1988).

44. On this point, Boltanski and Chiapello's analysis should be contrasted with those by Yves Clot, *Le Travail sans l'homme? Pour une psychologie des milieux de travail et de vie* (Paris: La Découverte, 1995) and Christophe Dejours, *Souffrance en France: la banalisation de l'injustice sociale* (Paris: Seuil, 1998).

45. Stéphane Beaud and Michel Pialoux, *Violences urbaines, violence sociale: genèse des nouvelles classes dangereuses* (Paris: Fayard, 2003), 144–45.

46. Linhart, *La Modernisation des* entreprises, 75ff.

47. Yves Clot, *La Fonction psychologique du travail* (Paris: Presses Universitaires de France, 1999), 7.

48. Beaud and Pialoux, *Violences urbaines, violence sociale*, 129.

49. Beaud and Pialoux, *Violences urbaines, violence sociale*, 173: "When they have not been able to remain at the same factory for more than a few months and when they have only been given short-term assignments, their work experiences leave the impression that they function within a professional world that appears to be, in its entirety, a 'trap,' or even 'perverted.' "

50. Sennett, *The Corrosion of Character*, chap. 4.

51. Sennett, *The Corrosion of Character*, 59.

52. Luc Boltanski and Ève Chiapello, *The New Spirit of Capitalism*, trans. Gregory Elliott (London: Verso, 2005), 122–25.

53. Sennett, *The Corrosion of Character*, 26–27.

54. See, for example, Alain Ehrenberg, *The Weariness of the Self: Diagnosing the History of Depression in the Contemporary Age* (Montreal: McGill-Queen's University Press: 2010).

55. This point has been particularly stressed in France by social convention theory; see for example Michael Storper and Robert Salais, *Worlds of Production: The Action Frameworks of the Economy* (Cambridge, MA: Harvard University Press, 1997).

56. In particular by Barrington Moore, Jr., *Injustice: The Social Bases of Obedience and Revolt* (White Plains, NY: M. E. Sharpe, 1978) and Alvin W. Gouldner, *Wildcat Strike* (Yellow Springs, OH: The Antioch Press, 1954).

57. Christophe Dejours, *Le Facteur humain* (Paris: Presses Universitaires de France, 1995), 59–61.

58. Christophe Dejours, *Travail, usure mentale* (Paris: Bayard, 2000).

59. Clot, *La Fonction psychologique du travail*, 7.

60. On this point and in the passages to follow, I take up arguments introduced by Ursula Holtgrewe, " 'Meinen Sie, da sagt jemand danke, wenn man geht?': Anerkennungs- und *Mischungsverhältnisse* im Prozess organisationaler Transformation," in *Anerkennung und Arbeit*, ed. Ursula Holtgrewe, Stephan Voswinkel, and Gabriele Wagner (Konstanz, Germany: Universitätsverlag Konstanz, 2000), 63–84.

61. Hermann Kocyba, "Der Preis der Anerkennung: Von der tayloristischen Missachtung zur strategischen Instrumentalisierung der Subjektivität der Arbeitenden," in *Anerkennung und Arbeit*, ed. Holtgrewe, Voswinkel, and Wagner, 127–40.

62. Axel Honneth, "Recognition as Ideology," in *Recognition and Power: Axel Honneth and the Tradition of Critical Social Theory*, ed. Bert Van Der Brink and David Owen (Cambridge: Cambridge University Press, 2007), 323–47; also available as "Recognition as Ideology: The Connection Between Morality and Power," in Axel Honneth, *The I in We: Studies on the Theory of Recognition* (Malden, MA: Politiy Press, 2012), 75–97.

63. On the circumstances surrounding collective deliberation within business, see Christophe Dejours, *Le Facteur* humain, 64–70.

64. In the following pages I will rephrase Axel Honneth's understanding of the connection between exclusion and recognition in "Zur Zukunft des Instituts für Sozialforschung," *Mitteilungen des Instituts für Sozialforschung*, Heft 12, 54–63.

65. For this critique of integration discourses, see Abdelmalek Sayad, "Qu'est-ce que l'intégration?," *Hommes et Migrations*, no. 1182 (December 1994): 8–14.

66. An illustration of this kind of application of the concept of disaffiliation can be found in Marie-Hélène Bacqué and Yves Sintomer, "Affiliation et désaffiliation en banlieue: réflexions à partir de Saint-Denis et d'Aubervilliers," *Revue Française de Sociologie* 42, no. 2 (May 2001): 217–49.

67. For a presentation of issues here, see Béatrice Appay, "Précarité, précarisation: réflexions épistémologiques," in *Précarisation, risque et santé*, ed. Virginie Ringa, Pierre Chauvin, Françoise Facy, and Michel Joubert (Paris: Inserm, 2001), 15–27.

68. Serge Paugam, *La Disqualification sociale: essai sur la nouvelle pauvreté* (Paris: Presses Universitaires de France, 1991).

69. For a review of the effects of "social support," see Emilio La Rosa, *Santé, précarité et exclusion* (Paris: Presses Universitaires de France, 1998), 183–88.

4. IDENTITY AS THE EXPERIENCE OF INJUSTICE

1. Both the positive and negative dimensions of critical moments when the question of identity arises are highlighted, for example, by Anselm L. Strauss, *Mirrors and Masks: The Search for Identity* (Glencoe, IL: Free Press, 1959), chap. 5.

2. Jean-Paul Sartre, *Anti-Semite and Jew: An Exploration of the Etiology of Hate*, trans. George J. Becker (New York: Schocken, 1948), 143.

3. Charles Taylor, *Multiculturalism and "The Politics of Recognition": An Essay* (Princeton, NJ: Princeton University Press, 1992).

4. Michael Walzer, "The Communitarian Critique of Liberalism," *Political Theory* 18, no. 1 (February 1990): 6–23.

5. John Rawls, *A Theory of Justice* (Cambridge, MA: Harvard University Press, 1970); Charles Taylor, "Le Juste et le bien," *Revue de métaphysique et de morale* 93, no. 1 (January-March 1988): 33–56.

6. Michael Walzer, *Interpretation and Social Criticism*, The Tanner Lectures on Human Values, 1985 (Cambridge, MA: Harvard University Press, 1987).

7. See Axel Honneth, ed., *Kommunitarismus: Eine Debatte über die moralischen Grundlagen moderner Gesellschaften* (New York: Campus Verlag, 1994). [Seven of the nine texts included in this volume are translated from English originals: articles by Michael Sandel, John Rawls, Amy Gutmann, Alasdair MacIntyre, Charles Taylor, Charles Larmore, and Michael Walzer. The other two texts are an introduction by Axel Honneth

and an article by Rainer Forst.] See also, within the Frankfurt School tradition, Rainer Forst, *Contexts of Justice: Political Philosophy beyond Liberalism and Communitarianism*, trans. John M. M. Farrell (Berkeley: University of California Press, 2002).

8. On the opposition between a constructivist approach and a reconstructive one, see Jürgen Habermas, *Between Facts and Norms*, trans. William Rehg (Malden, MA: Polity Press, 1997), 56–66; and Axel Honneth, "Recognition and Justice: Outline of a Plural Theory of Justice," *Acta Sociologica* 47, no. 4 (December 2004): 351–64. For the critique of Walzer, see Axel Honneth, "Formen der Gesellschaftskritik," in *Desintegration: Bruchstücke einer soziologischen Zeitdiagnose* (Frankfurt am Main: Fischer, 1994), 71–79.

9. Claude Dubar, *La Socialisation: construction des identités sociales et professionnelles* (Paris: Armand Colin, 1998), 109–28.

10. On the relation between the "Self," the "I," and the "Me," see George H. Mead, *Mind, Self and Society: From the Standpoint of a Social Behaviorist* (Chicago: University of Chicago Press, 1934), chap. 25.

11. Max Horkheimer and Theodor W. Adorno, *Dialectic of Enlightenment*, trans. John Cumming (New York: Seabury Press, 1972), 9–10, 32–34.

12. Bernard Lahire, *The Plural Actor*, trans. David Fernbach (Malden, MA: Polity, 2011), 37.

13. John Dewey, *Human Nature and Conduct (1922)*, The Middle Works of John Dewey, 1899–1924, vol. 14 (Carbondale: Southern Illinois University, 1988), part 1, section 2.

14. Dewey, *Human Nature and Conduct*, part 3, section 1.

15. William A. Gamson, "The Social Psychology of Collective Action," in *Frontiers in Social Movement Theory*, ed. Aldon D. Morris and Carol McClurg Mueller (New Haven, CT: Yale University Press, 1992), 53–76.

16. Sophie Béroud and Jacques Capdevielle, "Pour en finir avec une approche culpabilisée et culpabilisante du corporatisme," in *Faire mouvement: novembre-décembre 1995*, ed. Claude Leneveu and Michel Vakaloulis (Paris: Presses Universitaires de France, 1998), 71–101.

17. Avishai Margalit, *The Decent Society*, trans. Naomi Goldblum (Cambridge, MA: Harvard University Press, 1996), esp. chap. 3, "Honor."

18. Axel Honneth, "A Society without Humiliation?: Review Article," *European Journal of Philosophy* 5, no. 3 (December 1997): 306–24.

19. See the introduction to Theodor W. Adorno, *Negative Dialectics*, trans. Ernst Basch Ashton (New York: Seabury Press, 1973).

20. Karl Marx, *Critique of Hegel's 'Philosophy of Right,'* ed. Joseph O'Malley (Cambridge: Cambridge University Press, 1970), 78.

21. On this point see Étienne Balibar, "Three Concepts of the Political: Emancipation, Transformation, Civility," in *Politics and the Other Scene*, trans. Chris Turner (London: Verso, 2002), 1–39.

5. A DEFENSE OF IDENTITY POLITICS

1. Nancy Fraser, "Social Justice in the Age of Identity Politics: Redistribution, Recognition, and Participation," in Nancy Fraser and Axel Honneth, *Redistribution or Recognition?: A Political-Philosophical Exchange* (New York: Verso, 2003), 7–9.

2. See, for example, Marc Saint-Upéry, "El movimiento indígena ecuatoriano y la política del reconocimiento," *Iconos* 10 (April 2001): 57–67.

3. See, for example, Axel Honneth, "Redistribution as Recognition: A Response to Nancy Fraser," in Fraser and Honneth, *Redistribution or Recognition?*, 117–25, where he also articulates the preceding argument.

4. Étienne Balibar and Immanuel Wallerstein, *Race, Nation, Class: Ambiguous Identities* (London: Verso, 2010).

5. As an illustration, I can point to E. P. Thompson's analyses in *The Making of the English Working Class* (New York: Pantheon, 1964).

6. Saint-Upéry, "El movimiento indígena ecuatoriano y la política del reconocimiento."

7. This is Saint-Upéry's viewpoint in "El movimiento indígena ecuatoriano." .

8. This is Nancy Fraser's position in "Social Justice in the Age of Identity Politics."

9. Michel Maffesoli, *Du Nomadisme: vagabondages initiatiques* (Paris: Livre de Poche, 1997); Serge Gruzinski, *The Mestizo Mind: The Intellectual Dynamics of Colonization and Globalization*, trans. Deke Dusinberre (New York: Routledge, 2002).

10. For a discussion of this view, see Étienne Balibar, *We, the People of Europe?: Reflections on Transnational Citizenship*, trans. James Swenson (Princeton, NJ: Princeton University Press, 2004).

11. Jürgen Habermas, "Über Moralität und Sittlichkeit—Was macht eine Lebensform rational?," in *Erläuterungen zur Diskursethik* (Frankfurt am Main: Suhrkamp, 1991), 31–48; "Struggles for Recognition in the Democratic Constitutional State," in *The Inclusion of the Other: Studies in Political Theory*, ed. Ciaran Cronin and Pablo de Greiff (Cambridge, MA: MIT Press, 1998), 203–36, 287–89.

12. John Dewey, in his *Lectures in China* (Honolulu: The University of Hawaii Press, 1973), represents an exception to this rule.

13. Iris Marion Young, "Five Faces of Oppression," in *Justice and the Politics of Difference* (Princeton, NJ: Princeton University Press, 1990), 42–48.

14. See for instance Gayatri Spivak's concept of "strategic essentialism"—a concept she later criticized: Gayatri Chakravorty Spivak, "The New Subaltern: A Silent Interview," in *The Cultural Studies Reader*, ed. Simon During (New York, Routledge, 2006), 229–40. For another criticism of the political constructivist trap in feminist theory, see Iris Marion Young, "Gender as Seriality: Thinking about Women as a Social Collective," *Signs* 19, no. 3 (Spring 1994), 713–38.

15. Harbans Mukhia, "La Violence communautaire et la transmutation des identités," *Lignes* 25, no. 2 (1995), 174–85.

16. In the village of Mardhatan (Tamil Nadu), the Dalits live in small houses along the road, squeezed in between the sewers and the cocoanut groves or rice paddies. The higher castes barred access to the fields. The women were then sent to the police station: 'They chased us away, but once we came back with Nava Jyothi, the police listened to us respectfully.' The street theater practiced by Nava Jyothi is one of the best activist's tools for consciousness raising: for understanding one's status in society and taking action. Nava Jyothi is in the process of forming a union of agricultural workers bringing together men and women so that together they can defend their rights: a minimum wage, decent hours, days off, etc. The women's association, facilitated by Nava Jyothi, after long struggles (petitions, marches, . . .), has succeeded in obtaining for the Dalits running water and even faucets. This group

also made it possible to punish for the first time the rape of a Dalit child by a person of high caste. Naya Jyothi's action has made it possible for people to rediscover confidence in themselves.

(Frères des Hommes France, Réseau de Groupements d'Action Sociale (RGAS) Inde, and the Foundation for Educational Innovations in Asia (FEDINA), *En Inde, se mobiliser pour défendre ses droits* [a pamphlet, December 2002] (Paris: Frères des Hommes France, 2002).)

17. Michel Foucault, "The Subject and Power," in *Power: Essential Works of Michel Foucault, 1954–1984*, vol. 3, ed. James D. Faubion, trans. Robert Hurley (New York: The New Press, 2000), 328–330, and esp. 331, where he says that these struggles fight "against that which ties the individual to himself and submits him to others in this way (struggles against subjection, against forms of subjectivity and submission)," and that they attack "[t]his form of power that applies itself to immediate everyday life, categorizes the individual, marks him by his own individuality, attaches him to his own identity, imposes a law of truth on him that he must recognize and others have to recognize in him."

18. A theory of identity based upon the distinction between primary and secondary socialization can be found in Peter L. Berger and Thomas Luckmann, *The Social Construction of Reality: A Treatise in the Sociology of Knowledge* (New York: Doubleday, 1966), chap. 3. For a study of the historical dynamics of forms of identity, see Claude Dubar, *La Crise des identités: l'interprétation d'une mutation* (Paris: Presses Universitaires de France, 2007), 15–56.

19. Bernard Lahire, *The Plural Actor*, trans. David Fernbach (Cambridge, MA: Polity Press, 2011), 26–28.

20. Claude Dubar, *La Socialisation: construction des identities sociales et professionnelles* (Paris: Armand Colin, 1998), 109–28.

21. The phrase is Étienne Balibar's, from "Identité/Normativité," *Nous, citoyens d'Europe?* (Paris: La Découverte, 2001), 58. This idea is taken up, for example, in Judith Butler, *The Psychic Life of Power: Theories in Subjection* (Stanford, CA: Stanford University Press, 1997).

22. In certain respects, this line of argument can be found in Ernesto Laclau's analysis of identity in terms of difference in *Emancipation(s)* (New York: Verso, 1996).

23. Antonio Negri and Michael Hardt, *Empire* (Cambridge, MA: Harvard University Press, 2000), 143–46.

24. Luc Boltanski and Ève Chiapello, *The New Spirit of Capitalism*, trans. Gregory Elliott (New York: Verso, 2007).

25. William A. Gamson "The Social Psychology of Collective Action," in *Frontiers in Social Movement Theory* (New Haven, CT: Yale University Press, 1992), 56–57.

26. On this point, see Bruce Albert, " 'Ethnographic Situation' and Ethnic Movements: Notes on post-Malinowskian fieldwork" *Critique of Anthropology* 17, no. 1 (1997): 53–65.

27. Claude Corman, *Sur la piste des marranes: de Sefarad à Seattle* (Bègles, France: Éditions du Passant, 2000).

28. Jean-Loup Amselle, *Branchements: anthropologie de l'universalité des cultures* (Paris: Flammarion, 2001).

29. Pierre Bourdieu, *Outline of a Theory of Practice*, trans. Richard Nice (Cambridge: Cambridge University Press, 1977.

30. Alain Brossat, "Métissage culturel, différend et disparition," *Lignes* 6, no. 3 (2001): 28–52.

31. See, for example, the critique of the concept of ethnicity in Jean-Loup Amselle and Elikia M'Bokolo, eds., *Au Cœur de l'ethnie: ethnies, tribalisme et état en Afrique* , 2nd ed. (Paris: La Découverte, 1999).

32. On this point see the theory of social relations as "subsumption" in *The German Ideology*: " the class in its turn assumes an independent existence as against the individuals, so that the latter find their conditions of life predestined, and hence have their position in life and their personal development assigned to them by their class, become subsumed under it. . . . We have already indicated several times that this subsuming of individuals under the class brings with it their subjection to all kind of ideas, etc." (Karl Marx and Frederick Engels, *The German Ideology, Part One*, updated edition, ed. Christopher John Arthur (New York: International Publishers, 1974), 82.)

33. Pierre Bourdieu, *Pascalian Meditations*, trans. Richard Nice (Stanford, CA: Stanford University Press, 2000), 171–2.

34. Bourdieu, *Pascalian Meditations*, 155–59.

35. See on this point Alain Baubion-Broye and Violette Hajjar, "Transitions psychosociales et activités de personnalisation" (17–43) and Philippe Malrieu, "Transformation du moi dans les événements de vie" (195–217), both in , *Événements de vie, transitions et construction de la personne*, ed. Alain Baubion-Broye (Toulouse, France: Erès, 1998).

36. For a critique of socialization as internalization, see for example Christophe Dejours, "Réhabiliter la normalité?" *Le Passant Ordinaire* 45–46, (June-September 2003), 56–58.

37. Yves Clot, *La fonction psychologique du travail* (Paris: Presses Universitaires de France, 1999), 56.

38. On this point, see Emmanuel Renault, *Marx et l'idée de critique* (Paris: Presses Universitaires de France, 1995), 83–88.

39. Alain Touraine, *Critique of Modernity*, trans. David Macey (Oxford: Blackwell, 1995), 233.

40. Jürgen Habermas, *The Theory of Communicative Action, Volume One: Reason and the Rationalization of Society*, trans. Thomas McCarthy (Boston: Beacon Press, 1984), chap. 3.

41. See for example, Philippe Corcuff and Claudette Faye, "Légitimité et théorie critique: un autre usage du modèle de la justification publique" *Mana: Revue de Sociologie et d'Anthropologie* 2 (1996): 217–33.

42. See Theodor Adorno's 1966 "Postscriptum" (pp. 86–92) to his 1955 "Zum Verhältnis von Soziologie und Psychologie,"(pp. 42–85), both in *Soziologische Schriften*, vol 1 [= *Gesammelte Schriften*, vol. 8], ed. Rolf Tiedemann (Frankfurt am Main: Suhrkamp Verlag, 1972). [The original text has been translated in two parts as "Sociology and Psychology, Part I," *New Left Review* 46 (November-December 1967): 67–80 and "Sociology and Psychology, Part II," *New Left Review* 47 (January 1968): 79–97, but the Postscript is not included in this translation.]

6. SOCIAL CRITIQUE AS A VOICE FOR SUFFERING

1. Johanna Siméant, *La Cause des sans-papiers* (Paris: Presses de Sciences Po, 1998), 53.
2. This assessment of struggles of the deprived can be found in Jean-Louis Fournel and Jean-Claude Zancarini, "Analyse du discours politique : les 'sans,'" *Cités* 1 (2000): 211–17.
3. An illustration of this point of view can be found in Miguel Benasayag and Diego Sztulwark, *Política y situación: de la potencia al contrapoder* (Buenos Aires: De Mano en Mano, 2000), translated into French as *Du contre-pouvoir: de la subjectivité contestataire à la construction de contre-pouvoirs*, trans. Anne Weinfeld (Paris: La Découverte, 2000), 17ff.
4. For a study of the political use of hunger strikes, see Johanna Siméant, chapter 6 ("Le Corps de la protestation") in *La Cause des sans-papiers*, 277–355.
5. Siméant, chapter 2 ("Entrepreneurs, militants et réseaux") in *La Cause des sans-papiers*, 73–109. This notion of a "political entrepreneur" takes inspiration from the concept of "moral entrepreneurs," coined by Howard S. Becker, *Outsiders: Studies in the Sociology of Deviance* (New York: The Free Press, 1963), 147–63.
6. Jacques Guilhaumou, "Révolution française et tradition marxiste: une volonté de refondation," *Actuel Marx* 20 (October 1996): 171–92, at p. 178; Jacques Guilhaumou, *L'Avènement des porte-parole de la République (1789–1792): essai de synthèse sur les langages de la Révolution française* (Villeneuve d'Ascq, France: Presses Universitaires de Septentrion, 1998).
7. Jacques Guilhaumou, *La Parole des sans: les mouvements actuels à l'épreuve de la Révolution française* (Fontenay-aux-Roses, France: ENS Éditions, 1998).
8. Jacques Guilhaumou, "Les porte-parole de la lutte contre l'exclusion et la tradition civique marseillaise," in *Métropolisation, gouvernance et citoyenneté dans la région urbaine marseillaise* (Paris: Maisonneuve et Larose, 2001), 227–38.
9. On the political function of "word warriors," see James Tully, "The Struggle of Indigenous People for and of Freedom," in *Political Theory and the Rights of Indigenous People*, ed. Duncan Ivison, Paul Patton, and Will Sanders (Cambridge: Cambridge University Press, 2000), 36–59, esp. 50ff.
10. Didier Demazière and Maria Teresa Pignoni, *Chômeurs: du silence à la révolte (Sociologie d'une action collective)* (Paris: Hachette, 1998), 62, 169.
11. Olivier Voirol, "Lutte des réfugiés: contre le racisme institutionnel en Allemagne," *Le Passant ordinaire* 37 (November-December 2001), available at http://www.passant-ordinaire.com/revue/37-309.asp.
12. On this point, see Doug McAdam, John D. McCarthy and Mayer N. Zald, "Introduction: Opportunities, Mobilizing Structures and Framing Processes—Toward a Synthetic, Comparative Perspective on Social Movements," in McAdam, McCarthy and Zald, eds., *Comparative Perspectives on Social Movements: Political Opportunities, Mobilizing Structures, and Cultural Framings* (New York: Cambridge University Press, 1996), 9.
13. Pierre Bourdieu et. al., *The Weight of the World: Social Suffering in Contemporary Society*, trans. Priscilla Parkhurst Ferguson et. al. (Stanford, CA: Stanford University Press, 1999), 4.
14. Bourdieu et al., *Weight of the World*, 629.
15. A more detailed analysis of the positioning of the concepts of psychological suffering and social suffering, as well as a more thorough analysis of the criticisms raised against them, can be found in Emmanuel Renault, "La souffrance sociale: concepts,

usages sociaux, paradigms," *Histoire et Sociétés: Revue Européenne d'Histoire Sociale* 4 (2002), 51–64.

16. Christophe Dejours, ed., *Plaisir et souffrance dans le travail*, 2 vols. (Paris: Édition de l'AOCIP, 1987–1988).

17. Bourdieu et. al., *The Weight of the World*.

18. Serge Paugam, *La disqualification sociale: essai sur la nouvelle pauvreté* (Paris: Presses Universitaires de France, 1991).

19. Vincent de Gaulejac and Shirley Roy, eds., *Sociologies cliniques* (Paris: Desclée de Brouwer, 1993).

20. Pierre Bourdieu, *Pascalian Meditations*, trans. Richard Nice (Stanford, CA: Stanford University Press, 2000).

21. Serge Paugam, *Le Salarié de la précarité: les nouvelles formes de l'intégration profes-sionnelle* (Paris: Presses Universitaires de France, 2000).

22. *Rhizome: Bulletin National Santé Mentale et Précarité*, no. 5 (July 2001), ISSN 1622–2032. Available at: http://www.ch-le-vinatier.fr/orspere (accessed 14 March 2018).

23. Bourdieu et al., *The Weight of the World*, 629.

24. Bourdieu et al., *The Weight of the World*, 627–28.

25. Vincent de Gaulejac, "Introduction," in Gaulejac and Roy, *Sociologies cliniques* 13.

26. Sigmund Freud, *Civilization and its Discontents*, trans. James Strachey (New York: W. W. Norton, 1989), 37.

27. Bourdieu, *Pascalian Meditations*, 140–42, 164–65.

28. Bourdieu, *Pascalian Meditations*, 64, 160.

29. Patrick Declerck, *Les Naufragés: avec les clochards de Paris* (Paris: Plon, 2001); Oliv-ier Douville, "Mélancolie d'exclusion: quand la parole divorce du corps, et retour," *Psychanalyse et malaise social: Désir du lien?*, (Toulouse: Erès, 2001), 39–52.

30. Christophe Dejours, *Plaisir et souffrance*, vol. 1, 17.

31. For a defense of the concept of social pathology, see Axel Honneth, "Pathologies of the Social: The Past and Present of Social Philosophy," in *Disrespect: The Normative Foundations of Critical Theory* (New York: Polity, 2007).

32. Karl Marx, *Capital*, trans. Ben Fowkes (London: Penguin Books, 1990), Book 1, Chapter 14, § 5, 484.

33. Marx, *Capital*, 353ff, 484ff, 517ff, 610ff.

34. Marx, *Capital*, 354–56, 362, 365–67.

35. Marx, *Capital*, 356, 381 ("suffering"); 380–81 ("degeneration . . ."); 623 ("decay").

36. Christophe Dejours, "Note de travail sur la notion de souffrance," in *Plaisir et Souf-france dans le Travail*, vol. 1, 115: "health is not a stable state but rather a goal; what matters, once again, are the procedures employed to achieve it or to regain it when it has been lost. Suffering thus designates a first approach to the field that separates illness from health."

37. Theodore W. Adorno, *Negative Dialectics*, trans. Ernst Basch Ashton (New York: Seabury Press, 1973), 203.

38. Max Horkheimer, *Dawn: Notes 1926–1931*, in *Dawn and Decline: Notes 1926–1931 and 1950–1969*, trans. Michael Shaw (New York: Seabury Press, 1978), 36: "taking the risk of crossing that bridge might determine whether the overwhelmingly larger measure of injustice, the withering of human capacities, the lies, the senseless degradation, in short the unnecessary material and spiritual suffering is to disappear, or not. One has to fight for socialism, in other words." [from "Skepsis and Morality"].

39. Horkheimer *Dawn and Decline* 72 ["Power, Right, Justice"], translation modified.

40. Daniel Bensaid, "L'humanité au-delà du capital," *Actuel Marx* 31, no. 1 (2002): 139–46.

7. RECOGNITION AND PSYCHIC SUFFERING

1. Antoine Lazarus, "Annotations sur la Souffrance," in *L'Éthique de la souffrance*, ed. Miguel Benasayag and Samy Abtroun (Paris: Ellipses, 2000), 129–41.

2. Michel Joubert, "Précarisation et santé mentale," in *Précarisation, risque, et santé*, ed. Virginie Ringa, Pierre Chauvin, Françoise Facy, and Michel Joubert (Paris: INSERM, 2001), 15–35.

3. Olivier Douville, "Notes d'un clinicien sur les incidences subjectives de la grande précarité," *Psychologie Clinique* 7 (1999): 57–68; cited at 58–59.

4. Jean Furtos, "Épistémologie de la clinique psychosociale: (la scène sociale et la place des psy)," *Pratiques en Santé Mentale*, no. 1 (2000): 23–32.

5. Arthur Schopenhauer, *The World as Will and Representation*, 2 vols., trans. Judith Norman, Alistair Welchman, and Christopher Janaway (Cambridge: Cambridge University Press, 2010), Books 1 and 2.

6. As Michel Henry does in *The Genealogy of Psychoanalysis*, trans. Douglas Brick (Stanford, CA: Stanford University Press, 1993).

7. Schopenhauer, *The World as Will and Representation*, Book 4, §60.

8. Schopenhauer, *The World as Will and Representation*, §§57–59.

9. According to Michel Henry, what I am presenting here as a limit would rather constitute one of the key strengths of Schopenhauer's philosophy: shifting from a psychological conception to an ontological conception of affectivity. Schopenhauer would have grasped that life is essentially self-affection, and it is in this sense that it would be essentially suffering, understanding by suffering a distancing from oneself and work upon oneself in the immanence that is the ontological condition for the psychological phenomena of pleasure and pain. However, the Schopenhauerian philosophy, in contrast with Henry's, is a philosophy of forces rather than a philosophy of life. It aims for an interpretation of affects as energies rather than the elaboration of an ontological concept of affectivity.

10. On the centrality of conflict in Schopenhauer, who anticipates Nietzsche in this way, see *The World as Will and Representation*, Book 2, §§27–28.

11. I am referring here to a lecture presented by Christophe Dejours at the Collège international de philosophie on January 21, 2003, "L'Épreuve de soi entre théorie et clinique."

12. In a letter to Arnold Ruge, Marx notes, "But the existence of suffering human beings, who think, and thinking human beings, who are oppressed, must inevitably become unpalatable and indigestible to the animal world of philistinism which passively and thoughtlessly consumes. For our part, we must expose the old world to the full light of day and shape the new one in a positive way. The longer the time that events allow to thinking humanity for taking stock of its position, and to suffering mankind for mobilizing its forces, the more perfect on entering the world will be the product that the present time bears in its womb." Karl Marx, "Letters from the *Deutsch-Französische Jahrbücher*: 'M. to R., Cologne, May 1843,' " in Karl Marx and Friedrich Engels, *Collected Works*, vol. 3, *Marx and Engels: 1843–44*, trans. Jack Cohen, Richard Dixon, and Clemens Dutt (New York: International Publishers, 1975–2004), 141.

13. Karl Marx, "A Contribution to the Critique of Hegel's 'Philosophy of Right': Introduction," in *Critique of Hegel's 'Philosophy of Right,'* ed. Joseph O'Malley, trans. Annette Jolin and Joseph O'Malley (Cambridge: Cambridge University Press, 1970), 141–42.

14. Of course, the model of conflict and that of alienation are not the only two philosophical models of suffering. There is at least a third, the model of expenditure that could be attributed to authors such as Nietzsche and Georges Bataille (and it is to this third model that Max Scheler makes reference in "The Meaning of Suffering" when he argues, *pace* Schopenhauer, that suffering arises "not from want and need but form [sic: from] an increment of vitality, from growth." (Max Scheler, "The Meaning of Suffering," in *On Feeling, Knowing, and Valuing: Selected Writings*, ed. Harold J. Bershady (Chicago: The University of Chicago Press, 1992), 92.) Some have occasionally attempted to give psychological or metapsychological relevance to this model (see, for example, Alain Ehrenberg's rehabilitation of Pierre Janet *pace* Freud, which I will take up later).

15. Lucien Israël, in "Le mal-être" (in *Le Mal-Être: angoisse et violence*, ed. Jean Cournut, Lucien Israël, Augustin Jeanneau, and Jacqueline Schaeffer [Paris: Presses Universitaires de France,1997], 189–91), speaks of a "sacrifice—unconscious—of a highly developed psychic functioning in favor of a will—which could be called instinctive—to survive" (p. 190), in reference to Claude Smadja's contribution to the same collection ("Impensable douleur," 181–87), where this problematic is developed through an analysis of accounts of psychic and physical suffering in Nazi concentration camps. For an application of this problematic to forms of extreme disaffiliation, see Clément Bonnet and Michelle Fournial, "La psychiatrie face à l'exigence actuelle d'intervention psychosociale," *L'Information Psychiatrique* 75, no. 8 (October 1999): 805–25, esp. 811.

16. On this point, see for example Djemila Zeneidi, "Femmes SDF," *Le Passant Ordinaire* 27 (2000), 6.

17. Robert Castel, *From Manual Workers to Wage Laborers: Transformation of the Social Question*, trans. Richard Boyd (New Brunswick, NJ: Transaction Publishers, 2003).

18. The Freudian metapsychological theory is a theory of conflict, and the theory of suffering that it proposes falls within the model of conflict. In *Civilization and its Discontents*, what Freud terms suffering with social sources is ultimately explained by the superego's action upon the ego. In speaking of suffering with a social source, Freud paved the way for a study of the social processes that produce suffering and the specific sufferings that are a result of society. This has been done by authors such as Wilhelm Reich, Erich Fromm, and Herbert Marcuse. However we may take the contributions that they have made to the history of psychoanalysis and critical theory, it is clear that we can find nothing in their work that directly or indirectly resembles psychic suffering in the narrow sense, for two reasons: first, the Freudian concept of suffering with social origins is too broad for psychic suffering; second, the concept of psychic suffering designates specific symptoms produced by specific social processes, whereas Freud, Fromm, and Marcuse look at the symbolic causality of society taken as a whole.

19. Antoine Lazarus, ed., *Une souffrance qu'on ne peut plus cacher* (Paris: DIV & DIRMI, 1995), §§2.1 and 2.2.

20. Frédéric de Rivoyre, "Au-delà du principe de réalité: une recherche sur la psychopathologie de l'exclusion," *Psychologie Clinique* 7 (1999): 81–93.

21. Claude Dubar, *La Crise des identités: l'interprétation d'une mutation* (Paris: Presses Universitaires de France, 2007).
22. On the specific meaning of alcoholism in situations of extreme disaffiliation, see Jean Maisondieu, "Alcool, alcoolisme, exclusion et précarité," in Ringa, Chauvin, Facy, and Joubert, ed., *Précarisation, risque, et santé*, 377–93.
23. Olivier Douville, " 'Mélancolie d'exclusion': quand la parole divorce du corps, et retour," in *Psychanalyse et malaise social: désir du lien?* , ed. Frédéric de Rivoyre (Ramonville Saint-Agne, France: Érès, 2001), 48.
24. I take this distinction from Lucien Israël, "Le mal-être."
25. On social suffering understood in this sense, see Arthur Kleinman, Veena Das, and Margaret M. Lock, eds., *Social Suffering* (Berkeley: University of California Press, 1997).
26. For a study of how these different kinds of violence and of denial of recognition can lead to the destruction of a positive image of oneself, see the different aspects of shame brought to light by Vincent de Gaulejac by drawing upon an analysis of different life stories, in chap. 5 of *Les Sources de la honte* (Paris: Desclée de Brouwer, 1996), 61–73.
27. On this point see Christophe Dejours's analysis of the mechanisms of suffering at work in Christophe Dejours, "Note de travail sur la notion de souffrance," in Dejours, ed., *Plaisir et souffrance dans le travail* , vol. 1 (Orsay, France: AOCIP [Association pour l'ouverture du champ d'investigation psychopathologique], 1988).
28. Jean Furtos, "Épistémologie de la clinique psychosociale."
29. Olivier Douville, "Notes d'un clinicien sur les incidences subjectives de la grande précarité," 64.
30. Gladys Swain, *Le Sujet de la folie: naissance de la psychiatrie* (Toulouse: Privat, 1977).
31. Jean Maisondieu, "De l'exclusion pathogène au syndrome d'exclusion: [le coin du clinician]," *Rhizome* 4 (March 2001): 14.
32. On this latter point, see Didier Demazière's summary in *Sociologie du chômage* (Paris: La Découverte, 1995), chapter 5, "Vivre et exister en chômage," 90–102.
33. Jean-Marie Petitclerc, *La Violence et les jeunes* (Paris: Éditions Salvator, 1999).
34. Olivier Douville, " 'Mélancolie d'exclusion,' " 44–45: "What clinicians have also noticed regarding this feeling of shame—and this uniquely contradicts our altruistic ambitions—is that the subject, once accorded a semblance of dignity, can react with powerful rages. . . . And often, once shame has been overcome, we are dealing with a veritable clinic of hatred. . . . What is hatred? . . . It could be a montage that is created when the subject does not let go of the other. A subject who does not let go of the other, this is the topology of a subject that is not yet entirely excluded—one that, deep down, still believes that an other exists, but also believes, at the same time, that elsewhere—maybe only for others, people who aren't like him, strangers—there is still bodily dignity, language, culture."
35. Gabrielle Balazs and Jean-Pierre Faguer, "Une nouvelle forme de management: l'évaluation," *Actes de la Recherche en Sciences Sociales* 114 ("Les nouvelles formes de domination dans le travail"), no. 4 (1996): 68–78.
36. Olivier Douville, " 'Mélancolie d'exclusion,' " 43–44: "A good number of individuals, most often women, who appear to us as if they lived in a state of shamelessness are, quite to the contrary, caught up in great embarrassment about their own bodily existence (this is not merely a matter of their narcissistic self-image), which they

are no longer able to bear—like the character Jef, in Jacques Brel's eponymous (and very moving) song, who can no longer bear his heavy heart." For a critique of the so-called "absence of demands," see Sylvie Quesemand-Zucca, "Un + un = trois," in de Rivoyre, ed., *Psychanalyse et malaise social: désir du lien?*, 61–65, and *Rhizome* 2 (September 2000), entitled "Métamorphoses de la demande et engagement dans le soin."

37. Corinne Lanzarini, *Survivre dans le monde sous-prolétaire* (Paris: Presses Universitaires de France, 2000), 102ff. On the problematic of identity in situations of extreme disaffiliation, see also Anne M. Lovell, "Les fictions de soi-même ou les délires identificatoires dans la rue," in *La Maladie mentale en mutation: psychiatrie et société* (Paris: Odile Jacob, 2001), 127–61.

38. Douville, "Notes d'un clinicien," 64.

39. On the distinction between these two forms of shame, see de Gaulejac, *Les Sources de la honte*, 70–71.

40. Patrick Baudry, "Conflit, image du corps et rapport à la mort," in *Souffrances et violences à l'adolescence: Qu'en penser? Que faire?: Rapport à Claude Bartolone, Ministre Délégué à la Ville*, ed. Patrick Baudry et al. (Issy-les-Moulineaux, France: ESF Éditeur, 2000), 13–28.

41. Donald W. Winnicott, "The Antisocial Tendency," in *Deprivation and Delinquency*, ed. Clare Winnicott, Ray Shepherd, and Madeleine Davis (New York: Tavistock Publications, 1984), 120–131.

42. Patrick Baudry et al., "Introduction," in Baudry et al., ed., *Souffrances et violences à l'adolescence* , 11–12.

43. Christophe Dejours, *Souffrance en France: la banalisation de l'injustice sociale* (Paris: Seuil, 1998).

44. Carole Thiry-Bour et al., "Les conditions de travail des praticiens hospitaliers en psychiatrie publique," *L'Information Psychiatrique* 76, no. 10 (December 2000).

45. Michel Foucault, "Human Nature: Justice versus Power" [a debate with Noam Chomsky], in *Foucault and His Interlocutors*, ed. Arnold I. Davidson (Chicago: University of Chicago Press, 1997), 130.

46. Nicolas Frize, *Le Sens de la peine: état de l'idéologie carcérale* (Paris: Lignes/Éditions Léo Scheer, 2004), 65ff.

47. Olivier Douville, " 'Mélancolie d'exclusion,' " 41.

48. Quesemand-Zucca, "Un + un = trois," 62–63.

49. Quesemand-Zucca, "Un + un = trois," 63.

CONCLUSION: CRITIQUE AS A VOICE AGAINST INJUSTICE

1. The challenges raised by these three specifications are discussed by Gayatri Chakravorty Spivak, "Can the Subaltern Speak?", in *Marxism and the Interpretation of Culture*, ed. Cary Nelson and Lawrence Grossberg (Chicago: University of Illinois Press, 1988), 271–313.

2. Carol Gilligan, *In a Different Voice: Psychological Theory and Women's Development* (Cambridge, MA: Harvard University Press, 1982).

3. As in *Capital*, for example, when "[s]uddenly, however, there arises the voice of the worker, which had previously been stifled in the sound and fury of the production

process" (Marx, *Capital*, trans. Ben Fowkes (London: Penguin Books, 1990), Book 1, chap. 10, § 1, p. 342). Over the next page and a half, Marx lets this worker articulate his demands concerning the use of his labor power, and then notes: "During the great strike of the London building workers [1859–60] for the reduction of the working day to 9 hours, their committee published a manifesto that contained, to some extent, the plea of our worker" (p. 343n6).

4. Michel Foucault and Gilles Deleuze, "Intellectuals and Power," in *Language, Counter-Memory, Practice: Selected Essays and Interviews*, ed. Donald F. Bouchard (Ithaca, NY: Cornell University Press, 1977), 205–17.

5. Pierre Bourdieu, "Practical Sense and Political Labor," in *Pascalian Meditations*, trans. Richard Nice (Stanford, CA: Stanford University Press, 2000),182–88.

6. Bertrand Ogilvie, " Violence et représentation: la production de l'homme-jetable," *Lignes* 26, no. 3 (1995): 113–41.

INDEX

NEW DIRECTIONS IN CRITICAL THEORY

Amy Allen, General Editor

Narrating Evil: A Postmetaphysical Theory of Reflective Judgment, María Pía Lara

The Politics of Our Selves: Power, Autonomy, and Gender in Contemporary Critical Theory, Amy Allen

Democracy and the Political Unconscious, Noëlle McAfee

The Force of the Example: Explorations in the Paradigm of Judgment, Alessandro Ferrara

Horrorism: Naming Contemporary Violence, Adriana Cavarero

Scales of Justice: Reimagining Political Space in a Globalizing World, Nancy Fraser

Pathologies of Reason: On the Legacy of Critical Theory, Axel Honneth

States Without Nations: Citizenship for Mortals, Jacqueline Stevens

The Racial Discourses of Life Philosophy: Négritude, Vitalism, and Modernity, Donna V. Jones

Democracy in What State?, Giorgio Agamben, Alain Badiou, Daniel Bensaïd, Wendy Brown, Jean-Luc Nancy, Jacques Rancière, Kristin Ross, Slavoj Žižek

Politics of Culture and the Spirit of Critique: Dialogues, edited by Gabriel Rockhill and Alfredo Gomez-Muller

Mute Speech: Literature, Critical Theory, and Politics, Jacques Rancière

The Right to Justification: Elements of Constructivist Theory of Justice, Rainer Forst

The Scandal of Reason: A Critical Theory of Political Judgment, Albena Azmanova

The Wrath of Capital: Neoliberalism and Climate Change Politics, Adrian Parr

Media of Reason: A Theory of Rationality, Matthias Vogel

Social Acceleration: The Transformation of Time in Modernity, Hartmut Rosa

The Disclosure of Politics: Struggles Over the Semantics of Secularization, María Pía Lara

Radical Cosmopolitics: The Ethics and Politics of Democratic Universalism, James Ingram

Freedom's Right: The Social Foundations of Democratic Life, Axel Honneth

Imaginal Politics: Images Beyond Imagination and the Imaginary, Chiara Bottici

Alienation, Rahel Jaeggi

The Power of Tolerance: A Debate, Wendy Brown and Rainer Forst, edited by Luca Di Blasi and Christoph F. E. Holzhey